Alan Dunn's
Best of
Floral Sugarcraft

Culpitt

ALAN DUNN'S
BEST OF *Floral Sugarcraft*

Book One

Floral
WEDDING CAKES
& SPRAYS

Book Two

Sugar Flowers
For All Seasons

Floral
WEDDING
CAKES
& SPRAYS

Floral
WEDDING
CAKES
& SPRAYS

ALAN DUNN

Contents

*D*EDICATION

*With love to my Grandad, Ernest
Blair, and to the memory of Mitz,
the special dog with the very
alternative sense of humour!*

INTRODUCTION

Wedding cakes date back to Roman times when a basic fruit cake, made from food that was offered to the gods – rich fruit, nuts and honey cake – was used as part of the wedding ceremony. The cake was crumbled over the bride's head so that the gods would bless her with an abundance of everything. When Julius Caesar conquered Great Britain in 54 BC, the wedding cake, along with many other Roman traditions, was introduced and became part of our custom. It was only wealthy families at first who copied this practice, with poorer families scattering grains of wheat or corn over the bride, in the hope that their marriages too would be fertile. This custom carried on until about two hundred years ago.

The wedding cake has seen many changes since then, progressing very gradually to decorated cakes and then to multi-tiered centrepieces that many people now take for granted. To begin with, it was only royalty and the high society who could afford to have these tiered cakes, with the rest of the country having only single cakes decorated with perhaps a vase to add height to the display. The three-tier round cake became traditional, representing the three rings – the engagement, wedding and eternity ring. Soon the request for a three-tiered cake became fashionable amongst the middle classes, even if there was more cake than was actually needed for the guests. Consequently there was often a tier left over and, rather than use it immediately, it was often kept for the christening of the couple's first child.

Flowers too have been incorporated into celebrations and religious ceremonies since early times. So it therefore seems to have been a natural progression that flowers should feature quite predominantly in wedding cake designs. The styles of wedding cakes have evolved constantly over the years, with the fashions and trends of each period reflecting the cake design. In the past they were created as very grand formal tiered cakes, often inspired by architecture. Present day designs are more informal and less rigid in their design, and are often displayed on various types of cake stands. Flowers now, more than ever before, are often the main focal point of a wedding cake. The variation of sugar flowers and foliage used on cakes is vast, mainly due to the increased selection of flowers available to the florist which in turn can be offered to the bride.

In this book I have included a varied collection of some of the more unusual flowers, as well as many traditional flowers and foliage. The cake designs and floral combinations pictured in the pages that follow are offered only as suggestions and were never intended to be copied directly, more to be used as a starting point. Many of the cake designs shown, as in my last two books, feature quite large bouquets and arrangements. However, there are some cakes that require fewer flowers as well, for those people who have requested it! It is important to consider that a cake with large arrangements or a few bold flowers will make a far bigger impact at a wedding reception than a very delicate cake with small sprays and flowers.

Try using the various sugar flowers and foliages in different combinations, adding perhaps some of your personal favourites. Use them to create and experiment to produce work that is as individual as you are. Remember that beauty is in the eye of the beholder and the only limit to what you can achieve is your own imagination; so get started and have fun!

HEAVENLY SCENT

A very simple, pretty cake design intended for a small wedding reception. The arrangement includes a charming combination of tuberoses, roses, rue leaves and ivy.

Royal icing coloured with primrose paste food colouring
Plum, white and holly/ivy petal dust (blossom tint)
Fine willow green ribbon to trim cake
Broad green velvet ribbon to trim board

EQUIPMENT

Sugarpaste smoothers
36cm (14 in) oval cake board
Nos. 1 and 42 piping tubes (tips)
Embroidery side design template (see page 154)

FLOWERS

Heavenly Scent Arrangement (see page 11)

CORSAGE

1 half rose and 1 rosebud (see page 136)
5 ivy leaves (see page 114)
1 piece of rue (see page 11)

PREPARATION

1 Brush the cake with apricot glaze and cover with almond paste. Leave to dry overnight. Moisten the almond paste with clear alcohol and then cover with creamy-lemon sugarpaste, using sugarpaste smoothers to create a good finish to the surface of the cake.

2 Cover the cake board with creamy-lemon sugarpaste and position the cake on top. Use the sugarpaste smoothers again to achieve a neat join between the base of the cake and the board. Allow to dry overnight.

3 Colour the royal icing with a small amount of primrose colouring to match the sugarpaste coating. Pipe a shell border around the base of the cake using the royal icing in a piping bag fitted with a no. 42 tube. Attach a band of fine willow green ribbon just above the shell border. Glue the broad velvet ribbon to the cake board edge using a non-toxic glue stick.

SIDE DESIGN

4 Either pipe the embroidery directly on to the cake using the pattern on page 154 as a guideline, or trace the design on to greaseproof (wax) paper and scribe it on to the cake first. Use a no.1 tube to pipe the design. Broderie anglaise 'holes' are made using the pointed end of a celstick and then an outline piped in royal icing. Allow the design to dry. Highlight the roses with a very pale mixture of plum and white petal dust. Highlight the leaves with holly/ivy petal dust.

ASSEMBLY

5 Make the Heavenly Scent arrangement as instructed on page 11, and position carefully on top of the cake. Wire a small corsage with the remaining roses, ivy leaves and sprig of rue, and position next to the cake.

MATERIALS

25cm (10 in) oval cake
Apricot glaze
1.25kg (2½lb) almond paste (marzipan)
Clear alcohol (kirsch or vodka)
2kg (4lb) pale creamy-lemon sugarpaste

HEAVENLY SCENT ARRANGEMENT

This beautiful arrangement, taken from the Heavenly Scent cake on page 8, makes a useful alternative to a wired spray – giving the novice sugarcrafter a little more confidence as the flowers can easily be removed and re-arranged if a mistake is made first time round.

FLOWERS

3 stems of tuberoses (see page 12)
3 stems of ivy, plus some extras
(see page 114)
1 full rose, 3 half roses and
5 rose-buds (see page 136)
2 stems of rue (right)

EQUIPMENT

Florists' staysoft
Small oval acrylic board (HP)
Wire cutters
Fine pliers

PREPARATION

1 Fix the florists' staysoft to the acrylic board (because this is only a small arrangement, the paste will adhere itself sufficiently to the acrylic).

2 Cut each of the tuberose stems to the required length, make a hook at the end of each of the stems for support and then arrange them in the staysoft.

ASSEMBLY

3 Start by positioning the three stems of tuberoses and ivy in the staysoft to form the basic outline of the arrangement. Curve any of the stems if necessary to form a pleasing shape.

4 Position the large rose at the centre of the arrangement to form the focal point, then arrange the half roses and buds around the central rose.

RUE

Rue (*Ruta graveolens*) has very pretty foliage. The leaves are made using two sizes of triple-spreading 'E' cutters (Zimbabwean cutters). Insert a short length of 30-gauge wire into almost the full length of each leaf. Work the edges using the broad end of the dresden tool and then cup the back of each section using a small celstick. Pinch a central vein down each one. Dust with dark green, holly/ivy and white petal dust. Dip into a ¼ glaze. Tape leaves into groups.

5 To complete, add the rue leaves and some ivy leaves to fill in the gaps and frame the focal flower.

TUBEROSE

The tuberose (*Polianthes tuberosa*) probably originates from Mexico, but it has been cultivated in southern France for centuries for the perfume industry. There are both single and double forms of tuberose, although the latter is the most popular as a cut flower. The fleshy flowers and chubby bud arrangement add a wonderful charm to sprays and bouquets.

STAMENS

1 There are three slender stamens in a tuberose flower – I use artistic licence using six stamens to add more interest. Bend three seed-head stamens in half and either glue or tape them on to a 24-gauge wire. Dust the tips with primrose and lemon petal dust. Attach a small piece of paste to the base of the stamens to help the first petals stick.

FIRST AND SECOND LAYERS OF PETALS

2 Roll out a small amount of white flower paste and cut out one flower shape using the smallest of the six-petal pointed blossom cutters (N3). Place the shape on to a pad and soften the edges using the rounded end of a celstick. Using the broad end of the dresden tool, hollow out the length of each of the petals. Using the fine end of the tool, mark a few fine veins on each petal.

3 Moisten the paste on the wire below the stamens with fresh egg white, then thread the wire through the centre of the petal shape. Pinch and form the petals around the stamens to form a tight centre (thestamens should be able to be viewed, but not standing proud). Work on several flowers at a time, so that when you have completed the first layers of all of the flowers, the first flower should be ready to have the second layer of petals attached.

MATERIALS

Small white seed-head stamens
18, 24 and 26-gauge wires
White and green flower paste
Primrose, lemon, vine green, moss green, plum, white and dark green petal dust (blossom tint)
¼ glaze (see page 151)

EQUIPMENT

Six-petal pointed blossom cutters
(OP N1,2,3)
Dried corn on the cob husk
Leaf templates (see page 154)

4 Repeat steps two and three but this time use the larger six-petal cutter (N2). Attach to the first layer so that you have a petal positioned in between each on the previous layer. Make some of the centres tighter to represent newly open and fully open flowers. Dry slightly.

THIRD LAYER

5 Roll a ball of flower paste into a sausage shape and pinch out one end to form a pedestal shape. Place the flat part of the pedestal on a board and roll out the paste using a celstick, remembering that the tuberose has fleshy petals. Place the cutter (N1) down over the pedestal and cut out the petal shape.

6 Remove the flower from the cutter and place face down on to

the pad. Soften the edges of each of the petals, then turn the flower over and hollow out each of the petals on the upper side. Vein each petal as before.

7 Open up the centre using the pointed end of the celstick. Moisten the centre and then pull the first two layers on the wire through the centre of the flower, lining up the petals again so that each one is positioned as for the previous layer. Pinch the tips of the petals and curl some or all of them back slightly. Thin down the back of the flower if needed and remove the excess paste. Using a sharp scalpel, mark six lines as petal divisions on the back of the flower. Draw in some finer veins using the scalpel. Curve the back of the flower; firm up before dusting.

BUDS

8 Roll a ball of paste into a cone shape. Hook and moisten a 26-gauge wire and insert it into the base of the cone. Work the base of the cone down on to the wire to form the slender back. Using a cage with three 26-gauge wires, divide the surface to represent the outer petals of the bud. Pinch the tips of each of the sections to give them a subtle ridge. Vein the back of the bud as for the flower. Curve slightly. Repeat to make numerous buds of various sizes (sixteen buds pictured).

BRACTS

9 The buds and flowers are grouped in pairs down the stem and for each pair you will need to make a bract. They can be represented with floristry tape cut into a pointed shape, or preferably with paste. Roll out some pale green flower paste leaving a thick ridge down the centre (to give some support). Cut out a bract shape using a scalpel and one of the bract templates from page 154. Vein the surface of the paste using dried corn on the cob husk. Soften the edges and draw down a central vein on one side of the paste. Cut out as many bracts as you need and cover them with a plastic bag to prevent drying.

ASSEMBLY AND COLOURING

10 Tape two small buds on to the end of a ½-length of 18-gauge wire, using ½-width tape. Cut some strips of kitchen paper and wrap one around the stem and tape over. Remove a small bract from the plastic, moisten the inner part of the bract and attach to the stem at the base of the buds. Tape in the next two buds, thicken the stem with paper and again attach a bract. Con-tinue, gradually introducing the flowers. Dry a little before colouring.

11 Dust the backs of each of the flowers and buds with vine green and then a touch of moss and primrose petal dust on top. Dust the tips of the smaller buds with these colours as well. Tinge the buds and add a streak of colour using a mixture of plum and white. Dust the bracts with vine, moss and dark green. Dry. Paint with ¼ glaze. Dry.

LEAVES

12 Roll out pale green paste, leaving a thick ridge down the centre. Cut out the leaf shape. Insert a moistened 26-gauge wire. Vein using the husk veiner. Soften the edges and draw down a central vein. Firm up a little. Dust and glaze as for the bracts, then tape on to the main stem, pressing the leaf base around the stem for a neat finish.

ORCHID INSPIRATION

The subtle colours used in the bouquets on this two-tiered cake are very fashionable with brides at the moment. I have combined phaius orchids, arum lilies, palm and other foliage to create a very fresh modern wedding cake design.

MATERIALS

20cm (8 in) and 30cm (12 in) teardrop-shaped cakes
Apricot glaze
2.25kg (4½lb) almond paste (marzipan)
Clear alcohol (kirsch or vodka)
3.25kg (6½lb) champagne sugarpaste
Fine pale coffee ribbon to trim cakes
Broad pale coffee ribbon to trim boards
A small amount of flower paste
Caramel paste colouring

EQUIPMENT

Sugarpaste smoothers
25cm (10 in) teardrop-shaped board
and 40cm (16 in) oval cake board

Curved leaf and cornucopia cutters (ECC)
Tilting cake stand (CC)
Double-sided carpet tape
1 crystal pillar

FLOWERS

Orchid Inspiration Bouquet
(see page 16)
1 small crescent-shaped spray
(see page 17)

PREPARATION

1 Brush the cakes with apricot glaze and cover with almond paste. Leave to dry overnight. Moisten the surface of the almond paste with clear alcohol and cover with champagne sugarpaste, using sugarpaste smoothers to achieve a good finish. Cover the cake boards with champagne sugarpaste. Position the cakes on top, making sure you have a neat join between the bases of the cakes and the boards. Allow to dry overnight.

2 Attach a band of fine pale coffee ribbon around the base of each cake and a band of broad coffee ribbon to the edge of the cake boards.

SIDE DESIGN

3 Colour the flower paste with a touch of caramel paste colouring so that it matches the colour of the sugarpaste. Knead the paste to make it pliable and then roll it out quite thinly on to a non-stick board. Using the curved leaf and cornucopia cutters, cut out numerous shapes to decorate the sides.

4 Moisten the back of each of the shapes in turn with clear alcohol. Position them on to the cake surface, alternating the two shapes as shown in the main photograph.

ASSEMBLY

5 Place the tilting cake stand on the base board behind the indent of the large teardrop cake. Stick some double-sided carpet tape on the slope of the stand and position the smaller cake on top.

6 Assemble the bouquets as instructed on page 17. Insert the bouquet handle into a crystal pillar and then insert this into the top tier. (Do not position this too close to the edge of the cake.) Arrange the crescent-shaped spray on the right of the larger cake.

NOTE

If you are concerned that the top tier is too heavy to rest securely on the tilted stand, use a polystyrene dummy cake for the display and then provide a separate cake simply decorated for cutting.

ORCHID INSPIRATION BOUQUET

Orchids have long been used as bridal flowers to give an exotic and extravagant feel to a wedding celebration. Here phaius orchids have been teamed with cream arum lilies, eucalyptus and palm to give a very modern, dramatic finish to the bouquet.

FLOWERS

For the large bouquet
3 Good-Luck palm leaves
(see page 21)
3 stems of eucalyptus (see page 120)
5 phaius orchids (see page 18)
5 arum lilies (see page 36)
2 trailing stems of ivy, plus some
extra medium and large leaves
(see page 114)

For the small crescent-shaped spray
3 phaius orchids
3 arum lilies
2 stems of eucalyptus
3 stems of ivy

EQUIPMENT

18 and 20-gauge wires
Nile green floristry tape
Fine pliers
Wire cutters

PREPARATION

1 First of all strengthen any of the flower and foliage stems that will need extra support. To do this, tape 18 or 20-gauge wires (depending on the size of the piece) alongside the main stem.

ASSEMBLY

2 Decide how long you want the bouquet to be. The first palm leaf should measure at least two thirds the total length of the bouquet. Bend the stem to a 90 degree angle.

Add the other two palm leaves, bending each of them to the same angle and taping them together with ½-width tape, to form the basic structure and a handle to the bouquet. Next, add the three stems of eucalyptus in between the palm.

3 Start to tape in the phaius orchids, using the largest one to form the focal point. (Remember this flower should be higher in the bouquet than any of the others.) Position each of the orchids so that they are all facing different directions, as there is nothing worse than having all their faces pointing straight ahead.

4 Add the arum lilies, curving their stems to form an attractive shape to the bouquet. You need to use three flowers at the base of the bouquet and two at the top – forming a lazy 's' shape.

5 Finally fill in the gaps with the single and trailing ivy leaves. Neaten the handle of the bouquet using full width tape.

6 This is quite a large bouquet to use on a cake, therefore use a crystal effect plastic pillar to hold it in position, as the normal sized posy pick is too small.

7 Make the small spray in a similar way to the large bouquet, but form into a crescent, to fit in with the shape of the cake.

PHAIUS ORCHID

The phaius orchid (*Phaius tankervilleae*) was one of the earliest tropical orchids brought back from China to feature in British collections. They can also be found in tropical Asia and Australia, growing in swampy areas. I bought this orchid as a cut flower (which is probably a hybrid form) from a well known department store; it was reduced in price and looking very sorry for itself – but it still cost me £8! Although this orchid is not generally used in bridal work, I thought its unusual colour combination made it a useful flower as this type of colour has been a very popular colour scheme with brides recently: it would work very well with the rose called Leonardis which has a similar colouring.

COLUMN

1 Tape over a short length of 20-gauge wire with ¼-width white floristry tape. Form a small ball of white flower paste into a teardrop shape. Moisten the end of the covered wire with egg white and insert into the fine end of the teardrop, so that the wire is inserted into at least half the length. Using the rounded end of a small celstick, hollow out the upper part of the column, pinching the back of the column to form a subtle ridge. To form the pollinia, add a tiny ball of paste to the front of the column and divide it into two using a scalpel. Allow to dry thoroughly.

THROAT PETAL (LABELLUM)

2 Roll out some white flower paste thinly, leaving the central area slightly thicker. Place the throat petal template on top of the paste and cut out using a sharp scalpel. Vein the upper surface using the amaryllis veiner.

3 Double frill the scalloped edges using the broad end of the dresden tool, then soften the frill using the ceramic silk veining tool or a cocktail stick (toothpick) to frill over the top.

4 Place the petal on to a pad and cup the two outer sections of the petal. Apply a little egg white to the 'V' shape at the base of the petal. Place

MATERIALS

White and pale green
flower paste
18, 20, 24, 28 and 33-gauge wires
White, lemon, primrose, plum,
aubergine, tangerine, skintone,
red, brown, nutkin brown and
vine green petal dust
(blossom tint)
Deep magenta craft dust
Clear alcohol (vodka)

❀

EQUIPMENT

White and nile green
floristry tape
Phaius orchid templates
(see page 154)
Sharp scalpel
Single amaryllis veiner (Asi-es)
All veined lily petal veiner (GI)
Ceramic silk veining tool (HP)
Dried corn on the cob husk

the column on to the left hand side of the petal shape, starting at the base of the column about 1cm (½in) away from the pointed base of the petal. Wrap the right hand side over the top to hide the column. Curl back the edge of the right hand side of the petal. You should have some excess paste at the base of the petal, which needs to be squeezed into a pointed shape and curled underneath the petal to form a spur. Divide this spur into two using a pair of small scissors. Allow to firm up a little before colouring the lip.

COLOURING

5 Dust the base of the petal, starting just above the spur, with a mixture of white, lemon and primrose petal dust. If you are making a mature flower, increase the yellow colour and add some to the lip as well. Dust a small amount carefully deep into the throat. Dust a patch of plum and deep magenta craft dust in a curved shape on the lip. The more mature the flower is, the darker the

colouring will be. If you want to make it very dark, mix a little aubergine with plum and deep magenta, and then dilute with a small amount of clear alcohol. Paint some lines into the throat using a fine paintbrush. If the end result is too extreme, simply dust over the top to blend the lines in with the base colour. Dust the edges of the throat with a tiny amount of colour if desired. Dust a very pale patch of the deep magenta and plum mixture on to the underside of the throat.

PETALS AND SEPALS

6 Roll out some white flower paste thinly using a large celstick, leaving the central part slightly thicker. (You may use a grooved board if you wish.) Place the petal template on top of the paste and cut out the petal using a sharp scalpel.

7 Insert a short length of moistened 28-gauge white wire into the thick ridge of the petal, holding the paste firmly between your finger and thumb to prevent the wire piercing through to the surface of the paste. Vein the petal using the double-sided all veined lily petal veiner, then place on a pad and soften the edges a little using the rounded end of a large celstick. Do not try to frill the paste as this will make the orchid look untidy. Pinch the base and the very tip of the petal between your finger and thumb. Repeat to make a pair of petals, one dorsal and two

lateral sepals. Make sure that you keep them all covered to stop the surface of the paste drying out before you dust them.

COLOURING

8 The main problem with colouring the petals and sepals is that the backs of each of them should be white or creamy white and the upper surface a medium to dark reddish-brown. The only advice I can give is handle with care! Dust each petal/sepal in layers of tangerine, skintone, red and brown petal dust. The edges of each should be much paler. This colouring depends on the maturity of the flower and also the specific variety, and of course your own personal taste. To highlight the veins on the petals/sepals, brush a small amount of nutkin brown across the veins.

9 Allow each of the petals to semi-dry over a very gentle curve before assembling the flower.

10 Tape the narrow petals on to either side of the throat, using ½-width floristry tape. Next, tape in the dorsal and lateral sepals tightly behind the inner petals. While the paste is still pliable, re-shape the flower if needed. The stem from the back of the orchid to the main stem is a creamy colour, fleshy and has ridges on the back. I decided that this would make the flower difficult to arrange into sprays, so I have only

taped over the back a few times to represent the fleshy stem.

BUDS

11 The buds graduate in size down the stem. You will need to make at least seven buds varying between 1–3cm (½ –1¼ in) in length.

12 The small buds are basically teardrop-shaped pieces of white flower paste with a slight curve. Insert a hooked 24-gauge wire into the base of the teardrop. Divide up the surface of the bud using a cage to form the three sepals. The larger buds are made in exactly the same way, but when you have finished dividing the surface into three, you will need to pull out some of the paste in between the two lateral sepals to represent the spur. Divide the spur into two using scissors.

BRACTS

13 You will need to make a bract for every bud and flower on the stem, plus some extras to finish off the stem. These bracts will vary in size a little bit. Roll out some very pale green flower paste, leaving a thick ridge down the centre. Cut out the bract shape using a scalpel and the bract template. (You will find that with practice this shape can be cut out freehand – or you might have a cutter in your workbox that is roughly the same shape.) Insert a moistened 28-gauge wire into the thick ridge so that it supports at least half the length of the bract. Using the length of a packet of 33-gauge wires or a piece of dried corn on the cob husk, vein both sides of the bract. Place on to a pad and soften the edges then, using the broad end of the dresden tool, hollow out the inner part of the bract. Pinch the length of the bract between your fingers and thumb, then allow to dry with a slight curve. Dust lightly with vine green petal dust.

ASSEMBLY

14 Start the orchid spike with a small bud and bract. Tape on to an 18-gauge wire using ½-width nile green floristry tape, leaving part of the bud stem showing. Continue to add the buds and bracts down the stem, keeping them quite close together to begin with, then gradually space them a little more as you start using the larger buds. When you have added all of the buds, tape in the flowers. Leave quite a reasonable length on each of the flower stems, but continue to tape the bracts tightly at the axil between the flower stem and the main stem. On one spike of phaius, there can be up to fifteen flowers (a combination of buds and flowers). Add a couple more lengths of 18-gauge wire to give the stem more bulk and strength. Continue to add the remaining bracts down the stem at intervals.

15 Dust the buds and the main stem with vine green petal dust; the smaller the bud, the greener it will be – but you must keep the colouring very subtle throughout. Bend the stem in shape and then steam to remove the dry dusted appearance. The leaves are very long and not suitable for use on cakes.

GOOD-LUCK PALM

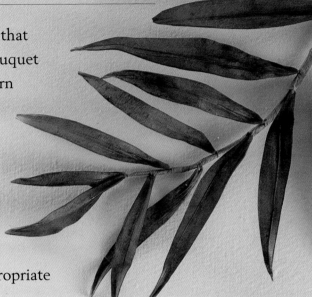

Palms provide a very bold foliage that instantly give an arrangement or bouquet a very exotic, dramatic and modern appearance. Good-Luck palm (*Chamaedrea elegans*), often known as the Parlour palm, originates from Mexico. Although it is not commonly used in bridal work, it is a good size for the flower maker to replicate in sugar and because of its common name it seemed appropriate for wedding cakes.

MATERIALS

Mid-green flower paste
20, 24 and 33-gauge wires
Aubergine, dark green and
holly/ivy petal dust
(blossom tint)
¼ or ½ glaze (see page 151)

EQUIPMENT

Leaf templates (see page 154)
or fresh palm leaves
Long leaf cutters (TT665,666)
Sharp scalpel
Piece of sponge
Nile green floristry tape

TOP LEAVES

1 Roll out some mid-green flower paste, leaving a thick central ridge. Place the template or fresh palm on top of the paste and cut out the shape using a sharp scalpel. Insert a moistened 24-gauge wire into the thick ridge of the leaf. Use the fresh leaves to vein the paste if possible. Alternatively, press the length of a packet of 33-gauge wire on to the paste. Pinch the tips of the leaf, then place on a piece of sponge to firm up.

2 Repeat this process until you have cut out enough leaves to make a complete piece. Some of the leaf sizes can be cut out using the long leaf cutters, but this won't make all of the sizes.

COLOURING

3 Dust the edges of each leaf with aubergine and then over-dust heavily with dark green and holly/ivy petal dust. Allow to dry. Dip into either a ¼ or ½ glaze, depending on your own taste, shake off excess and leave to dry.

ASSEMBLY

4 Tape the leaves on to a 20-gauge wire, alternating them from side to side. Add extra wire to support the weight and to add length to the palm. Dust the main stem with the holly/ivy and dark green petal dust and then bend the whole stem into shape using pliers.

NOTE

As these leaves are very fragile, make sure the wire is inserted into a good length of each leaf. Another method that is very useful for long leaves is to roll out a long piece of paste thinly on to a grooved board. Moisten the wire and lie it on the paste where the groove is to sandwich the wire and then fold over the excess paste, re-roll and cut out as normal. With this method, the wire will be running the whole length of the leaf.

It is also a very useful method for bluebell, daffodil and orchid leaves, and also useful for very reflexed lily petals.

American-style Gerbera Wedding Cake

Here, a very unusual combination of pink gerberas, bells of Ireland and red ink plant have been used in two informal sprays on a pink American-style tiered cake to create an attractive, bold and fun alternative wedding cake design.

MATERIALS

15cm (6 in), 20cm (8 in) and 25cm (10 in) oval cakes
Apricot glaze
2.5kg (4¾lb) almond paste (marzipan)
Clear alcohol (kirsch, cointreau or vodka)
3kg (5½lb) pale pink sugarpaste
Picot edge dusky pink ribbon
Pale cream royal icing

EQUIPMENT

15cm (6 in) and 20cm (8 in) thin oval boards

38cm (15 in) oval cake board
Sugarpaste smoothers
No. 42 piping tube (tip)
1 crystal pillar (cut down to size)

FLOWERS

For the large spray
3 gerberas, one larger than the others (see page 28)
3 stems of bells of Ireland (see page 89)
3 stems of red ink plant and foliage (see page 26)
3 stems of eucalyptus (see page 120)

For the small spray
1 gerbera
½ stem of bells of Ireland
2 stems of red ink plant and foliage
2 stems of eucalyptus

PREPARATION

1 Position the two smaller cakes on to the thin boards of the same size. Brush all the cakes with apricot glaze and cover with almond paste. Cover the largest tier without a board. Allow to dry overnight. Moisten the almond paste with clear alcohol and cover with pale pink sugarpaste (the thin cake boards will be hidden).

2 Cover the large cake board with pale pink sugarpaste and position the large cake on top. Use sugarpaste smoothers to neaten the join between the base of the cake and the board. Place the other two tiers on top of the base tier, again make sure that you have a neat join between each of the cakes.

3 Using pale cream coloured royal icing and a piping bag fitted with a no. 42 piping tube, pipe a shell border around the base of each of the cakes.

ASSEMBLY

4 Glue the pink ribbon to the large cake board edges. Cut a crystal pillar down to the depth of the middle tier. Wire up the flowers, berries and foliage into a spray (see page 25) and insert into the pillar. Insert the arrangement into the cake before the surface of the paste has dried. Wire up the smaller spray and position next to the base tier to form a balanced design.

NOTE

This type of stacked cake can be very heavy to transport. The cakes can be transported separately, then assembled and piped at the venue.

GERBERA TABLE ARRANGEMENT

This arrangement has been designed as a piece to decorate the top table at a wedding alongside the wedding cake; perhaps two arrangements could be made, one to sit at either end of the table. This would probably only be suitable for a close family wedding, as the flowers used are very time-consuming to make. Another idea is to use the flowers from the wedding cake, re-constructed into this arrangement, to keep as a memento of the wedding day.

FLOWERS

5 stems of red ink plant, with foliage
(see page 26)
3 stems of bells of Ireland
(see page 89)
3 gerberas, one larger than the others
(see page 28)

EQUIPMENT

18-gauge wires
Florists' staysoft
Small black spherical vase
Pliers
Wire cutters

PREPARATION

1 First strengthen any of the flowers that need extra support by taping an 18-gauge wire alongside the flower stem. Place a clump of staysoft into the vase, pressing it firmly down to make sure that it is secure and also that the weight is even to support the arrangement.

ASSEMBLY

2 Start by arranging the stems of red ink plant in the staysoft to form the basic outline and height of the arrangement. (The height should be at least one and a half times the height of the vase.) Add the three stems of bells of Ireland, following the curves of the red ink plant.

3 Place the largest gerbera at the centre of the arrangement to form the focal point. Place the two gerberas one at either side of the large flower to form a line. At this stage it is best to stand back and look at the arrangement and perhaps add extra foliage, like the eucalyptus used on the cake, if required.

RED INK PLANT OR VIRGINIAN POKEWEED

The berries of this perennial climbing herb make a striking addition to arrangements and bouquets. Although in its native America the red ink plant (*Phytolacca Americana*) is considered a weed or wild flower, it can be grown in gardens in the British Isles. The plant is poisonous, but despite this it has been used in the past to colour food and wines, and as a substitute for red ink. The berries start to form during the summer months and progressively turn into rich red-purple berries that have such a dark hue that they look black when fully ripened. They are available from florists from the end of July through to October.

MATERIALS

Pale green and ruby flower paste
18, 24, 26 and 30-gauge wires
Spring green, deep purple, black, moss green, dark green and aubergine petal dust (blossom tint)
Deep magenta craft dust
Full and ½ glaze (see page 151)

EQUIPMENT

Tiny Zimbabwean calyx cutter or small blossom cutter
Physalis leaf veiners (GI)
White and nile green floristry tape

BERRIES

1 Cut several short lengths of 30-gauge wire. Make a hook in the end of each of the wires. Roll small balls of pale green flower paste, graduating the size a little. Flatten the balls. Moisten the hooked wire and pull through the centre of each berry, so that the hook is embedded.

2 Using a sharp scalpel, mark deep striations, radiating them from the centre of the berry. Repeat the

26

process using the ruby coloured flower paste, but this time you will need to make the berries larger.

Calyx

3 The calyx is optional. You can either roll out some ruby paste, cut out the calyx using the cutter and stick it on the back. Or you can simply snip five sepals on the back of each berry with a small pair of sharp scissors.

Leaves

4 Roll out some pale green flower paste on to a grooved board. Cut out the leaf shape free-hand or make a template and cut out with a sharp scalpel.

5 Insert either a 26-gauge or 24-gauge wire depending on the size of the leaf. Vein the leaf using the physalis leaf veiner. Place on a pad and soften the edges using the rounded end of a large celstick. Pinch the whole length of the leaf from behind to emphasize the central vein and to give some shape to the leaf. Pinch the tips a little more into shape. Allow to dry on a slight curve until they are at the leather hard stage before dusting. Tape over each of the stems with ½-width nile green tape.

Colouring and Assembly

6 Tape over each of the berry stems with ¼-width floristry tape. Tape the berries on to a 24-gauge wire to begin with, starting with the small green berries and graduating in size through to the ruby berries to form the fruit racemes. To thicken the stems as you work further down the fruit cluster, add a few more lengths of 24-gauge wire.

7 Dust the main stem and the short stems with deep magenta craft dust. Dust the small berries with spring green petal dust. Add a touch of deep magenta to some of the larger green berries and then dust the ruby berries to a bright pink. Finally, over-dust the large and medium sized berries with deep purple and lots of black. Dip the whole stem into full glaze, shake off the excess and leave to dry.

8 Dust the leaves with spring green, then moss, and a touch of dark green. Dust the edges with a mixture of deep magenta and aubergine. Brush some of this mixture into the central vein at the base of the leaf, tapering off towards the tip. Dip into a ½ glaze, shake off the excess and leave to dry.

9 To make a long trailing stem, tape the leaves, starting with a small one, on to an 18-gauge wire. Continue to tape in the leaves, graduating in size down the stem. Add a fruit raceme and tape in a leaf at the axil.

GERBERA

The ancestors of these cheerful cultivated daisies were native to South Africa – mainly the Transvaal and Cape Province, hence its common name the Transvaal daisy. The gerbera flowers (*Gerbera jamesonii*) can be single or double varieties and some of the newer cultivars have fringed petals. The spectacular colour range includes white, pink, red, yellow, orange and purple. Some gerberas have black eyes and others have green. When they are bought as a cut flower, they are sold without their leaves.

MATERIALS

18, 30 and 33-gauge white wires
White or pink, ruby and
mid-holly/ivy flower paste
Small seed-head stamens
Aubergine, plum, dark green
and holly/ivy petal dust
(blossom tint)
Mimosa sugartex

EQUIPMENT

Sharp scalpel
Cymbidium orchid sepal cutters
(TT20,23) or narrow daisy petal
cutters (TT612,613,614)
Nile green floristry tape

CENTRE

1 Bend an 'L'-shaped hook in the end of an 18-gauge wire. Hold the hook halfway down with pliers and curl it back inside itself to form a coil. Bend the whole coil over so that it is at right angles to the wire and forms a ski-stick shape. Roll a ball of white or pink flower paste, moisten the hook on the wire and insert the hook into the ball. Flatten the top of the ball and pinch some of the paste down on to the wire.

2 Using a small pair of sharp curved scissors, snip around the centre to form lots of tiny hairs. Indent the centre using the rounded end of a celstick. Allow to dry.

3 Roll out a length of ruby flower paste quite thinly. Cut out a long rectangular shape using a sharp scalpel. Next, make lots of narrow cuts along one side of the rectangle so that it looks like a comb. Soften the edges a little by pressing each of the sections with the broad end of the dresden tool. Cut the tips off several seed-head stamens and cut the lengths to form lots of shorter strands. Moisten each of the strands with a little egg white. Attach along the cut side of the paste so that part of each of the stamens extends beyond the edge of the paste.

4 Moisten the base of the rect-angle and wrap around the dried centre, overlapping the paste if necessary. Repeat this process three or four times, until the centre is large enough. Trim the stamens if they are a little too long. Allow to dry.

5 Dust the first part of the centre with aubergine petal dust, so that it is very dark. If the colour is not strong enough, steam and re-dust. Dust the outer parts of the centre with the colour of the finished flower. Paint the tips of the stamens with fresh egg white and dip them into some mimosa sugartex. Dry.

PETALS

6 The cutters used for this flower can either be the cymbidium orchid sepal cutters or narrow daisy petal cutters. Whichever you decide to use, they will need to be squashed into the correct shape. The cymbid-ium orchid cutters will need to be made narrower and the daisy petal cutters will need to be pulled out slightly to make them broader.

7 Roll out ruby flower paste, leaving a thick ridge down the centre. Cut out a petal using either of the cutters. Insert a moistened 30-gauge or 33-gauge wire, depending on the petal size you are working with.

8 Place the petal on a pad and soften the edges (do not frill). Hollow out the back of the petal using either the celstick or the broad end of the dresden tool. Turn the petal over and, using the fine end of the dresden tool, draw down a series of fine veins from the base to the tip of the petal. Pinch the base and the tip of the petal, then place to one side to firm up a little.

9 You will need to make a lot of petals to complete a flower – this will depend on how large your finished centre is and also if you are planning to make a double variety, in which case you will have to make a lot of small petals as well. I find it easier not to count the petals when I am making this type of flower. Do not allow the petals to dry totally before you assemble the flower. If they are drying out too quickly, cover them with a plastic bag to stop them being exposed to the air.

COLOURING AND ASSEMBLY

10 Dust each of the petals with your chosen colour. The underside of each of the petals should be much paler – I usually fade the colour out towards the tips on the upper side.

11 Tape the petals around the stamen centre using ½-width nile green tape, starting with the smaller petals (if using) and gradually adding the larger petals. Leave a little of the wire showing underneath the centre as this helps to give the flower more movement and longer petals.

12 Thicken the stem with the addition of a couple more 18-gauge wires and strips of absorbent kitchen paper wrapped around the stem. Tape over and rub the stem with the sides of a pair of scissors to smooth the tape out.

CALYX

13 Roll a ball of pale green flower paste into a cone shape, then hollow out the broad end using the rounded end of a celstick. Moisten the centre and thread on to the back of the flower. Remove any excess. The calyx is made up from lots of separate sepals. Roll numerous pointed strands of green paste. Flatten and vein the centre. Attach them over the base of the calyx so that they completely cover it. Pinch each of the sepals as you attach them to create a slight ridge on each one. Dust the calyx and the stem with a touch of dark green and lots of holly/ivy dust.

GERBERA 2

The alternative method used for this gerbera centre is slightly different to the one described on page 28. It is simpler to create and represents another type of gerbera. This method is not to be used for competition work as glue is not allowed to be used at all.

MATERIALS

Pale melon and holly/ivy
flower paste
18 and 30-gauge white wires
White seed-head stamens
Primrose, lemon, moss green,
apricot, dark green and holly/ivy
petal dust (blossom tint)

EQUIPMENT

Hi-tack non-toxic craft glue
Cymbidium orchid sepal cutter
(TT23) or narrow daisy
petal cutter (TT613)
Nile green floristry tape
Glue gun and glue sticks
(optional)

CENTRE

1 Repeat the first part of the centre as described in steps 1 and 2 on page 28. Allow to dry thoroughly.

2 Line up the tips of a complete bunch of small white seed-head stamens and hold them firmly between your finger and thumb. Using a cocktail stick (toothpick), spread some of the non-toxic glue over the length of the stamens on both sides. Blend the glue into the strands to bond them together. (Although it dries fast, this glue will not attach you to the stamens so do not worry.) Place the stamens to one side and allow the glue to set a little – if you allow the glue to dry completely, it will curl and buckle the stamens.

3 Cut the stamens in half, cutting across the length of the stamens. Now you can either glue the stamens with some more hi-tack glue or with some melted glue from a glue gun – I usually use the hi-tack, but you must be sure that the centre is completely dry otherwise you will just end up with a sticky mess. Wrap the stamens around the centre so that they are a little higher. Squeeze the stamens against the dried paste to secure the two materials firmly

together. Allow to dry and then trim away the excess stamens. The finished centre should not be too deep as this will make the flower difficult to assemble.

4 Make the petals as described on page 28 and tape around the stamens.

5 Dust the very centre gently with a mixture of primrose and a touch of lemon petal dust. Mix together some moss green with more primrose petal dust and colour the centre gently. The outer part of the centre and the stamens need to be dusted with the flower colour. The stamens should be slightly darker than the colour of the petals. Add the calyx as on page 29.

NOTE

The gerberas used on the Floral Romance wedding cake on page 146 were made as a set flower, ie unwired petals. To make these flowers, cut out the petals in layers, using first a carnation cutter and then two sizes of sunflower cutter (TT669,673). Soften the petals and vein as described on page 29. Attach in layers, positioning the petals in between the previous layer.

PURE ELEGANCE

A very elegant two-tier off-set wedding cake with beautiful arum lilies, jasmine and
ivy hand-tied bouquets. The delicate brush embroidery design on the sides of the
cakes complements the floral sprays beautifully.

MATERIALS

20cm (8 in) and 30cm (12 in)
kidney-shaped cakes
Apricot glaze
2kg (4lb) almond paste (marzipan)
Clear alcohol (kirsch or vodka)
3kg (6lb) white sugarpaste
White royal icing
Fine aqua ribbon to trim cakes
Broad aqua ribbon to trim boards
Holly/ivy, dark green, primrose and
lemon petal dust (blossom tint)

EQUIPMENT

Sugarpaste smoothers
25cm (10 in) and 38cm (15 in)
oval cake boards
Nos. 1 and 42 piping tubes (tips)
Brush embroidery templates
(see page 155)
Paintbrush
Twisted silver-finish candlestick

FLOWERS

Arum Lily Hand-tied Bouquets
(see page 34)

PREPARATION

1 Brush the cakes with apricot
glaze and cover with almond
paste. Allow to dry overnight.
Moisten the almond paste with clear
alcohol and cover with white sugarpaste, using sugarpaste smoothers to
achieve a good smooth finish. Cover
the cake boards with white sugarpaste. Place the cakes on top, making
sure that they are central and that

there is a neat join between the base
of the cakes and the boards. Allow to
dry for a few days.

2 Using white royal icing and a
piping bag fitted with a no. 42
piping tube, pipe a shell border
around the base of each cake.
Attach a band of fine aqua ribbon
around both of the cakes just above
the shell border.

SIDE DECORATION

3 Trace the arum lily design templates on page 155 on to greaseproof (parchment) paper. Place the pattern on to the side of the cake and scribe the design on to the surface of the cake. Study the design carefully before you start piping – it is very easy to start piping and then realize that one part of the design should be tucked behind the flower that you are working on.

4 Using white royal icing and a piping bag fitted with a no. 1 tube, start piping a substantial line to outline part of a leaf or flower. Using the largest paintbrush that the design will take, moisten with water and brush the icing from the edge to the centre of the flower or central vein of a leaf using very firm strong brush strokes. Repeat to complete the design.

5 With a flower like an arum lily, pipe heavier along the lines that are at the forefront of the flower and again brush to soften the area where the edge joins the main body of the flower. Allow to dry.

6 Paint in the main colour and detail in each piece using petal dust mixed with a small amount of clear alcohol.

ASSEMBLY

7 Attach the broad aqua ribbon to the cake board edges using a non-toxic glue stick.

8 Tape together the two hand-tied bouquets (see page 35) and tie with broad white ribbon. Position on the top of the cakes.

9 Place the twisted candlestick at the back of the base tier and place the smaller cake on top.

NOTE

As arum lilies are a very popular flower for bridal bouquets at Eastertime, this beautiful wedding cake with an arum lily theme makes an ideal choice at this time of year.

Arum Lily Hand-tied Bouquet

This style of bouquet has become very popular with brides over the last few years. The advantage of this type of fresh flower bouquet, rather than the traditional wired bouquet, is that the flowers can be placed straight back into water after the wedding ceremony. The hand-tied bouquet is very easy for the sugarcrafter to copy as long as you have sufficient flowers and foliage to complete the design.

FLOWERS

For the large bouquet
3 trailing stems of Chinese jasmine
(see page 38)
7 arum lilies (see page 36)
1 long stem and two shorter stems
of ivy (see page 114)
3 stems of eucalyptus (see page 120)

For the small bouquet
3 short stems of Chinese jasmine
5 arum lilies
3 stems of ivy
2 stems of trailing ivy
2 stems of eucalyptus

EQUIPMENT

18-gauge wires
Pliers
Wire cutters
Nile green floristry tape
Broad white silk ribbon

PREPARATION

1 First of all, strengthen any of the stems and foliage that may need some extra support, by taping in additional 18-gauge wires, making sure that each of the stems is neatly finished.

ASSEMBLY

2 Tape together at one point, a long trailing stem of jasmine, a small arum lily and a long stem of ivy using ½-width nile green floristry tape. A florist would usually tie the flowers together using raffia, ribbon or string – it is easier for the sugarcrafter to use tape.

3 Next tape in two arum lilies, slightly behind and one either side of the first one, with their points to either side of the bouquet. Tape in a long piece of eucalyptus

underneath the arum lily on the right hand side (when you hold the bouquet to wire it together it will be on the left hand side). Again tape all of these pieces at one point.

4 Continue to add the arum lilies, alternating them from side to side in the bouquet. One of the larger flowers should be positioned a little more centrally than the others to form the focal point. As you work down the bouquet, continue to add jasmine stems, eucalyptus and ivy. When the bouquet has been completed, tape over the area where the last flowers join to neaten the finish. Trim the stems and then tie a silk ribbon into a bow with long trails to hide the floristry tape.

5 The smaller spray on the top of the cake is made in the same way as for the larger bouquet, creating a little more of a curve and some height at the top of the spray.

ARUM LILY

To be correct this is not an arum or a lily, but it is commonly known as an Arum or Calla lily (*Zantedeschia*) by florists. They originate from Africa and have for a long time, since 1687, been cultivated in Europe. There are many varieties covering a colour range of white, yellow, pink, green, red, burgundy and almost black. The white varieties are most commonly used in bridal work, often thought to symbolize purity. My favourite forms have large spathes coloured with strong green streaks. Arum lilies, whatever the colour, give a bridal bouquet a very strong, modern, uncluttered appearance. The flower shown here is a copy of a medium sized creamy coloured flower that has a dark burgundy eye at the base of the spathe.

SPADIX

1 Tape over a length of 18-gauge wire with ½-width nile green floristry tape, then moisten the end with a small amount of egg white. Roll a piece of white flower paste into a medium sized ball and insert the wire into it. Work the paste firmly and quickly between your fingers and thumb to cover about 4.5cm (1¾in) of the wire. Smooth the shape down between the palms of your hands, then remove any excess paste from the base. Attach another piece of paste at the base of the spadix to give the base of the flower more padding.

MATERIALS

White or pale bitter lemon and mid-green flower paste
18 and 20-gauge wires
Aubergine, white, moss green, primrose and dark green petal dust (blossom tint)
Mimosa yellow sugartex
¾ glaze or glaze in an aerosol can (see page 151)

EQUIPMENT

Nile green floristry tape
Arum lily templates
(see page 155)
Extra large amaryllis veiner (GI)
Lords and ladies leaf cutter
(TT604)
Arum lily leaf veiner (GI)

2 While the paste is still fresh, dust over the top of the spadix with aubergine petal dust. (This is only if you are trying to create this specific variety of arum lily. If you are making the more common white variety, dust with lemon petal dust.) Moisten

the surface of the spadix with fresh egg white and then roll in the mimosa yellow sugartex. Allow to dry.

SPATHE

3 Roll out some white or pale bitter lemon flower paste; not too finely as this is quite a fleshy flower. Place the arum lily template on top of the paste and cut around using a sharp scalpel. Place the spathe into the double-sided amaryllis veiner and press the two sides together firmly. Remove the paste from the veiner, place on a pad and soften the edges using a large celstick.

4 Using the fine end of a dresden tool, draw down a few central veins on the upper side of the spathe.

5 While the paste is still fresh, dust a patch of aubergine petal dust on to the upper surface as pictured. (As before, this will depend on the variety you are making – the more common white form does not have this colouring at the base.) Moisten the base of the spathe and place the spadix on either the left or the right hand side of the spathe. (This will depend on the variety and sometimes you can have two flowers of the same variety that wrap in opposite directions.) Gently roll the two together, being very careful not to get pollen on the surface of the spathe. Curl the edges back a little, especially the long edge that over-laps. Pinch the tip of the spathe to form a fine point. If you are working on a very large flower, it is best to hang the flower upside down until the paste is firm enough to re-arrange. Remember, in a spray you will need to have some flowers wrapped tighter than others. Allow to firm up before dusting.

COLOURING

6 Dust the base and part of the back of the spathe with a mixture of white, primrose and moss green petal dust. Dust the tip carefully with this mixture as well. You can also add a touch to the centre of the flower. Steam gently to give a slightly waxy appearance.

7 To thicken the stem, cut some absorbent kitchen paper into strips and wrap around the wire, taping over the top with ½-width floristry tape. Dust with a mixture of primrose and a lot of moss green.

LEAVES

8 Tape over a piece of 20-gauge wire with ½-width tape. Repeat this several times leaving 4cm (1½in) untaped, so that the majority of the wire has more bulk.

9 Roll out some mid-green flower paste, leaving a thick ridge down the centre. Cut out a leaf using the lords and ladies leaf cutter. Insert the moistened wire into the thick ridge and place the leaf into the leaf veiner. Press the two sides together firmly. Remove the leaf, place on a pad and soften the edges. Allow to dry slightly before dusting.

COLOURING

10 Dust the leaf with dark green, then moss green. Dust the edges with a touch of aubergine. Allow to dry thoroughly. Glaze using a ¾ glaze, shake off excess and allow to dry. If you wish you can etch away the main and some of the finer veins using a scalpel.

Chinese Jasmine

Chinese jasmine (*Jasminium polyanthum*) is a wonderful filler flower for the sugarcrafter; it is very simple to make and gives a very delicate finish to a spray or bouquet. Used with its slender foliage, trailing stems and groups of flowers and buds, a very unusual, elegant bouquet or arrangement can be made. Try using this plant as the main feature for a winter wedding cake. It makes the ideal starting flower for the inexperienced flower-maker.

MATERIALS

White and mid-holly/ivy
flower paste
24, 28, 30 and 33-gauge
white wires
Fine stamens (optional)
Moss, dark green, plum, pink and
holly/ivy petal dust
(blossom tint)
¼ glaze (see page 151)

EQUIPMENT

Small stephanotis cutter (TT568)
Simple leaf cutters (optional)
Nile green floristry tape

Buds

1 I tend to use many more buds than flowers, as they have a softer, prettier appearance, and more importantly, they are quicker to make! Form a tiny ball of white flower paste into a cone shape, and insert a dry 33-gauge wire into the broad end. (There is no need to use egg white with such a small piece.) Hold the base of the bud between your finger and thumb, then gradually thin down the bud using a rubbing motion. Try to keep the tip of the bud very pointed.

Flower

2 Form a small ball of white flower paste into a teardrop shape. Pinch out the broad end between your fingers and thumbs to form a pedestal. Place the shape down on a board and roll out the paste finely using a small celstick. Place the stephanotis cutter over the thick part of the pedestal and cut out the flower. Rub your thumb over the cutter before removing the flower to make sure you have a clean cut to the edges of the petals.

3 Place the flower on a pad and, using the rounded end of the small celstick, soften the back of each petal, working half on the paste and half on the pad. Using the pointed end of the tool, open up the throat of the flower. Moisten the end of a 28-gauge wire and pull it through the flower, until the end is just hidden.

4 If you wish you may insert a fine stamen in the throat of the flower. Move the petals around a little to add some movement. The flower has such a very fine calyx that it is unnecessary to add one for general work; if anything, mix a little moss and dark green petal dust and dust at the base of each flower.

Leaves

5 The leaves grow in groups of five, seven or nine, and the top leaf is always larger than the others. I use a quick method for these leaves when they are needed for wedding cakes, as you will need to make quite a few to make an impact. (In my last book I made the leaves using squashed simple leaf cutters, which gives a good effect but takes too long.)

6 Form a teardrop-shaped piece of mid green flower paste and insert a moistened 30 or 33-gauge wire. Place the teardrop on to the board and, using the flat side of any rubber veiner, flatten the leaf to make it finer and form the leaf shape. (This will take a little practice before you achieve the correct shape.)

7 Soften the edges of the leaf using a small celstick, then pinch the leaf firmly with your finger and thumb to form a central vein and make the leaf look more natural. Make lots of leaves to complete a full stem. Allow to firm a little before dusting.

Colouring and Assembly

8 Group the buds and flowers into mixed clusters, taping them together with ¼ width green floristry tape.

9 Dust the upper surfaces of the buds with plum or pink petal dust. The flowers have less colour on them, again only on the upper surface (it tends to be where they are exposed to the light). Dust a patch of moss and dark green at the base of the flowers and buds.

10 Tape together the leaves using ¼-width tape again, starting with the large one and then taping the others in pairs down the stem. Dust the upper surfaces heavily with dark green and then over-dust with moss or holly/ivy. Dip into a ¼ glaze, shake off the excess and leave to dry.

11 To form a climbing stem, tape over a 24-gauge wire with ½-width tape, and then tape the leaves on to it so that you have two groups coming out at either side of the stem. The flowers and buds always appear out of these leaf axils. Continue to build up the stem until it is the length you need.

MAGICAL

This exquisite three-tier wedding cake, with its masses of delicate sweet pea flowers, trailing stems and entwining tendrils, would delight any bride who wants a magical, almost fairytale-style wedding reception. The actual cake has been kept very simple in form, with only some abstract bumble bees and delicate shading to break up the surface.

MATERIALS

20cm (8 in), 25cm (10 in) and 30cm (12 in) elliptical-shaped cakes
Apricot glaze
3kg (6lb) almond paste (marzipan)
Clear alcohol (kirsch or vodka)
5kg (10lb) white sugarpaste
Fine pale pink ribbon to trim cakes
Lilac ribbon to trim board
Small amount flower paste
Plum, deep purple, pearl white and white petal dust (blossom tint)

EQUIPMENT

20cm (8 in), 25cm (10 in) and 40cm (16 in) elliptical-shaped cake boards
Sugarpaste smoothers
2 long crystal pillars
2 posy picks
Pliers
Wire cutters
Bumble bee cutter (HH)

FLOWERS

18 stems of sweet peas (see page 46)
Numerous stems of sweet pea foliage with tendrils

PREPARATION

1 Attach the two smaller cakes to cake boards of the same sizes with a little softened sugarpaste. Brush the three cakes with apricot glaze and cover with almond paste. Allow to dry overnight. Brush the cakes with clear alcohol and cover with white sugarpaste, then neaten with sugarpaste smoothers.

2 Cover the large cake board with white sugarpaste and transfer the large cake on top.

3 Attach a band of fine pink ribbon around the base of each of the cakes. Glue the lilac ribbon to the base cake board using a non-toxic glue stick.

ASSEMBLY

4 Place the middle tier, off set, on top of the base tier. Insert the two crystal pillars into the back of the middle tier. Position the top tier on top of the middle tier and rest it against the two pillars.

5 Arrange the sweet peas and foliage into the crystal pillars behind the top tier, trailing them over the top of the small cake and then down over the middle tier. Insert a couple of posy picks into the bottom tier and arrange the remaining sweet peas into them. Try to make the arrangements as wild and informal as possible.

6 Cut out several small bumble bees from flower paste using the bumble bee cutter. Stick in position using a little clear alcohol. Dust with plum and deep purple, diluted with pearl white and white petal dust. Shade the edges of the cake using a pale mixture of the petal dust.

Sweet Pea Candlestick and Napkin Ring

This elegant candle arrangement harmonizes beautifully with the Magical wedding cake: perhaps several arrangements could be made to decorate the wedding couple's and guests' tables. The pretty napkin ring decoration could also be used to carry the sweet pea fairytale theme throughout the reception.

FLOWERS FOR THE CANDLE ARRANGEMENT

1 stem of purple sweet peas
(see page 46)
1 stem of pale pink sweet peas
1 stem of dark pink sweet peas
1 stem of sweet pea foliage
with tendrils
3 stems of trailing Chinese jasmine
(see page 38)

FLOWERS FOR THE NAPKIN RING

1 stem of purple sweet peas
1 stem of sweet pea foliage

EQUIPMENT

1 beeswax candle
1 candlestick
24-gauge wire
Nile green floristry tape
Pliers
1 napkin ring
1 napkin

CANDLE ARRANGEMENT

1 Position the candle on to the candlestick. Tape over several lengths of 24-gauge wire using ½-width nile green floristry tape.

2 Place the sweet pea foliage on to the candlestick and wrap the 24-gauge wire around both the stem and the stick. In turn, add the sweet pea flowers and foliage and jasmine, and fasten each with the 24-gauge wire. Bend the various pieces around so that they form an interesting shape around the candlestick. Be careful not to let the sugar flowers get too close to the flame!

NAPKIN RING

1 Fold the napkin into a rectangle and then roll it into a cylindrical shape. Thread into the napkin ring.

2 Place the napkin and ring on to the plate, alongside the cutlery, and then attractively decorate with the sweet peas.

Sweet Pea Garland Headdress

This garland is not intended as a practical suggestion – you can imagine what would happen if it rained! This is purely a practice piece for the sugarcrafter, although there is nothing to stop a bride wearing or carrying sugar flowers if she chooses to do so. At sugarcraft exhibitions there is a trend at the moment to include a headdress in both the competition classes and on branch tables. On one occasion, I produced a garland similar to this one, but using roses and agapanthus instead of sweet peas, and displayed it as part of the wedding cake design!

FLOWERS

10 stems of sweet peas (see page 46)
Lots of sweet pea foliage,
with tendrils
20 stems of lily-of-the-valley
(see page 54)

EQUIPMENT

1 glass head
18-gauge wires
Nile green floristry tape
Fine pliers
Wire cutters
Broad gold chiffon ribbon
A length of white chiffon

PREPARATION

1 Measure the circumference of the head. Make the basic frame on which the headdress will be built, using 18-gauge wires. The final length of the headdress should be 4cm (1½in) longer than the circumference of the head. Tape several lengths of wire together using ½-width nile green floristry tape, overlapping some of the wire in order to form a circle.

ASSEMBLY

2 Tape the sweet pea leaves and tendrils on to the frame at intervals using full-width tape. Next, tape in the lily-of-the-valley stems so that some of the stems point upwards and some downwards.

3 Carefully entwine the sweet pea stems around the frame to secure them into place. Continue to add sweet peas to bulk out the headdress, keeping the circle balanced.

4 Finally, add extra foliage and lily-of-the-valley to fill in any gaps. Tie a bow with trails at the back of the headdress. Arrange a length of white chiffon over the head. Place the garland on to the head and relax the flowers a little if required.

Sweet Pea

Sweet peas have to be one of the best loved flowers, with their instantly recognizable butterfly winged flowers, structured stems and clinging fine tendrils. They are usually taught as a beginner's flower. Here I have turned the traditional method for sweet peas on its head by wiring each of the petals which makes a much more realistic and less fragile flower. Although sweet peas can be used with other flowers, they tend to speak for themselves and so look best when used by themselves with their own foliage and wonderful tendrils. The sweet peas that I have copied have quite large, frilly petals and were based on a florist's cut flower; home grown sweet peas tend to have smaller flowers, shorter stems and much, much more scent. They were a joy to make!

MATERIALS

White and mid-green flower paste
20, 24, 28 and 30-gauge wires
Primrose, spring green, white,
moss green, dark green, plum and
deep purple petal dust
(blossom tint)
¼ glaze (see page 151)

❀

EQUIPMENT

Scalpel
Rose petal cutters
(TT278,279,280)
Nile green floristry tape
Small rose calyx cutter (R13a)
Sweet pea cutters or templates
(see page 156)
Ceramic silk veining tool (HP)
Fine pliers
Fresh sweet pea foliage
or peony veiners

CENTRAL PETALS OR 'KEEL'

1 There are actually two petals fused together at the base that contain the stamens. This section is known as the 'keel'. In the past I have cut out petals to form this section, but in this version I create the keel as a solid piece, as it is quicker; also when the flower is assembled there is very little difference between the two. Roll a ball of white flower paste into a teardrop shape with a slight point at the rounded end as well. Flatten the shape with your fingers to form a pasty shape. Moisten a hooked 24-gauge wire and insert into the base of the shape. Pinch a sharp angle to the edge of the rounded part.

2 Using a sharp scalpel, indent and open up the straight edge to represent the opening for the stamens. Curve the straight edge back a little. You will need to make a keel for each of the flowers and buds.

BUDS

3 The keel for some of the smaller buds should obviously be smaller than those for the flowers. Roll out some white flower paste thinly and cut out two rose petal shapes using the cutters. Using a sharp scalpel, cut out a very narrow, deep 'V' shape from one of the petals. Frill the edges using the ceramic tool. Moisten the base of the petal and attach to the flat side of the keel.

4 Frill the second rose petal, draw down a central vein and stick on top of the split petal. Pinch the whole piece together at the base to secure and then curl back the outer petal a little.

CALYX

5 Form a ball of mid-green flower paste into a teardrop shape, then pinch out the base to form a small pedestal shape. Place the shape, flat side down on to the board and thin out the paste using a small celstick. Cut out the calyx using the small rose calyx cutter. Elongate each of the sepals, by rolling them with the celstick. Place the calyx on a pad, flat side down, and hollow out the centre of each of the sepals using the broad end of the dresden tool. Open up the centre of the calyx using the pointed end of a celstick. Moisten the centre and thread on to the back of the flower. Try to position two of the sepals on to the back of the outer petal shape. Pinch and curl the tips of the calyx back slightly.

6 Tape over the stem with ½-width nile green tape. To bend the stem, hold the point of the stem directly behind the calyx using fine pliers. Hold the wire at the end and bend this end over in a long swoop. This gives a neat curve to the stem.

FLOWER (WING PETALS)

7 Roll out a piece of white flower paste, leaving a slightly thicker area down the centre (this should measure only half the length of the wing petal and be very subtle). Cut out a wing petal using either the wing petal cutter or the template

from page 156 and a sharp scalpel.

8 Hook and moisten the end of a 30-gauge wire and insert it into the base of the thick area on the petal. Pinch the base to secure the petal.

9 Place the petal, ridge side up, back on to the board. Vein the surface of the paste using the silk veining tool, keeping the point of the tool to the point of the petal, working in a fan formation. You might also need to soften the frill, by rolling over with a cocktail stick (toothpick). Repeat the process so that you have left and right wing petals. Allow them to firm up a little – it does not matter about drying them on too much of a curve as they should be taped on to the keel well before they have had a chance to

dry. They can be manipulated into the correct shape at a later stage.

STANDARD PETAL

10 Roll out some more paste, again leaving a thick ridge. Cut out the petal using either a cutter or the template for the standard petal on page 156. Insert a hooked 28-gauge white wire at the base of the petal (do not insert the wire too far).

11 Vein the petal and frill using the silk veining tool again. Place the petal on a pad and draw down a central vein on the upper side of the petal. Turn the petal over and, using the broad end of the dresden tool, hollow out two small indents, one either side of the central vein at the base of the petal (this in

turn should create two raised areas on the front of the petal). Allow to firm up with a gentle curl.

ASSEMBLY AND COLOURING

12 Tape the two wing petals on to either side of the keel, using ¼-width nile green floristry tape. The long side of each petal should be uppermost. As the petals are still wet, you can now re-shape them to give a really good natural appearance.

13 Tape the standard petal tightly on to the back of the flower. Squeeze the base of the petals together to form a tight, neat join, then curl the standard petal back a little; the more mature the flower is, the further back this petal will be.

Allow to dry to the leather hard stage before dusting.

14 Mix a small amount of the primrose and spring green together with a touch of white petal dust. Dust the tip of the keel gently and in at the base of each of the petals. Dust the petals with your chosen colour, starting at the edge and working down towards the base. I used plum and white for the pale pink flowers, plum and a touch of deep purple for the darker pink flowers and deep purple mixed with a touch of plum dust for the purple flowers. Dust the back of the standard petals with a flush of the green mixture. Attach the calyx as for the bud. Dust the calyx with spring and moss green with a touch of white petal dust. Bend the stem as for the bud, but not so extreme.

LEAVES

15 When you buy sweet peas from the flower shop as a cut flower, they don't have their foliage with them. I have included them here, because I feel they set off the flowers to their best. Roll some mid-green flower paste, leaving a ridge down the centre (or use a grooved board). Place a leaf template or fresh leaf on top of the flower paste and cut out the leaf shape – with prac-

tice and for speed, you can cut these leaves out free-hand. Insert a moistened 28-gauge wire into the thick ridge. Vein preferably with a fresh leaf or with a suitable veiner. (The leaves in this step-by-step have been veined with fresh leaves, but the leaves on the Magical sweet pea cake have been veined using the peony veiner.)

16 The next step depends on the variety of sweet pea you are making, as some have frilly edges and others have flat edges. Frill partially with the broad end of the dresden tool and then over-frill with a cocktail stick (toothpick). Pinch the leaf to emphasize the central vein and then allow to firm up before dusting. You will need to make the leaves in pairs.

17 Dust to various degrees using dark green, white, moss and spring green petal dust. The leaves are not shiny, so you have the option of simply steaming them when they are dry or alternatively dipping them into a ¼ glaze. (The leaves pictured here were steamed and the leaves on the cake were glazed.)

BRACTS

18 At the base of each of the leaf stems, where they join

the main stem, there are two bracts. These are very simple to make. Cut several short lengths of 30-gauge wire. Roll a small teardrop piece of mid-green paste. Insert the dry wire into the broad end of the teardrop and flatten using the smooth side of a rubber veiner (or something similar). Pinch the bract a little and dry.

TENDRILS

19 The tendrils grow from leaf stems (a common mistake is to tape them on to the flower stems). They just add character to the whole display. Use ¼-width nile green tape twisted back on itself to form fine strands. You will need three tendrils to form one group. Tape the three tendrils together on to a 24-gauge wire. Some tendril groups then go on to have another few tendrils below these three.

ASSEMBLY

20 Tape the flowers and buds into the stems with three or four flowers on them. Use a 20-gauge wire to form the main stem and leave a short length of each of the flower stems showing. The actual stems on a sweet pea are ridged – you do not need to worry about that sort of detail for cakes.

LILY-OF-THE-VALLEY WEDDING CAKE

Lily-of-the-valley has long been a traditional flower for bridal bouquets and wedding cakes, so it seemed appropriate to use these flowers on a royal-iced cake to give a formal, elegant design.

MATERIALS

15cm (6 in), 20cm (8 in) and 25cm (10 in) round cakes
Apricot glaze
2.5kg (5lb) almond paste (marzipan)
1.5kg (3lb) pale cream royal icing
Primrose, moss and white petal dust (blossom tint)
A small amount of clear alcohol (kirsch or vodka)
White royal icing (see page 152)
Picot edge cream ribbon to trim boards

EQUIPMENT

20cm (8 in), 25cm (10 in) and 38cm (15 in) round cake boards
Greaseproof (parchment) paper
No.1 and 0 piping tubes (tips)
Thick card
A4 plastic file pocket
Lace and embroidery design templates (see page 155)
Scriber
Crystal candle holder
Small and medium perspex dividers

FLOWERS

40 stems of lily-of-the-valley for the top arrangement (see page 54)
5 lily-of-the-valley leaves
9 stems of ivy (see page 114)
15 stems of lily-of-the-valley for the smaller groups
3 small stems of ivy

PREPARATION

1 Brush the cakes with apricot glaze and cover the tops with almond paste. Cut a long strip of almond paste and cover the sides of the cakes. Allow to dry thoroughly.

2 Coat the tops of the cakes and then the sides with at least three layers of royal icing until a smooth finish is obtained with a sharp, clean top edge. Attach each of the cakes to their boards with a little royal icing and allow to set. Coat the boards several times, then allow to dry.

3 Pipe a fine snail trail around the base of each of the cakes using royal icing and a piping bag fitted with a no. 1 tube. Glue a length of cream ribbon to the board edges.

SIDE DECORATION

4 Trace the heart lace design on page 155 several times on to a piece of tracing paper. Cut a piece of thick card to a size that will slide into an A4 plastic file pocket. Insert the card along with the tracing paper into the pocket so that the design shows through the plastic.

5 Pipe over the lace design using white royal icing and a piping bag fitted with a no. 0 piping tube. Allow to dry.

6 Scribe a fine line on to the cake, either freehand or using a template, to help position the embroidery and lace. Using either a no.1 or 0 tube and white royal icing, pipe the lily-of-the-valley buds and flowers on to the cake. Allow to dry. Paint in the main and flower stems using a mixture of primrose, moss and white petal dust, diluted with a small amount of clear alcohol. Colour some of the smaller buds with this mixture as well. Finer detail can be added using a slightly darker mixture.

7 Attach the lace pieces to the cake with royal icing, piping two dots to hold each piece. In between each piece, pipe another dot. Follow the scribed line up to the top edge of the cake and then follow the edge of the cake until the scribed mark at the other side of the cake is reached.

ASSEMBLY

8 Make three small groups of lily-of-the-valley and tie them together using a stem of ivy. You will need one group of three, one of five and one with seven stems. Attach to the centre of the cake design at the base of each of the cakes.

9 Make a larger group of lily-of-the-valley and trailing ivy stems and insert into the candle holder.

10 Assemble the wedding cake using the perspex dividers instead of pillars. Position the cake top arrangement carefully on top of the small cake.

LILY-OF-THE-VALLEY FAVOURS

Wedding favours can often be very fancy in appearance. If you want to give gifts that are more individual, try decorating small boxes filled with chocolates or sugared almonds with sugar flowers. The box pictured here is pretty but very simple, with only a few stems of lily-of-the-valley tied on to the box with a piece of dark green ribbon. On the opposite page is a variation on a theme. Here the guests may pick up their own almonds at their leisure from a plate decorated with a glass container of lily-of-the-valley.

FLOWERS FOR THE TABLE FAVOURS

40 stems of lily-of-the-valley (see page 54)
5 lily-of-the-valley leaves
9 stems of ivy (see page 114)
15 smaller stems of lily-of-the-valley and extra ivy leaves

EQUIPMENT

Crystal glass candle holder
Fine pliers
Wire cutters
30cm (12 in) round misted glass plate or dish
Good quality white sugared almonds

ASSEMBLY

1 Arrange the 40 stems of lily-of-the-valley, leaves and ivy into the crystal glass candle holder.

2 Place the arrangement on the centre of the glass plate. Empty out the almonds around it.

3 Place the smaller stems of lily-of-the-valley in sprays around the base of the plate at regular intervals.

LILY-OF-THE-VALLEY FAVOURS BOX

Line the favour box with some fine white or pale green tissue paper. Place some sugared almonds inside and wrap the paper over the top. Close the lid.

Tape together three stems of lily-of-the-valley and a short stem of ivy, using ½-width nile green floristry tape. Tie the lily-of-the-valley to the top of the box with dark green ribbon, then tie the ribbon into a bow to secure it in place.

LILY-OF-THE-VALLEY

Lily-of-the-valley (*Convallaria majalis*) flowers during May, but it is available at a price from the florist all year round for use in bridal headdresses and bouquets. There are both single and double forms, and also some with pink flowers! My favourite is the single white flowering variety. They are very useful for softening the edges of bouquets and look wonderful by themselves in tied bunches or small vases.

MATERIALS

24 and 33-gauge white wires
White and mid holly/ivy
flowerpaste
Primrose, moss and dark green
petal dust (blossom tint)
Leaf templates (see page 155)
¼ glaze (see page 151)

❀

EQUIPMENT

Tiny six petal blossom (OP)
or five petal plunger cutter
(PME)
Nile green floristry tape

FLOWERS

There are many methods to make lily-of-the-valley – I have tried most of them and I still prefer this quick method which produces very dainty flowers, fast! I have adapted an original method developed by my friend Tombi. I now use a very small six petal blossom cutter which wasn't available when she made her version. The method is based on an idea that Faberge used to create these wonderful flowers using flakes of mother of pearl attached to pearls to decorate eggs.

1 Cut several lengths of 33-gauge wire into 4cm (1½ inch) lengths. Bend a tiny hook on the end of each piece. Holding several pieces of wire at a time enables you to bend the hooks at a faster rate. I use 10-15 buds and flowers combined to complete a stem. I use any combination of the two as it depends what stage of flowering you are trying to achieve!

2 Roll a small ball of white flower paste. Roll out a small amount of paste thinly and cut out a flower shape. You will find that the paste sticks in the cutter. To remove it,

simply press it against the small ball of paste. Remove the cutter and the two should have formed a bond (you will not need to use any egg white for this.) Using the pointed end of a celstick, hollow out the centre of the flower. Press the sides of the flower against the stick to join the two pieces together securely. Moisten the hook on a wire and thread through the flower, embedding the hook into the sides of it. Repeat as many times to produce approximately 5-7 flowers for each stem.

BUDS

3 Make lots of small balls in grad-uating sizes. Insert a dry hooked wire into each one. Re-shape the balls to make them a definite round shape.

ASSEMBLY

4 Start with a tiny bud and tape on to a 24-gauge wire. Continue to tape in the buds, leaving a small amount of each of their stems showing. Alternate the buds and also use graduating sizes down the stem. Next add the flowers, again leaving a short stem on each. When you have added the last flower, bend each of the buds and flowers down using nipping motions with your pliers. Curve the whole stem.

5 Dust the main, bud and flower stems with a mixture of primrose and moss green petal dust, then dust the buds, gradually making them paler as they get closer to the flowers.

LEAVES

6 The leaves are also used by the florist, mainly because the plant is provided with its leaves and is very expensive. The leaves vary in their tone and depth of green and there are also some with variegated leaves.

7 Roll out a long strip of green paste on to a grooved board. Moisten a 24-gauge wire and lay it

down the centre, over the groove. Pull back the paste above the wire and fold it over the top to sandwich the wire. Re-roll the paste to bond the two sides of paste together. Using the template from page 155, cut out the basic leaf shape using a scalpel. Remove the leaf from the groove and flatten the ridge.

8 Place the leaf back against the board and use a packet of 33-gauge wires to vein the length of the leaf. The veins should follow the curve of the edge of the leaf on both sides.

9 Place the leaf on to a pad and then soften the edges using the rounded end of a large celstick. Pinch the central vein and overlap the two edges at the base of the leaf. Allow the leaf to firm up before colouring.

10 Dust with dark green and moss petal dust. Dip into a ¼ glaze, shake off the excess and allow to dry.

Midsummer Wedding

A very striking colour combination of wild blue cornflowers and formal yellow roses has been used here to create a stunning summer wedding cake. The addition of honeysuckle and sprigs of rosemary help to marry the two very intense colours together.

MATERIALS

15cm (6 in), 23cm (9 in) and
30cm (12 in) round cakes
Apricot glaze
3kg (6lb) almond paste (marzipan)
Clear alcohol (kirsch or vodka)
5kg (10lb) pale egg
yellow sugarpaste
Fine willow green ribbon
to trim cakes
Broad willow green ribbon
to trim boards

EQUIPMENT

23cm (9 in) cake card
23cm (9 in) and 43cm (17 in)
round cake boards
Sugarpaste smoothers
Antique finish candle holder
2 long tapered crystal pillars

FLOWERS

2 Midsummer Bridal Bouquets,
one slightly larger (see page 58)

PREPARATION

1 Brush the cakes with apricot glaze and cover with almond paste. Allow to dry overnight. Attach the 23cm (9 in) cake to the cake card. Moisten the almond paste with alcohol, then cover the cakes and boards separately with pale yellow sugarpaste, using smoothers to obtain a good finish. Position the largest and smallest cakes on the boards, then place the 23cm (9 in) cake on top of the base tier, making sure that you have a neat join.

Attach the fine willow green ribbon around the base of each of the cakes and the broad ribbon around the cake board edges.

2 Make two Midsummer Bridal Bouquets as described on page 58; the spray for the base tier should be slightly larger.

ASSEMBLY

3 Position the candle holder on to the centre of the middle tier of the cake. (Place a thin cake card, the same size as the base of the holder, underneath the holder to separate it from the sugar-paste, if preferred.) Place the top tier on to the candle holder, making sure that the whole display looks balanced.

4 Measure the length of the crystal pillars to the depth and angle at which they are to be inserted into the cakes, then cut them down to size using a hack saw. Wash the pillars in very hot water, dry and insert into the cakes. Position the sprays into the pillars. Using pliers, re-position any of the stems that have moved while being inserted into the cake.

MIDSUMMER BRIDAL BOUQUET

This bouquet adorns the base tier of the Midsummer Wedding cake on page 56. It was intentional to make this bouquet a little on the sparse side – I wanted to create a wild, country-style cake with space for the flowers and foliage to breathe. If a more structured bouquet is required, simply add plenty of trailing ivy stems. The top bouquet is a slightly smaller version of the bouquet described.

FLOWERS

4 stems of honeysuckle flowers
(see page 62)
5 stems of honeysuckle foliage
6 sprigs of rosemary (see page 65)
1 full rose, 3 half roses and
3-4 rosebuds (see page 136)
5 cornflowers and 5 cornflower buds
(see page 60)

EQUIPMENT

18-gauge wire
Nile green floristry tape
Fine pliers
Wire cutters

PREPARATION

1 First of all strengthen any of the flower stems, if necessary, by taping on an additional 18-gauge wire alongside the main stem.

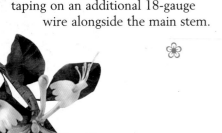

ASSEMBLY

2 Decide how long you want the finished bouquet to be. The first long stem of honeysuckle needs to measure at least two-thirds the total length of the bouquet. Bend the stem to a 90 degree angle. Next add another length of honeysuckle foliage, to form the remaining third of the bouquet. Bend its stem and tape in securely – the basic shape should now be an 'S' shape. Continue to add the remaining honeysuckle foliage and flower stems in the same way, along with the rosemary sprigs to form a complete outline of the bouquet shape.

3 Wire in the largest rose to form the focal point (this should be slightly higher than any of the other flowers in the bouquet). Add the three half roses around the focal flower and then taper off at both ends with one rose bud at the base of the bouquet and two rose buds at the tip.

4 Finally, thread and tape in the cornflowers and buds to complete the bouquet. Neaten the handle by taping over using full width floristry tape.

NOTE

Use a crystal effect pillar instead of a posy pick to hold this bouquet on the cake.

CORNFLOWER

The intense blue of the cornflower (*Centura cyanus*) is very hard to resist. There are some forms that provide white, pink and purple flowers, but it is the blue flowers that I am most fond of. They are very time-consuming to make, but the end result is very satisfying.

MATERIALS

Fine lace-makers' cotton thread
24, 28, 30 and 33-gauge
white wires
Black seed-head stamens
Ultramarine craft dust
White and green flower paste
Deep purple, black, moss green,
white, skintone, dark green and
holly/ivy petal dust
(blossom tint)
Cyclamen liquid food colouring

EQUIPMENT

Nile green floristry tape
Zimbabwean eight-petalled
jasmine cutter

STAMENS

1 Wrap some white thread several times around two fingers to form a loop. Twist the loop into a figure of eight, then bend in half to form a smaller loop. Bend a short length of 28-gauge wire through the centre. Tape over the base of the thread and down on to the wire using ¼-width tape. To make two sets of stamens, bend another short length of wire through the opposite side of the stamens and tape over as before. Cut the thread in half to make two sets.

2 Trim the length of the stamens if they look too long. Tape in some black stamens around the thread centre and trim their seed-head tips

off. Dust the thread with ultramarine craft dust, deep purple and a touch of black petal dust. Using tweezers, bend out the stamens and curl them. The centre of a fresh cornflower is actually much more complicated than this, but this is quite adequate.

FLORETS

3 I have tried several methods for making the florets and have found that by wiring each of them although time-consuming, produces a more realistic and less fragile flower. Form a small ball of white flower paste into a teardrop shape. Pinch out the base of the teardrop to form a pedestal shape. Place the pedestal on to the board, flat side down, and thin out the paste by rolling it with a small celstick. Place the eight-petalled jasmine cutter over the top and cut out the flower. (If you cannot obtain an eight-petalled jasmine cutter, try a six-petalled pointed blossom cutter.) Remove the floret gently from the cutter. Because it is so fine, this cutter has a tendency to pull off a few of the petals from time to time.

4 Place the floret back on to the board and elongate the petals a little using the celstick. Four of the petals at one side need to be elonated a little more than the others.

5 Open up the throat of the floret using the pointed end of a celstick, pressing the sides of the paste against the celstick to thin them out.

6 Place the floret on your finger, with the petals uppermost, and vein each of the petals down the centre with the fine end of the dresden tool. Pinch the tips of the petals and angle some of them back slightly. Bend a hook in the end of a short length of 33-gauge wire and moisten the end. Pull the wire through the centre of the floret, embedding the hook deep into the centre. You will need to make at least eight florets to make a complete flower. (This is based on the wild cornflower rather than a hybrid form which usually has many more florets.)

COLOURING AND ASSEMBLY

7 Dust each of the florets on the inside and the backs with ultramarine craft dust. Add depth to the centre of each one with a touch of deep purple. The more mature the flower is, the paler the blue it will be. Tape eight florets around the stamens, using ¼ -width nile green tape. Cut off the excess wire, leaving only a few, plus the 28-gauge wire

from the stamens. The thick section at the top will be hidden under the calyx. Tape two or three 24-gauge wires on to the main stem to give support.

CALYX

8 Roll a ball of pale green flower paste into a cone shape, then hollow out the broad end using the rounded end of a small celstick. Moisten the centre and thread on to the back of the flower. Thin down the base of the calyx and trim off any excess. To form the scaled effect of the calyx, snip the individual scales using a small pair of curved scissors. Be very careful not to damage the florets as you do this.

9 Dust the calyx with a mixture of moss green and white petal dust. Dust a small amount of skintone petal dust at the top of the calyx at the base of the florets. To define the scales, mix a small amount of cyclamen liquid colouring with a tiny amount of black, then paint in the lines using a fine paintbrush.

BUDS

10 Wire a single floret on to a 24-gauge wire. Squash the floret up to make it look like an opening flower. Dust as for the flower and then add a smaller version of the calyx on the back.

LEAVES

11 Insert a 33-gauge or 30-gauge wire into a small sausage of pale green paste. Work the paste down the wire, forming a slight point at the tip. Place it down on the board and, using the flat side of a veiner (or similar object), flatten the paste to thin it out and form a leaf.

12 The leaves have slight serrations on the edges which can be made by flicking the edge of the leaves with a scalpel. Draw down a central vein and pinch the tip.

13 Dust with a touch of dark green and then over-dust with white and holly/ivy petal dust. Tape on to the bud and flower stems, then dust over the stems using the same colours. Steam the flower heads.

Japanese Honeysuckle

There are over 180 different species of honeysuckle and many garden varieties. This form of honeysuckle has been naturalized in Britain where it flowers between July and September. Japanese honeysuckle (*Lonicera japonica*) is simpler to make as you do not need as many flowers and buds to create an impact compared with the more familiar honeysuckle where the flowers grow in clusters. They are easier and more effective to include in a bridal bouquet because of the trailing slender stems. The flowers can be white at first, becoming yellow later and occasionally tinged with a strong pink.

MATERIALS

Fine or small white
seed-head stamens
20, 26 and 28-gauge white wires
Skintone, lemon, moss green,
primrose, dark green, plum
and aubergine petal dust
(blossom tint)
Pale melon or white and
mid-green flower paste
¼ glaze (see page 151)

EQUIPMENT

Nile green floristry tape
Glue gun and glue sticks
Honeysuckle cutters
(OPHS1,2,3)
Simple leaf cutters (TT225-232)
Rose leaf veiner

Stamens

1 The stamens in the flower are very small 'T' bar shaped anthers – these can be made in sugar, but they are very time-consuming. The following method has become a standard procedure where commercial stamens are used to represent the stamens, and the 'T' bar anthers are forgotten in favour of completing a wedding cake in time! Bend three stamens in half to form six. Pull one of the stamens so that it is a little longer than the others, for the pistil. Glue or tape the stamens on to a 26-gauge wire using ¼-width nile green floristry tape.

2 Dust the tips of the stamens with a mixture of skintone and lemon petal dust. Dust the tip of the pistil with a touch of moss and primrose. Curl the stamens slightly.

Flower

3 Roll a small ball of pale melon flower paste into a long teardrop, then pinch out the base between your fingers and thumbs to form a pedestal. Using a celstick, roll out the base of the pedestal to make it much finer. Cut out the flower shape using the honeysuckle cutter.

4 Elongate the four upper petals by rolling them against the board with a small celstick. Roll the single long petal a little, trying not to elongate it as much as the other four as this will weaken the paste and make the flower too fragile. Pick up the flower and open up the throat using the pointed end of the celstick.

5 Rest the flower on the side of your finger and, using the broad end of a dresden tool, press several times on the central section of the four upper petals to give a slightly hollowed out appearance.

6 Moisten the base of the stamens and thread the wire through the centre of the flower. Thin down the back slightly and then bend it gently into either a lazy 'S' or 'C' shape. Do not mix the two shapes. Curl the long petal and the upper ones back.

7 Each flower has a tiny calyx at the base. This is made by attaching a small ball of paste at the base of the flower. Form the sepals by snipping several times with sharp scissors. Dust with moss green dust.

BUDS

8 Roll a ball of pale melon paste into a cone and insert a moistened 28-gauge wire into the broad end. Thin down the cone shape between your fingers and thumb, then bend it into the same shape as the flower back. Attach a calyx as before. Make the buds in pairs.

LEAVES

9 Roll out some mid-green flower paste on a grooved board. Cut out leaves in pairs of various sizes using the cutters. Insert a moistened 28-gauge wire into the thick ridge. Vein using a rose leaf veiner. Place on a pad and soften the edges. Pinch the back of each leaf from the tip to the base to reinforce the central vein. Dry the leaves on a curve.

10 Dust the leaves with moss and a little dark green. Glaze with a ¼ glaze, shake off excess and allow to dry. Add a touch of plum petal dust at the base, tapering into the central vein (see page 64).

COLOURING AND ASSEMBLY

11 Dust the underside and a little of the base on the upper surface of each bud and flower with a mixture of lemon and primrose. Colour the upper side of the buds and flowers with plum petal dust. The smaller buds should be paler. Dust the tips of the buds with a touch of aubergine petal dust.

12 Tape the buds and flowers into pairs and, if you have a lot of tiny leaves, tape two leaves at the base of each of the pairs.

13 To form a long stem, tape two small leaves on to the end of a 20-gauge wire using ½-width tape. Add the leaves in pairs, graduating the sizes. When the stem is started sufficiently, add the buds. Tape two pairs of buds, one either side of the main stem, and tape in a single leaf on both sides of the join. Graduate the size of the buds and leaves, then introduce the flowers in the same fashion. Bend the stem to shape.

14 Dust the main stem with moss green and over-dust with plum petal dust.

COMMON HONEYSUCKLE

Common honeysuckle (*Lonicera periclymenum*) is the form of honeysuckle that most people are familiar with. It has creamy-white flowers that mature to yellow, and can be tinged with apricot or plum or purple colouring. The flowers and leaves are made like the Japanese honeysuckle, then arranged into clusters.

LEAVES

1 The shape of the foliage depends on the exact variety of honeysuckle you are making; follow the instructions for the leaves on the Japanese honeysuckle (see page 63), inserting the wire into either the pointed or the rounded end as described. Dust and glaze as before.

COLOURING AND ASSEMBLY

2 Tape the buds in clusters of about ten, taping first the small buds together and then adding the larger ones. Add three to five flowers to each cluster.

3 It is easier to colour the flowers and buds at this stage as you can get a better balance of colour to the overall cluster. Dust the underside, then a little at the base of each bud and flower. Dust the upper sides of each bud and flower, starting at the tip with apricot, plum and then a touch of aubergine petal dust.

4 Tape two leaves below each bud and flower cluster, adding a 20-gauge wire if any of the flower clusters need extending.

MATERIALS

Small white seed-head stamens
20, 26 and 28-gauge white wires
Skintone, lemon, moss green, primrose, dark green, apricot, plum and aubergine petal dust (blossom tint)
Melon and mid-green flower paste
¼ glaze (see page 151)

❀

EQUIPMENT

Nile green floristry tape
Honeysuckle cutters (OPHS1,2,3)
Simple leaf cutters (TT225-232)
Rose leaf veiner

5 To form a complete stem, tape the leaves in pairs, starting with two small leaves, on to a 20-gauge wire using ½-width tape. Add a bud cluster, then two leaves at the axil. Add the clusters, then gradually the flower clusters again, adding two leaves where the smaller stem joins the main stem. Dust the stems with moss green and the upper surface of the stems with plum petal dust.

ROSEMARY

Aromatic rosemary (*Rosemarinus officinalis*) is not only used in cooking, it is also popular with florists for use in wedding displays, bouquets and button holes. Traditionally it has been used to represent remembrance. The only problem with making this plant is that you need hundreds of very small narrow leaves to make a visual impact, which is why it is often ignored by the sugarcrafter if requested. If you decide to make rosemary, give yourself plenty of time. During the summer months rosemary produces pretty pale blue flowers, which could also be made if the plant is to be a main feature on a cake or of a design.

MATERIALS

Pale holly/ivy flower paste
22 and 33-gauge white wires
Dark green, holly/ivy, white and skintone petal dust (blossom tint)
Confectioners' glaze

EQUIPMENT

Nile green floristry tape
Small palette
Fine paintbrush
Any medium-sized veiner

1 I mentioned that this form of foliage is very time-consuming to make – that is true! It is also very repetitive and, I am tempted to say, boring. (My only suggestion to solve this problem if you are asked to make rosemary is to rent several good videos to watch as you are making them!) Although it sounds as if I dislike rosemary, I think the finished sugar foliage is wonderful and once I had finished making it for this book, I was very pleased with the end result.

2 Cut several lengths of 33-gauge white wire into fifths or sixths. Insert a moistened wire into a small sausage of pale green flower paste. Work the paste on to the wire and remove any excess length. Using a firm flat object (I usually use the back of a leaf veiner), flatten the paste against the board to form a leaf shape. If you have used too much paste the end result will be too thick and wide; to remedy this, simply trim off the excess paste with a pair of small scissors.

3 Pinch the leaf between your finger and thumb to form a central vein. Repeat the process many times until you have the amount that you need, remembering to graduate the sizes. Allow to dry.

4 Mix together a small amount of confectioners' glaze and green petal dusts in a palette to form a thick paint. Using a paintbrush, give only the upper surface of each leaf one coat. The smaller leaves should be a slightly fresher green to represent the new growth.

5 Tape the leaves in groups of two and three on to a 22-gauge wire until you have the length of stem you need. Dust the backs of the leaves with white petal dust and add patches of skintone on to the stem. When you have finished, breathe a sigh of relief!

FLORAL RHAPSODY

Ranunculus make a wonderful alternative to the ever popular rose as a wedding flower. Here they have been used to create a cake that would be suitable for a small reception. The delicate embroidery complements the sprays of flowers perfectly to form a very fresh and pretty wedding cake design.

MATERIALS

23cm (9 in) heart-shaped cake
Apricot glaze
1kg (2lb) almond paste (marzipan)
Clear alcohol (kirsch or vodka)
1.5kg (3lb) champagne sugarpaste
Ivory royal icing (see page 152)
Fine orange ribbon to trim cake
Green velvet ribbon to trim board
Apricot, tangerine, red, holly/ivy and
primrose petal dust (blossom tint)

EQUIPMENT

32cm (13 in) heart-shaped
cake board
Nos. 0 and 42 piping tubes (tips)
Side design template (page 156)
Nile green floristry tape
2 posy picks

FLOWERS

9 sprigs of rosemary (see page 65)
3 stems of ivy, plus a few extra single
leaves (see page 114)
9 ranunculus (mixed sizes) and
10 ranunculus buds (see page 72)
5 stems of rue (see page 11)

PREPARATION

1 Brush the cake with apricot glaze and cover with almond paste. Allow to dry overnight. Moisten the almond paste with clear alcohol and cover with champagne sugarpaste, using smoothers and the pad method (see page 153) to achieve a smooth finish. Cover the board with champagne sugarpaste and transfer the cake on top. Allow to dry.

2 Pipe a shell border around the base of the cake using a piping bag fitted with a no. 42 piping tube and ivory coloured royal icing. Attach a band of fine orange ribbon slightly above the shell border.

SIDE AND TOP DESIGN

3 The side and top design can be piped directly on to the cake free-hand using a no. 0 piping tube or the design can be scribed on to the surface using the design on page 156 as a template. Once the embroidery has dried, petal dust with an apricot, tangerine and red mixture for the flowers and holly/ivy and primrose for the leaves.

SPRAYS

4 Use the rosemary and ivy to form the basic outline of the semi-crescent spray. Bend the stems at an angle of 90 degrees to create a handle. Tape together using ½-width nile green floristry tape. Cut off any excess wire.

5 Add the ranunculus, using the largest flower to form the focal point of the spray. Next add the buds and then the rue leaves to soften the overall appearance. Add a few extra ivy leaves to add depth to the centre spray.

6 Wire up a small straight spray using a small flower, a couple of buds and some mixed foliage.

7 Attach the green velvet ribbon to the cake board edge. Insert the sprays into posy picks, then into the cake.

NOTE

Inform the person who is to cut the cake that there are two posy picks in the cake.

Floral Rhapsody Table Arrangement

This pretty arrangement has been created using the flowers from the Floral Rhapsody cake, with some roses added. Quite often the bride and groom like to keep the floral decorations from the wedding cake as a memento. To re-arrange the flowers into a suitable container gives a more permanent and decorative piece for the home. However, it is best to suggest that a glass or perspex case is made to protect the flowers from dust, and also that they are kept away from moisture and direct sunlight as food colours will fade eventually.

FLOWERS

8 sprigs of rosemary (see page 65)
5 stems of ivy, various lengths
(see page 114)
5 short stems of rue leaves
(see page 11)
9 ranunculus flowers of various sizes
(see page 72)
9 ranunculus buds
5 half roses (see page 136)
5 rosebuds

EQUIPMENT

Florists' staysoft
Small verdigris effect container
(or other suitable container or vase)
20-gauge wires
Nile green floristry tape
Fine pliers
Wire cutters

PREPARATION

1 Place a clump of staysoft in the base of the chosen container. Flatten the top of the staysoft. If any of the flower or foliage stems need strengthening or lengthening, tape in an extra 20-gauge wire alongside the main stem.

ASSEMBLY

2 Start by forming the outline of the arrangement using the sprigs of rosemary. You will need to make the height of the arrangement at least one and a half times higher than the container. To give the arrangement some depth, add the stems of ivy and the rue leaves.

3 Add the largest ranunculus flower next to form the focal point. Continue to add the ranunculus flowers evenly positioned around the focal flower. Try to position each of the flowers so that they face different directions. Add the ranunculus buds to the outer parts of the arrangement.

4 Last of all, add the roses, starting with the half roses which should be positioned deep into the arrangement around the large ranunculus. Fill in any gaps with extra ivy or rue leaves. Once the arrangement is complete, stand back and take an overall look at the position of the flowers and, if needed, move or relax them a little.

RANUNCULUS KNIFE SPRAY

I often have flowers left over when I am working on a wedding cake and these can be used to make a small spray to decorate the wedding cake knife. This spray can be just a collection of flowers and foliage or a single flower, such as a rose or an orchid. They are generally only used as a decorative item for the cake cutting ceremony photograph.

FLOWERS

1 large, 1 medium and 1 small ranunculus flowers (see page 72)
3 ranunculus buds
2 small stems of jasmine, with foliage (see page 38)
1 stem of rosemary (see page 65)
2 stems of ivy (see page 114)
1 sprig of rue (see page 11)

EQUIPMENT

1 cake knife
20, 22 and 24-gauge wires
Nile green floristry tape
Pliers
Wire cutters
Ivory silk ribbon

PREPARATION

1 Clean and polish the cake knife. Lengthen any of the flower stems, if necessary, with 20-gauge or 22-gauge wire.

THE SPRAY

2 Start the spray by taping together the three ranunculus buds with nile green floristry tape. Next, add a group of jasmine with foliage, then add the small ranunculus flower, using ½-width floristry tape.

3 Add and tape in the stem of rosemary and the longer of the two stems of ivy. Trim off any excess wire

from the handle and tape over the top. Next add the medium ranunculus, then the large one, accompanied by a group of jasmine and rue leaves. Last of all, add the second stem of ivy, which should curve away from the front of the spray. Trim off the excess wire and tape over to neaten the handle.

ASSEMBLY

4 Take a couple of lengths of 24-gauge wire and thread them through the main body of the knife spray. Position the spray over the cake knife and bind the wire around the cake knife handle. You will need to bind the wire around the knife two or three times to secure it in place. Twist the remainder of the wire together to tighten the whole piece, then cut off the excess wire.

5 Tie a ribbon bow with trails around the knife and the spray to hide the join. Trim the ribbon ends to sharp angles using a pair of large scissors. Place the decorated knife next to the wedding cake ready for the cake cutting ceremony.

NOTE

You can buy small perspex and wooden stands to hold the knife in position if required.

RANUNCULUS

The genus name derives from the Latin *Rana*, meaning frog, which refers to the swampy places where these flowers are found in the wild. Ranunculus (*Ranunculus asiaticus*) have often been referred to as the up-market buttercup, sometimes known as the Persian buttercup; they are in fact from the same family. They are one of the most cheerful, colourful flowers and yet, at the same time, have a delicacy because of the fine petals. They are available for most of the year from the flower shop, but are at their best during the spring months which is when they are in season. Ranunculus come in all shades of pink, red, orange, yellow, peach, burgundy, purple and white; the size of both the flower heads and stems also varies. The flower shown here is a smaller flower.

CENTRE

1 Tape over a ½-length of 20-gauge wire with ½-width nile green floristry tape and bend an open hook in one end. Roll a ball of poppy (or your chosen colour) coloured flower paste, moisten the hook and insert it into the base of the paste. Flatten the top of the ball and pinch the paste down on to the wire to secure it in place.

2 Using a sharp scalpel, mark the surface of the paste to represent the inner petals, working from the centre to the edges. You will need to work quickly before the paste dries and the surface starts to crack. Indent the centre a little more by increasing the pressure when you cut the inner petals. Allow to dry.

MATERIALS

Poppy and pale green
flower paste
20, 24 and 26-gauge wires
Primrose, moss green, apricot,
tangerine, red and dark green
petal dust (blossom tint)
¼ glaze (see page 151)

EQUIPMENT

Nile green floristry tape
Sharp scalpel
Australian rose petal cutters
(TT351,350,349)
Ceramic silk veining tool (HP)
Nasturtium calyx cutters
(448,661)
Leaf templates (see page 156)
Veining tool (PME)

PETALS

3 Roll out some poppy coloured flower paste not too thinly at first, as you will need a little bit of

thickness to allow the petals to be veined. Cut out many petals using the smallest of the Australian rose petal cutters (351). I cannot tell you how many petals to cut out, as it depends on the size of the flower you are planning to make and on the size of the prepared centre. If you look at a bunch of ranunculus flowers, each one seems to have a different number of petals. It is therefore best to start by cutting out six or seven petals, attaching them to the centre and deciding whether to attach more or stop and use the next size. (There are too many petals on a fresh flower to try and copy exactly, so all you are doing is creating an impression.)

4 Vein and, at the same time, broaden each of the petals using the ceramic silk veining tool. Roll the tool across the petal in a fan formation, applying quite a lot of pressure. Place each of the petals on a pad and soften the edges. Moisten the base of the petals and start attaching them to the dried centre. Some of the petals interlink and some do not on one flower.

5 Repeat the above process with the two larger rose petal cutters, adding the petals and stopping only when you feel the flower looks finished. Remember you will need to make some of the flowers so that they look as if they are only just forming. As you apply some of the larger petals, try to pinch them into place to create a slightly cupped appearance. Allow to firm up before colouring.

COLOURING

6 Dust the tight centre of the flower with a mixture of primrose and moss green petal dust. Then colour the petals using your chosen colours – in this case I have used apricot, tangerine and red. The back of each of the petals should be paler

than the upper surface. You will need to make the petals closer to the centre slightly darker, so increase the red petal dust. If you are trying to achieve a very concentrated colour, steam the flower and re-dust. Steam the flower again to completely remove the dusted appearance.

CALYX

7 Roll out a small piece of pale green flower paste not too thinly, leaving a thicker raised section at the centre. Cut out the calyx using either the small or large nasturtium calyx cutters, depending on the size of the finished flower. Place on a pad, soften the edges and hollow out the length of each of the sepals. Moisten the centre and thread on to the back of the flower, trying to position each sepal so that they cover a join between two petals. The sepals should curve back with their tips curling towards the petals. Pinch the tips of each of the sepals into a point. Dust with a mixture of moss and primrose petal dust. Thicken the stem with shredded absorbent kitchen paper and tape over the top with ½-width nile green tape.

LEAVES

8 Roll out some pale green flower paste, leaving a thick ridge down the centre. Place a leaf template on top and cut out with a sharp scalpel. Insert a moistened 26-gauge or 24-gauge wire into the thick ridge, depending on the size of the leaf. Place the leaf on a pad and

soften the edges. Using the veining tool, draw some fine veins on the surface of the leaf. Pinch the leaf down the centre and curl some of the ends back a little. Allow to firm up before dusting.

9 Dust the tips of the leaf with a little red petal dust. Using moss green and dark green petal dust, dust the leaf from the edge down on to the main section of the leaf, fading out the colour as you get to about two thirds from the tip. Dust the whole leaf with a mixture of moss and primrose petal dust. Dip into a ¼ glaze, shake off the excess and allow to dry.

MEDIEVAL WINTER WEDDING

The rich red amaryllis, roses and red-tinged hypericum berries combined with the ivy, dark green dusted boards and the red, gold and green braiding, make this cake a perfect centrepiece for a medieval-style December wedding.

MATERIALS

20cm (8 in) and 30cm (12 in)
teardrop-shaped cakes
Apricot glaze
2kg (4lb) almond paste (marzipan)
Clear alcohol (kirsch or vodka)
750g (1½lb) sugarpaste, coloured
with holly/ivy paste colouring
2.25kg (4½lb) sugarpaste, coloured
with autumn leaf paste colouring
Red, gold and green braid
to trim cakes
Green velvet ribbon to trim boards
Holly/ivy and dark green petal dust
(blossom tint)

EQUIPMENT

25cm (10 in) and 40cm (16 in)
teardrop-shaped cake boards
Broad flat paintbrush
Sugarpaste smoothers
Tilting cake stand
Double-sided carpet tape
1 crystal pillar
Pliers

FLOWERS

Medieval Winter Wedding Curved
Bouquet (see page 77)
A few extra stems of large dark
green ivy (see page 114)

PREPARATION

1 Cover both cake boards with holly/ivy sugarpaste. Allow to dry overnight. Dust the surface of the paste with a broad, flat paintbrush using holly/ivy and dark green petal dusts (the finished result should be streaky).

2 Brush the cakes with apricot glaze and cover with almond paste. Allow to dry overnight. Moisten the surface of the almond paste with clear alcohol and cover with autumn leaf coloured sugarpaste, using smoothers to achieve a good finish. Transfer the cakes to the boards, making sure that there is a neat join between the base of the cakes and the boards. Attach a band of braid around the base of both of the cakes using a small amount of green icing to hold them in place. Glue the green velvet ribbon to the cake board edges using a non-toxic glue stick.

3 Make the Medieval Winter Wedding Curved Bouquet as described on page 77.

ASSEMBLY

4 Position the small cake on to the tilting cake stand using double-sided carpet tape to hold it in place. Place the larger cake next to the small one so that the shapes fit neatly together. Insert the long crystal pillar into the base tier and place the handle of the curved bouquet into it. Using pliers, re-position any of the pieces that need adjusting. Add a few extra stems of ivy to frame the edge of the top tier.

NOTE

If you are concerned that the top tier might slide off the stand, decorate a polystyrene dummy for the wedding display and provide a simply decorated cutting cake which can be kept behind the scenes.

MEDIEVAL WINTER WEDDING CURVED BOUQUET

The curved shower bouquet is my favourite shape for a bridal bouquet as it lends itself very easily to cakes. This style of bouquet can curve either to the left or right, but one side of the bouquet must be slightly heavier with flowers and foliage.

FLOWERS

1 long stem and 6 shorter stems of large trailing ivy (see page 114)
3 stems of hypericum berries (see page 78)
3 small amaryllis (see page 80)
3 rosebuds and 3 half roses (see page 136)

EQUIPMENT

18-gauge wires
Nile green floristry tape
Fine pliers
Wire cutters

PREPARATION

1 First of all, strengthen any of the stems that are to be very long or that are particularly heavy, by taping in additional 18-gauge wires.

ASSEMBLY

2 Decide how long you want the bouquet to be in length. The first long stem of ivy needs to measure at least two-thirds the total length of the bouquet. Bend the stem to a 90 degree angle. Add the other shorter stems of ivy, bending each to the same angle and taping in each piece with full width nile green floristry tape. You will also need to decide which way the bouquet is to curve and make the appropriate side slightly heavier. Add the hypericum berries next, making sure they are evenly spaced. This should form the basic outline of the bouquet.

3 Next, tape in the three amaryllis, starting with the largest flower at the focal point (this should be positioned slightly higher than any of the other flowers). The three amaryllis should form a diagonal line in the bouquet.

4 Finally, tape in the roses to fill in the gaps in the bouquet. Cut off the excess wire from the handle, then neaten by taping over the top with full width tape.

Hypericum

Hypericum produces yellow five-petalled flowers with masses of golden yellow stamens. However, it is the fruit that is mainly used as a filler in bouquets and arrangements. There are many varieties of hypericum, each producing berries of a different size, slightly different shape and variations in the colour of the fully ripened fruit. They are available for most of the year as a cut flower from florists' shops.

MATERIALS

18, 26 and 28-gauge wires
Pale green flower paste
Moss green, primrose, red,
aubergine and dark green petal
dust (blossom tint)
Full and ½ glaze (see page 151)

❀

EQUIPMENT

Sharp scalpel
Nile green floristry tape
Medium and small stephanotis
cutters (TT56,568)
Leaf template (see page 158)
or fresh hypericum leaves

Berries

1 Cut a length of 28-gauge wire into four. Take a small piece of pale green flower paste and roll it into a ball, then into an egg shape. Moisten the end of a piece of wire and insert it into the base of the shape, so that it almost pierces through the tip. Squeeze the paste between your fingers and thumb to form a fruit with three sides. Pinch the tip of the fruit into a sharp point.

2 Using a sharp scalpel, mark very fine striations on to the surface of the fruit. Repeat the process to make numerous berries of slightly

different sizes. Place into a plastic bag to stop them drying out before dusting.

COLOURING

3 Dust each of the berries to various depths; starting with the smaller berries, dust with a mixture of moss and primrose and a tinge of red petal dust. As the berries mature, increase the amount of red and also add some aubergine. Allow to dry. Dip each berry into a full glaze, shake off excess and allow to dry. Tape over each of the stems with ¼-width nile green floristry tape.

CALYX

4 Roll out a small piece of green flower paste, leaving a bump at the centre. Cut out a calyx shape using either of the two sizes of stephanotis cutter (this will depend upon the size of the berry). Imagine

the shape as a figure and, using a celstick, broaden the head and legs, using a rolling action. Place the shape on to a pad and soften all of the sepals.

5 Dust the edges of the calyx with the primrose and moss green mixture. Moisten the centre of the calyx with egg white and thread on to the back of the berry. Pull all of the sepals back. Allow to dry.

LEAVES

6 Roll out some green flower paste, leaving a thick ridge down the centre. Place either the template or fresh hypericum leaf on top of the paste and cut out the shape using a sharp scalpel. Insert a moistened 28-gauge or 26-gauge wire, depending on the size of the leaf, into the thick ridge. You will need to insert the wire into at least half the length of the leaf.

7 Place the leaf on to the back of the fresh hypericum leaf and press the two together using the flat part of your hand. Place the leaf on to a pad and soften the edges. Reinforce the central vein by pinching the leaf on the back from the tip to the base. Allow to firm up before dusting.

8 Dust with moss and dark green petal dust, making the back very pale. Dust a little aubergine petal dust on to the edges and at the base of each leaf. Dip into a ½ glaze, shake off the excess and allow to dry. Using a sharp scalpel, etch some fine veins on to the leaf.

ASSEMBLY

9 Tape the berries together into groups of two and three. Join two groups together and add two leaves at the axil. Repeat this process several times to form lots of groups. Start a main stem with one of the groups taped on to an 18-gauge wire using ½-width nile green floristry tape. Tape some pairs of leaves at intervals down this stem. Repeat and make another stem. Join these two together, taping two leaves at the axil again. Continue this method until you have completed the required length. Dust the stems with aubergine, red and moss green petal dust. Bend each of the stems into shape using pliers.

AMARYLLIS

Originally botanists grouped this flower (*Hippeastrum*) with the true amaryllis (*Amaryllis belladonna*): unfortunately the name has stuck. Amaryllis originate from tropical and subtropical rainforests of South America and the Caribbean. They are often given as gifts at Christmastime as pot plants and it is in this form that most people associate them. However, they are also used as cut flowers and in bridal bouquets during the winter season. The variety pictured here is one of the smaller types of amaryllis, making it more suitable for wedding cakes.

MATERIALS

White, poppy and pale green flower paste
18, 24 and 26-gauge wires
Lemon, red, aubergine, dark green, vine and moss green petal dust (blossom tint)
Scarlet craft dust

EQUIPMENT

Fine-nosed pliers
White and nile green floristry tape
Amaryllis petal templates (see page 156)
Small narrow and side of petal amaryllis veiners (GI)
Large wide amaryllis veiner (GI)
Sharp scalpel

STAMENS

1 Cut two lengths of 26-gauge wire into thirds. Using a pair of fine-nosed pliers, bend a flat hook at one end of the wire, then hold the hook halfway down its length with pliers and bend it again to form a 'T' bar shape. Thicken the length of each stamen with a few layers of ¼-width white floristry tape, making them finer towards the anther. Repeat to make six stamens.

2 Attach a small sausage of white flower paste over the 'T' bars to form anthers. You will not need to use egg white for this. The size of the anther depends on how mature the flower is – a mature flower would have smaller anthers. Using a scalpel, indent a line on to the upper surface of the anther. Dust the anthers with lemon petal dust. Dust the length of the stamen with either red petal dust or scarlet craft dust (the latter gives a much richer red colour).

PISTIL

3 Roll a ball of poppy-coloured flower paste and insert a 24-gauge wire. Work the paste firmly and quickly between your finger and thumb to cover a good length of the wire. The pistil should not be longer than any of the petals. Smooth the pistil between the palms of your hands and trim off the excess paste. Using a small pair of scissors, cut the end of the pistil into three sections. Round off the sides of each of the sections, then curl them back a little. Bend the whole length of the pistil into a very lazy 'S' shape (see photograph). Dust the pistil with red or scarlet craft dust, leaving the end much paler to allow the base colour to show through. Allow to dry.

4 Tape the six stamens on to the pistil using ½-width green floristry tape, making the pistil a little longer. Using pliers, bend each of the stamens to follow the shape of the pistil.

PETALS

5 I find that when I am making red flowers, it is better to start off a lot paler than I want the finished flower to be. If the paste is coloured deep red to begin with, then the end result is too dense and artificial. Roll out some mid-poppy coloured (or whatever your chosen colour is) flower paste, leaving a thick ridge down the centre (use a grooved board if you wish). Using a scalpel and the amaryllis templates made from the outlines on page 156, cut out the left, right and central petals.

6 Insert a moistened 26-gauge wire into the thick ridge of each, making sure that the wire supports at least half the length of the petals. Vein the left and right petals using the medium curved veiner from the small amaryllis set. Remove from the veiner, place on a pad and soften the edges gently using the rounded end of a large celstick (do not frill them).

7 Pinch each petal at the tips and at the base, and occasionally curl the edges at the base in slightly (this adds some interest and gives

variation). Allow the petals to firm a little before dusting.

8 Vein the central petal using the narrow veiner in the set. Soften and dry as before.

9 Repeat the process for the larger outer sepals. You might need to use a 24-gauge wire for these sepals. Vein using the large amaryllis veiner from the larger set. Soften the edges of the sepals and then draw down a central vein using the dresden tool. Pinch the base and the tips of the sepals. Dry as before.

COLOURING AND ASSEMBLY

10 Dust each of the petals and sepals using either red petal dust or with scarlet craft dust (as shown). Start by dusting the edges of the petals/sepals and then gradually bring the colour down to cover the majority of the paste. Dust the base of each of the petals/sepals with aubergine and catch the edges with a tiny amount of aubergine, just to break up the red a little. When you have done this, there should be a little aubergine left on the brush. Use this to dust across the veins on each petal to highlight them.

11 Tape the left and right petals on to the stamens, so that the stamens curl towards them. Add the narrow petal underneath the stamens. Position the large sepals behind and in between each of the petals and tape the flower together tightly using ½-width nile green floristry tape. As the paste is still soft, you should be able to adjust the petals to give a more natural, relaxed finish. Tape an 18-gauge wire along-side the existing stem to strengthen the flower.

BUDS

12 Tape over a half length of 18-gauge wire with green floristry tape. Bend a large hook on the end. Roll a large ball of poppy coloured flower paste into a teardrop shape, moisten the hooked wire and insert it into the fine end of the teardrop. Allow to dry.

13 Roll out and cut out three sepals as for the flower, but this time do not wire them. Vein and soften as before. Moisten the teardrop and attach the sepals to the cone. Pinch from the tips of the sepals down to the base, so that you form a ridge on each of the sepals. Dust as for the flower.

ASSEMBLY

14 Thicken the flower and bud stems with strips of absorbent kitchen paper and tape over with full-width floristry tape. Group the flowers and buds into groups of a maximum of five. Dust the stems with dark green, vine and moss green petal dust.

NOTE

Amaryllis come in a range of different shades and combinations of red, pink, peach, burgundy, green and white. Some varieties have very strong, striped designs on their petals. For most of the other coloured flowers, use cream or white flower paste, then dust to the required finish.

RUSCUS

Ruscus has very curious flattened stems that look like leaves called cladodes. It is from the centre, often on the back of each of the cladodes, that the plant produces its insignificant flowers and more substantial red fruit. Sometimes the fruit is still in place when you buy the foliage from a florist shop. There are several varieties of ruscus, some with more oval shaped leaves and others like the one shown here with very pointed leaves. It is only the plant's 'leaves' that are used in floristry, and these are simple to make in sugar. To make things easier they will be referred to as leaves in the text.

MATERIALS
Mid-green flower paste
Dark green petal dust
(blossom tint)
20 and 28-gauge wires
¾ glaze (see page 151)

EQUIPMENT
Ruscus cutters (CC)
Fresh or dried ruscus
Sharp scalpel
Nile green floristry tape

LEAVES

1 Roll out a small piece of mid-green flower paste thinly, leaving a thicker central ridge. Cut out the leaf (cladode) using either the ruscus cutters or by using a fresh piece of ruscus as a template. Insert a moistened 28-gauge wire into the thick ridge, so that it supports at least half the length of the leaf.

2 Using the fresh or dried ruscus, vein the paste. You will need to apply pressure on to the paste as the veining is very subtle. Pinch the leaf from the tip to the base on the back. Repeat the process to make numerous leaves in various sizes.

3 Dust heavily with dark green petal dust on the upper surface and a little on the back. When the leaves are dry, dip them into a ¾ glaze. Shake off the excess and allow to dry. Tape the leaves together into groups of two and three. Then tape them on to a 20-gauge wire, starting with one set of leaves and then spiral further groups down the main stem. Dust the main stems with the dark green mixture.

SUMMER GARDEN WEDDING

This spectacular wedding cake was designed and decorated by Tony Warren and displayed on the Table of Honour at the International British Sugarcraft Guild Exhibition 1997. I have rearranged the floral display to include cosmos and other flowers. It would form a magnificent centrepiece for a reception held in a garden marquee.

MATERIALS

20cm (8 in) and 30cm (12 in) teardrop-shaped cakes
Apricot glaze
2kg (4lb) almond paste (marzipan)
Clear alcohol (kirsch or vodka)
3kg (6lb) champagne sugarpaste
Pink royal icing
Apricot, fuchsia, white and pearl white petal dust (blossom tint)
Fine colonial rose ribbon to trim cakes
Picot edge ivory and green braid ribbon to trim boards

EQUIPMENT

Sugarpaste smoothers
28cm (11 in) and 38cm (15 in) teardrop-shaped cake boards
Broad flat paintbrush
No. 1 piping tube (tip)
Home-made tilting stand and 45cm (18 in) thin oval base
Sage green material
Pot of velverette fabric glue

Double-sided carpet tape
Perspex separator
Florists' staysoft
Florists' binding tape

FLOWERS

3 oriental hybrid lilies and 1 bud (see page 91)
5 pink cosmos (see page 86)
2 stems of agapanthus (see page 98)
5 stems of sweet peas (see page 46)
7 roses (see page 136)
4 stems of Solomon's seal (see page 100)
3 stems of bells of Ireland (see page 89)
10 stems of ivy (see page 114)

PREPARATION

1 Brush the surface of the cakes with apricot glaze and cover with almond paste. Allow to dry overnight. Moisten the surface of the almond paste with clear alcohol and cover with champagne sugarpaste, using smoothers to obtain a good finish. Cover the cake boards with champagne sugarpaste. Transfer the cakes to the boards, making sure that you have a very neat join between the base of the cakes and the boards. Allow to dry.

2 Mix together apricot, fuchsia and white petal dust, and then dilute with clear alcohol. Using a broad, flat paintbrush, paint uneven strokes of colour on to the sides of the cake and on the board. Allow to dry, then dust over with pearl white petal dust (optional).

3 Attach a band of fine rose ribbon around the base of both of the cakes, then pipe a snail trail over the top using royal icing and a piping bag fitted with a no. 1 piping tube. Glue the picot edge ivory ribbon to the edge of the boards using a non-toxic glue stick.

ASSEMBLY

4 Adhere the sage green material on to the thin oval board using the velverette fabric glue. Stretch the material to make a smooth neat surface and glue the excess neatly to the underside of the board. Attach the band of green braid to the board edge. Place the bottom tier of the cake on to this board. Position the top tier on to the tilting part of the stand, held in place with double-sided carpet tape.

5 Place the perspex separator upside down behind the base tier. Attach a clump of staysoft and hold in place using florists' binding tape. Attractively arrange the flowers and foliage in a free-style unstructured manner into the staysoft to complete the design.

Cosmos

Cultivated in Europe since the eighteenth century, the cosmos (*Cosmea sulphureaus*) is a bright, showy and very popular summer garden flower. It comes in a range of different colours which include pink, red, white, lavender, orange and yellow. (There is also another species that has dark brown burgundy flowers with a scent of chocolate. However this is much smaller and has a different type of foliage – see page 88.) The size of cosmos flowers varies – the one that I have made is a slightly smaller species. There are also double forms of cosmos flowers. This is one of the easiest and most effective flowers I have ever made.

MATERIALS

White seed-head stamens
20, 24, 28 and 30-gauge
white wires
Cyclamen liquid food colouring
Lemon, plum, aubergine, moss
and dark green petal dust
(blossom tint)
Deep magenta craft dust
Pale ruby, white, pale and
mid-green flower paste

EQUIPMENT

Nile green floristry tape
Small stencil brush
Australian rose petal cutters
(TT349-352)
Small cosmos veiner (GI)
Pointed daisy cutter (TT106)

*S*TAMENS

1 Take ¼ - ⅓ of a bunch of seed-head stamens and bend them in half to double the amount. Try to keep the tips at roughly the same height. Tape them on to a 24-gauge wire, making sure that they are not too long. Trim away any excess stamen from the base and tape down to the end of the wire. Using cyclamen liquid colouring and a stiff stencil brush, colour the stamens. While the tips are still damp, dip them into some lemon petal dust to form the pollen. Shake off any excess and allow the stamens to dry thoroughly.

*P*ETALS

2 First of all bend each of the Australian rose petal cutters to make them a more narrow shape, by simply pressing the sides together with your fingers and thumb. Roll out some ruby coloured flower paste, not too thinly on to a grooved board. Cut out eight petals using

your chosen size of cutter (I tend to use a mixture of sizes in an arrangement). Cut several lengths of 28-gauge wire into thirds, moisten the end of the wire and insert it into at least half the length of each petal. Pinch the base of each petal to secure it and form a slightly pointed shape. To make a larger flower, stretch the petal at this stage.

3 Vein each of the petals using the double-sided cosmos petal veiner. Remove from the veiner and place back on the board. Using the broad end of the dresden tool, work the edges to pull out three subtle points. Place the petal on to a pad and soften the sides using a celstick. Pinch each petal into shape and allow to firm with a slight curve at the end.

COLOURING AND ASSEMBLY

4 The colouring depends on your personal taste; some of the flowers have only a patch of colour at the base and others are very bright and bold. My preference is to use deep magenta craft dust or plum petal dust to colour the main part of the petal, and then to dust a patch of aubergine at the base. In an arrangement where the cosmos is the main flower, use a mixture of various pinks and white.

5 Tape the petals around the stamens using ½-width nile green floristry tape. Add a 20-gauge wire to lengthen and strengthen the stem. As the petals should be still wet at this stage, you can now re-shape them or squash them together to form a partially open flower. Allow to dry, then steam to remove the dusty effect.

CALYX

6 The cosmos has a double calyx. The first layer is made by forming a ball of pale green flower paste into a mexican hat shape. Place the shape, flat side down, on to a board.

Roll out the paste using a celstick and then cut out the calyx shape with the daisy cutter. Before you remove the paste from the cutter, rub your thumb over the paste against the cutter to give a clean, neat cut to the calyx.

7 Re-roll the sepals using a celstick, then hollow the centre out using the pointed end of the tool. Place the calyx on to a pad and draw down a central vein on the inside of each of the sepals using the fine end of the dresden tool. Moisten the centre of the calyx with egg white and thread on to the back of the flower, removing any excess paste from the base.

8 To form the second layer of the calyx, roll eight very fine strands of mid-green flower paste; these should be pointed at one end. Using the flat side of a veiner, flatten each of the sepals. Attach them to the first calyx using egg white, positioning each of them in between each of

the sepals on the previous layer. Curl the tips back slightly. This method makes a very pretty but extremely fragile calyx. A simpler and safer method is to use floristry tape. Cut the tape into ¼ width and twist it back on itself to form a fine strand. Cut eight pieces and then tape on to the first layer using ½-width tape. Dust with a mixture of dark and moss green petal dust.

Buds

9 Form a ball of pale green paste and insert a hooked, moistened 24-gauge wire into the base. Divide the surface of the ball into eight sections using a sharp scalpel. Flatten each alternate section using the broad end of the dresden tool. Dust with moss green and aubergine petal dust. Add the outer calyx as described for the flower.

Leaves

10 In the past I have made these leaves in sugar, however they are very fragile and look a little too thick compared with those of the fresh flower. I now use floristry tape to achieve a more realistic and robust leaf. Using ½-width nile green

tape, start by taping the end of a piece of 30-gauge wire. When you reach the end of the wire, continue to twist the tape back on itself to form a fine strand. Add another four pieces of twisted tape (no wire) to this main wire to form one leaf section. Repeat this to make another two leaf sections. Tape the three sections together to form one set of leaves. Dust with dark green and moss green petal dust.

Assembly

11 Tape together the buds and flowers of various sizes, adding a set of leaves every time you join them together. Continue to add sets of leaves to cover the length of the stem you require. Dust the main stem with a mixture of moss and dark green petal dust, and add a touch of plum and aubergine petal dust here and there.

Note
CHOCOLATE COSMOS

I mentioned that this flower smells of chocolate – it actually smells more like drinking chocolate to me!

To make the flower, use one of the smaller Australian rose petal cutters and pale brown flower paste. Cut out eight petals, vein and work as described for the cosmos pictured. The petals should be cupped rather than being dried flat.

The stamens are made in the same way as the flower described, this time using a smaller group of stamens and omitting the addition of pollen to the tips.

Dust the petals in layers of aubergine, brown and nutkin brown petal dust – predominantly aubergine. Assemble the flower as before and add the calyx.

The leaves do not have a fern-like structure like the ones pictured, but are tri-lobed in shape and a greyish green in colour.

Bells of Ireland

This unusual plant (*Moluccella laevis*) derives its name from the large green bell-like calyces. The flower is very small in comparison to the calyx and is the shape of a nettle flower. Bells of Ireland used to be eaten as a vegetable and has been cultivated in Europe since the sixteenth century. Florists use the plant in both its fresh and dried state to add height and interest to arrangements and bouquets.

MATERIALS

White, pale holly/ivy and mid-green flower paste
18, 24, 26, 28 and 30-gauge wires
Vine green, holly/ivy, dark green, moss green and aubergine petal dust (blossom tint)
½ glaze (see page 151)

EQUIPMENT

Small set of rose petal cutters (TT)
1 fresh stem of bells of Ireland with leaves
Nile green or white floristry tape

Calyx

1 It is unusual to start with the calyx instead of the flower, but it is the calyx that provides the decoration in this instance. Bend a small hook on the end of either a 26-gauge or 24-gauge wire (this will depend upon the size of the calyx). Moisten the hook and attach a small cone of white paste. Mark the surface in half using a scalpel. You will need to make one of these buds for each calyx. Dry.

2 Roll a ball of pale green flower paste into a cone shape, then pinch the base out to form a mexican hat shape. Place the hat down on to the board and thin out the base using a celstick. Cut out the calyx shape using a rose petal cutter, making sure that the majority of the paste is at the pointed end of the rose petal shape.

3 Hollow out the base and the centre of the calyx using the pointed end of a large celstick to form the characteristic bell shape. (It would be a good idea to buy a fresh stem to form the correct shape.) Continue to press the sides of the calyx, using your thumb against the celstick, until you have made the edges of the calyx quite fine.

4 Pinch a few points around the edges of the calyx, using your

finger and thumb. Moisten the base of the bud and thread through the centre of the calyx. Curl back the edges if required to form a more attractive shape. You will need to make lots of calyces to complete a stem of bells of Ireland. The fresh stem has rings of six to eight calyces in graduating sizes from the tip to the base.

5 Dust the calyces to various degrees using vine, holly/ivy and a touch of dark green (the outer surface of each of the calyces should be much paler). Allow them to dry overnight.

6 Using a sharp scalpel, etch some fine veins on the inside of each of the calyces. This is optional as it can be very time-consuming – it does however look very good when completed.

FLOWERS

7 The flowers are not essential, but do add a little interest even if you only include a few on a whole stem! I have often bought this plant from the florist where it has either not come into flower yet or it is past its best and the flowers have dropped off. A flower-arranger recently told me that the flowers are often removed to enhance the appearance and to make them last a bit longer.

8 Form a ball of white flower paste into a teardrop shape. Using a fine pair of scissors, cut the teardrop in half to form two petals. Flatten each petal between your finger and thumb. Next divide the base of one of the petals into two and then trim the sides to form the petal shape. Frill and thin out the edges using the broad end of the dresden tool. Pinch a ridge down the centre using tweezers.

9 Hollow out the top to form a hood petal using a small celstick. Position inside a calyx using a small amount of egg white. Sometimes the flowers have a pink tinge to them.

LEAVES

10 Roll out some mid-green paste, leaving the centre slightly thicker. Using a fresh leaf as a template, cut out the leaf shape with a scalpel. Insert a 30-gauge or 28-gauge wire into the thick ridge. Use the fresh leaf to vein the paste. Pinch the central vein and allow to dry. You will need to make various sizes to complete a stem. The fresh bells of Ireland has a group of leaves at the top of the stem and is then followed by the rings of calyces, which have two leaves attached, one at either side at the base of each of the rings. As with the flowers, sometimes the florist and flower-arranger removes the leaves – this is an option that the sugarcrafter can happily pick up on.

11 Dust with holly/ivy and dark green petal dust. Glaze using a ½ glaze, shake off excess and leave to dry.

ASSEMBLY

12 If you are using leaves, start the stem with two tiny leaves. Tape in a few more pairs of leaves in graduating sizes using ½-width white or nile green floristry tape. Next, tape in a ring of small calyces and a pair of leaves (if using). Leave a gap on the stem and then add a slightly larger ring of calyces (and leaves.) As you tape down the stem you might need to add another couple of 18-gauge wires and some shredded absorbent kitchen paper to thicken and strengthen the stem. When you have completed the length of stem required, dust with a pale mixture of greens similar to those used on the calyces. Catch the edge of the calyces here and there with a touch of aubergine petal dust. Steam the whole stem to remove the dusty appearance left by the colour. Bend the stem into the required shape; real stems often twist to follow the light.

Oriental Hybrid Lily

The oriental hybrid lilies originate from crosses made from *L. auratum*, *L.speciosum* and *L. rubrum*. They have predominantly white or pink flowers, with spots or speckling. The lily pictured is based on a variety called *Le rêve* which has pale pink flowers and only a small amount of speckling on each petal. The oriental lilies are always a popular choice for bridal bouquets, mainly due to their showy, exotic appearance and heavy scent.

Stamens

1 Use a third of a length of 26-gauge white wires for each stamen. You will need six of these. Using a pair of fine-nosed pliers, bend a flat hook at one end of the wire, then hold the hook halfway down its length with the pliers and bend it again to form a 'T'- bar shape. Thicken the length (filaments) of each stamen with a few layers of ¼-width white floristry tape making them finer towards the anther. Dust with a pale mixture of primrose, moss green and white petal dust.

2 Attach a sausage of white paste over the 'T' bar to form the anther. Mix together some mimosa sugartex with skintone and lemon petal dust to form a pollen mixture. Paint the anthers with a little egg white, then dip into the pollen mix. Allow to dry thoroughly.

Pistil

3 Roll a ball of pale green flower paste and insert a moistened 24-gauge wire. Work the paste firmly between your finger and thumb in a rubbing motion and try to cover a

MATERIALS

18, 24 and 26-gauge white wires
Primrose, moss green, white, skintone, aubergine, deep purple, plum, fuchsia, pink, lemon and dark green petal dust (blossom tint)
White, pale and mid-green flower paste
Mimosa sugartex
Egg white
½ glaze
Cyclamen liquid food colouring

EQUIPMENT

Fine-nosed pliers
White and nile green floristry tape
Medium casablanca lily cutters (TT)
Casablanca lily veiners (GI)

good length of the wire. (The pistil should measure at least the length of one of the petals.) Smooth the pistil between the palms of your hands and then trim away any excess paste. Flatten the top of the pistil and then using a pair of tweezers, pinch the end into three sections. Flatten the top again if needed, then divide the upper surface into three using a sharp scalpel. Bend the whole pistil slightly to make it more natural looking. Attach another piece of green paste at the base to represent the ovary. Divide into six using a sharp scalpel.

4 Colour the pistil with a mixture of moss and primrose petal dust, making the ovary stronger in colour. The tip of the pistil is coloured with a touch of aubergine and deep purple. To make a mature pistil, add a drop of glaze to the tip.

5 Tape the stamens around the pistil, making the pistil higher than the stamens. Bend the stamens into the required position.

PETALS

6 Roll out some white flower paste, leaving a thick ridge down the centre. Using the wide petal cutter, cut out three petals. Insert a moistened 24-gauge wire into each

petal, taking the wire up into at least half the length of the petal.

7 Vein each of the petals using the large casablanca veiners, pressing the two sides together firmly to give a good impression. Place the petals on a pad and soften the edges using the rounded end of a celstick. Pinch down the centre of the each petal, especially at the tips. Repeat the process to cut out three narrow petals. Dry over a curve until firm enough to handle.

COLOURING

8 Dust the base of each petal with primrose, and then over-dust half of this area with moss green. The main depth of colouring of the flower depends on your personal taste as there are slight variations. Mix together plum, fuchsia or pink with white petal dust, and colour the petals using a flat brush. Keep the pink away from the primrose at the base otherwise you will end up with a slight orange tone. The narrow petals have less colour on them.

9 Using a fine paintbrush and a little cyclamen liquid colouring, paint on the specks of colour. (It is a good idea to have a fresh flower or good photograph to copy at this stage.)

10 Dust the tips of the petals with the brush you used for the primrose and moss green. The colour should be very pale; cleaning your brush with cornflour (cornstarch) will help to give a more subtle finish.

ASSEMBLY

11 Start by taping the larger petals around the base of the stamens using ½-width nile green floristry tape. Add the smaller petals in between each of the larger ones, slightly recessed. As the petals

should be still slightly soft at this stage, you can now re-curl them if needed. Dust the back of the flower with the moss and primrose mixture, making it darker at the base. Tape each flower on to an 18-gauge wire for strength.

BUDS

12 Tape over an 18-gauge wire with ½-width nile green floristry tape. Bend a large open hook in one end and moisten with egg white. Roll a large sausage of paste and insert the wire into one end, making sure that it is firmly fixed.

13 To mark an impression of the petals, make a 'cage' using three 24-gauge wires taped at the base. Open the cage and insert the bud, tip first. Arrange the wires equally and close them together so that they press into the paste and mark it equally into three sections. Release the cage and move each of the wires a few millimetres to one side. Close the cage again to form three ridges down the length of the bud. Remove the cage and then, using your finger and thumb, pinch a deep ridge on the paste between each pair of division lines.

14 Dust the bud with a small amount of the flower colour,

and then over-dust with the primrose and moss green mixture. The base of the bud should be slightly darker so increase the moss green at the base. The smaller the buds are, the more green they should be.

15 Steam both the flowers and buds to give a waxy appearance and to seal the colour on to the petals (see page 151).

LEAVES

16 Roll out some mid-green paste, leaving a thick ridge down the centre. Cut out the leaves using a sharp scalpel. Insert a moistened 24 or 26-gauge wire depending on the size of the leaf into at least half the length of the ridge on each leaf. Place each on a pad and soften the edges using the largest celstick. Vein either by marking with the fine end of the dresden tool or with a double-sided veiner, or with the fresh leaf. Allow to dry until firm enough to handle.

17 Dust the leaves with dark green and moss green petal dust. The smaller leaves should be more of a lime green in colour. Dip each leaf into a ½ glaze, shake off excess and leave to dry.

HEARTS ENTWINED

This dramatic creation offers an unusual alternative for a single-tiered wedding cake design. The idea is that it represents two hearts – one with the heart-shaped cake and the other with curved stems of the flowers and foliage.

MATERIALS

23cm (9 in) heart-shaped cake
Apricot glaze
1kg (2lb) almond paste (marzipan)
Clear alcohol (kirsch or vodka)
1.5kg (3lb) white sugarpaste
Fine celadon green ribbon
to trim board
175g (6oz) green sugarpaste

EQUIPMENT

23cm (9 in) heart-shaped cake board
23cm (9 in) heart-shaped thin
cake board (optional)
Rectangular bonsai dish

FLOWERS

Hearts Entwined Arrangement
(see page 97)
2 stems of Solomon's seal
(see page 100)
A few extra pieces of ivy
(see page 114)

PREPARATION

1 Place the heart cake on to the reverse side of the 23cm (9 in) cake board and adhere with a little softened sugarpaste. Brush the cake with apricot glaze and cover with almond paste. Leave to dry for 1 week. Brush the surface of the almond paste with clear alcohol and cover the cake with white sugarpaste, using sugarpaste smoothers and the sugarpaste pad method to achieve a good smooth finish (see Note). Allow to dry.

2 You now need to decide whether or not you want to cover the silver cake board at the back or not. You can leave the back of the cake with the silver board showing; trim the board edge with fine green ribbon, if liked. Alternatively, cover the 23cm (9 in) heart-shaped thin board with white sugarpaste. Crimp the edge if preferred. Allow to dry. Attach some double-sided tape on to the back of the thin board and stick it to the silver side of the cake board on the back of the cake.

ASSEMBLY

3 Roll out some green sugarpaste and line the rectangular bonsai dish. Position, embed and secure the cake on its side into the green paste.

4 Place the Hearts Entwined Arrangement in front of the cake and curve the stems more if required to follow the shape of the cake. Insert two stems of Solomon's seal in the sugarpaste behind the cake, arching their stems over the cake to complete the design. Add a few extra pieces of ivy at the base.

NOTE

As well as using smoothers, a good way to achieve a silky smooth finish on sugarpaste is to flatten a ball of sugarpaste in the palm of your hand and to smooth it over the paste. This is especially good for smoothing the top edges of cakes.

HEARTS ENTWINED ARRANGEMENT

This beautifully elegant arrangement can be taken directly from the Hearts Entwined wedding cake after the reception and used as a room decoration as a reminder of the wedding day.

FLOWERS

2 stems of Solomon's seal
(see page 100)
1 oriental hybrid lily (see page 91)
2 stems of agapanthus (see page 98)
Several pieces of ivy (see page 114)
3 pink half roses and 2 pink
rosebuds (see page 136)
11 stems of lily-of-the-valley
(see page 54)
Extra leaves/foliage

EQUIPMENT

Florists' staysoft
Green oval bonsai dish
Glue gun and glue sticks
18-gauge wire
Nile green floristry tape
Pliers
Wire cutters

PREPARATION

1 Position a ball of florists' staysoft offset on to the bonsai dish, using a small amount of glue from the glue gun. Strengthen any of the longer flower stems, using 18-gauge wire alongside the main stems.

ASSEMBLY

2 First of all, hook the end of the tallest stem of Solomon's seal (this will help it stand in such a small amount of staysoft). Insert it into the staysoft, arching its stem over to form an attractive outline. Next insert the small stem of Solomon's seal to form a basic 'L' shape.

3 Trim the length of the lily stem, hook the end and position it centrally into the staysoft to form the focal point.

4 Hook the ends of the agapanthus stems and insert them, one next to each of the Solomon's seal stems.

Add some ivy leaves behind the lily to add depth to the arrangement.

5 Cut the half roses and rosebuds to the required length. Hook the ends and arrange them around the lily to fill in some of the gaps. Use the rosebuds towards the edge of the arrangement.

6 Finally insert the lily-of-the-valley in groups into the staysoft at three separate points of the arrangement. Add any extra foliage to fill in any gaps in the design.

AGAPANTHUS

If I am asked to include a blue flower on a wedding cake, this is the flower that immediately springs to my mind! Its name translated from the Greek means the flower of love (*agape* – love, *panthus* – flower) so it is an appropriate choice as a bridal flower. Orginating from South Africa but mainly cultivated in Holland, agapanthus is not a difficult flower to make. It covers a large range of different shades of blue, but for those who do not like blue there is also a white form.

MATERIALS

White seed-head stamens
18, 24 and 28-gauge wires
Primrose, deep purple, lavender, white, bluebell, moss and vine green petal dust (blossom tint)
White or pale cream flower paste
Clear alcohol (kirsch or vodka)

EQUIPMENT

Nile green floristry tape
Agapanthus cutter (TT516)

STAMENS

1 Tape six stamens on to a 24-gauge wire using ¼-width nile green floristry tape. Add an extra stamen to represent the pistil (in the fresh flower this is shorter than the stamens – I tend to make it longer as it makes the flower look prettier). Dust the tips of the stamens first with primrose, then over-dust with a touch of deep purple. Curl the stamens slightly.

FLOWER

2 Roll a ball of white or pale cream flower paste into a cone shape. Pinch the broad end of the cone between your fingers and thumb to thin out the base and form a pedestal shape. Place the flat part of the pedestal against the board and roll out using a celstick. Try to form a neat waistline around the thick area of the pedestal.

3 Cut out the flower using the agapanthus cutter. Before you remove the paste from the cutter, rub your thumb over the paste against the cutter to make sure the petals have cleanly cut edges.

4 Place the flower flat side down on a board. The agapanthus has three petals broader than the other three – this is reflected in the cutter shape. However you will still need to broaden each of the six petals slightly using a celstick and a rolling motion.

5 Open up the centre of the flower using the pointed end of the celstick. Press the base of each petal against the stick to form a graceful shape to the back of the flower.

6 Place the flower on to a pad and, using the fine end of the dresden tool, draw down a vein on the back of each petal. Turn the flower over and draw a vein on the front in exactly the same position as the veins on the back. Pinch the tips of each flower slightly.

7 Moisten the base of the stamens and pull them down into the centre of the flower. Neaten the back of the flower and remove any

excess paste. Arrange the petals so that the broader ones are slightly higher in position. Curve the whole flower so that the stamens are closer to one side.

COLOURING

8 Dust the flower with a mixture of lavender, white and bluebell, starting at the edges and dusting towards the centre of the flower (keep the centre white). Over-dust the edges with deep purple. Dust the centre and the back of the flower with a small amount of primrose and moss green petal dust.

9 Each of the petals has a darker line running down the centre. Dilute some deep purple petal dust with a small amount of clear alcohol. Paint a strong vein down the centre of each of the petals.

BUDS

10 Hook and moisten the end of a 24-gauge wire. Roll a ball of paste into a cone shape and insert the hooked wire into the fine end. Neaten the base of the cone again. Form the broad end of the cone into a slight point to form the tip. Using a cage with three 28-gauge wires, insert the bud tip first. Mark the petals and then move each of the wires slightly to one side and mark again to form three narrow ridges. Pinch the broad sections slightly, between your finger and thumb. You will need to make many buds of various sizes to form a complete umbel. Dust the buds with the same combination as the flowers, using more green on the smaller buds.

ASSEMBLY

11 Agapanthus flowers are often used as individual pipped flowers in sprays and corsages, but if you want to create more impact in an arrangement or bouquet, use them as a complete umbel. Tape the buds on to an 18-gauge wire using ½-width floristry tape (the smaller buds will have shorter stems). Next add the flowers (you will need between five and seven flowers at least). Thicken the stem with a couple more 18-gauge wires and also tape in some shredded absorbent kitchen paper to form more bulk. Dust the stem with a mixture of moss and vine green.

12 The leaves are very long and straplike, and are not used generally in floral arrangements.

NOTE

Agapanthus is available for many months of the year, with a peak during the summer. There can be as many as 200 flowers on one umbel of agapanthus. Fortunately this is not required by the sugarcrafter!

SOLOMON'S SEAL

It is not known for certain why Solomon's seal (*Polygonatum*) has its rather grand name. One theory is that it was because of the medicinal value of the plant for 'sealing' wounds and healing broken bones, and also as a cure for black eyes. It is traditionally said that the biblical King Solomon approved of its use! The flower shown here has been based on a garden variety. They can also be obtained as a cut flower from the florist. Solomon's seal can either be used as long trailing stems or they can be pipped and used individually in sprays and bouquets.

MATERIALS
Fine white stamens
18, 24, 26, 30 and 33-gauge wires
Primrose, moss, holly/ivy and
dark green petal dust
(blossom tint)
White and mid-green
flower paste
¼ glaze (see page 151)

EQUIPMENT
Nile green floristry tape
Six petal pointed blossom
cutters (N6,N7)
Solomon's seal leaf veiners (GI)

STAMENS

1 Tape six fine stamens on to the end of a short length of 30-gauge wire using ¼-width nile green floristry tape. Dust the tips with a touch of primrose petal dust. Place to one side and wash your hands because you need the flowers to be white not pale yellow!

FLOWER

2 Form a ball of well kneaded white flower paste into a teardrop shape. Pinch out the broad end of the teardrop to form a pedestal shape. Place the pedestal, with the flat side down, on to a board. Thin out the paste using a small celstick.

3 Cut out the flower shape using either of the two sizes of six petal blossom cutters – you will need a mixture of sizes to complete a stem. The backs of the flowers are

quite heavy and, because of this, you would be advised to place the back of the pedestal into a hole on the firm side of a celpad. Place the cutter over the flat section of paste and cut out the flower. Remove the cut out flower from the hole.

4 Soften the edges of each of the petals to thin them out a little. Open up the throat of the flower using the pointed end of a small celstick. Press the sides of the flower against the stick to thin them out and to give the flower more of a bell shape. The flower should be bulbous at the base, then have a waistline and then the petals should flair out a little at the base.

5 Place the flower, face side up, against your finger. Draw down a central vein on each petal using the fine end of the dresden tool. Pinch the tips of each of the petals and then arrange them so that it looks as if three of the alternate petals are on the inside layer and three on the outside. Curl their tips back a little. You will need to make a lot of flowers as they are grouped in twos and threes down the stem.

6 Dust the tips of the petals and the base of each flower with a mixture of primrose and moss green.

BUDS

7 Tape over several short lengths of 33-gauge wire with ¼-width nile green floristry tape. Bend a small hook in the end of each one. Roll a small ball of white flower paste into a cone shape and insert the hooked wire into the base. Roll the cone shape so that it resembles the shape of the flower but it needs to have a slight point at the tip too. Dust the tips and the base of each bud as for the flower.

LEAVES

8 Roll out a piece of mid-green paste, leaving a thick ridge down the centre. Using one of the Solomon's seal leaf veiners, press the flat side on top of the paste to leave an imprint of the basic outline. Cut out the leaf shape using a scalpel.

9 Insert a moistened 26-gauge or 24-gauge wire, depending on the size of the leaf, into the thick ridge. Place in between the two sides of the leaf veiner and press firmly to achieve a defined impression. Place the leaf on a pad and soften the edges using the rounded end of a large celstick. Pinch the leaf at the back from the tip to the base to shape the leaf. Allow to firm up over a slight curve before dusting.

COLOURING AND ASSEMBLY

10 Dust the leaf in layers with moss, holly/ivy and some dark green petal dust. Dip into a ¼ glaze, shake off the excess and allow the leaf to dry.

11 Tape the buds and flowers into sets of two and three, using ¼-width nile green tape. To form a long arched stem, tape a smaller leaf on to the end of an 18-gauge wire using ½-width nile green tape. Add a couple more slightly larger leaves, alternating them on the stem. Start adding the groups of buds, which should dangle below the stem. Every time you add a set of buds or flowers, you need to tape in a leaf at the axil. As you work down the stem you might need to add more 18-gauge wire to give strength to the stem.

12 Dust the main and shorter stems with a mixture of the various greens used on the leaves. Bend the flowers down and the leaves up using pliers, then bend the whole stem into its characteristic arched shape.

CHEERFUL HARMONY

This two-tiered cake with its wonderful tangled mass of
Iceland poppies would be most suited to a couple who
would like their wedding just that little bit different.
The design conjures up an immediate representation
of hot summer days, mainly due to the glorious colour
combination of orange, peach, red and yellow. This is
the cake that I created for the Table of Honour at the
International British Sugarcraft Guild Exhibition 1997.

MATERIALS

15cm (6 in) and 30cm (12 in)
oval cakes
Apricot glaze
2kg (4lb) almond paste (marzipan)
Clear alcohol (kirsch or vodka)
3kg (6lb) champagne sugarpaste
Fine red ribbon to trim cakes
Royal icing
Broad burnt orange ribbon
to trim boards
Tangerine, red, green and skintone
petal dust (blossom tint)

EQUIPMENT

Sugarpaste smoothers
23cm (9 in) and 40cm (16 in) oval
cake boards
Border stencil design (SL)
Firm soft medium paintbrush
Sharp scalpel
Fine paintbrush
Thin perspex disc
Small fleur-de-lys candle holder
Florists' staysoft
Two small perspex discs

FLOWERS

12 Iceland poppies, assorted colours
(see page 107)
about 14 Iceland poppy buds

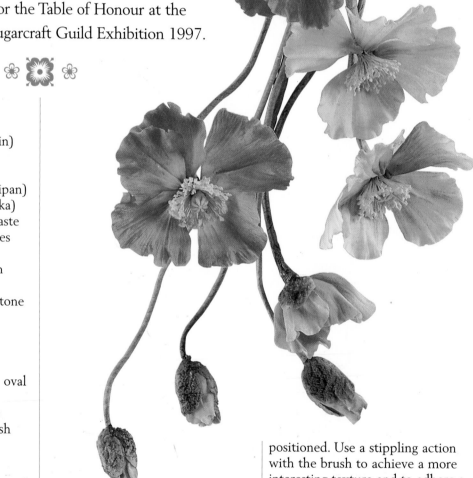

PREPARATION

1 Cover both cake boards with
champagne sugarpaste and allow
to dry. Using tangerine petal dust
and a firm soft paintbrush, colour
the area of the boards that will
be exposed once the cakes are

positioned. Use a stippling action
with the brush to achieve a more
interesting texture and to adhere a
strong colour to the boards. Over-
dust with red petal dust using the
stippling action again (some of the
tangerine base colour should show
through). Dilute a little of the red
petal dust with a small amount of
clear alcohol (if you have too much
alcohol the finished result will be
patchy and very sticky). Place the
stencil on top of the dusted board

102

and, using the stippling action again, apply the diluted red colour. (The stencil design I used was quite complicated so I picked out parts of the design to simplify and create an individual design.) Allow to dry. Using as sharp scalpel, etch around the edges of each of the stencilled shapes to highlight and define the design.

2 Brush the cakes with apricot glaze and cover with almond paste. Allow to dry overnight. Moisten the surface of the almond paste with clear alcohol and cover the cakes with champagne sugarpaste, using sugarpaste smoothers to achieve a good finish. Position the cakes on the cake boards and allow to dry for a few days.

3 Using the same stencil as before, add a design to the top of both cakes. This time use the orange and red petal dusts mixed with alcohol to create the design. Add extra hand-painted details using a finer paintbrush and orange, red and green dusts diluted with alcohol.

4 Fasten two bands of red ribbon around the base of each cake using a small amount of royal icing. Attach the broad burnt orange ribbon to the board edges using a non-toxic glue stick.

ASSEMBLY

5 Position the thin perspex disc on to the centre of the bottom tier and place the fleur-de-lys candle holder on top. Position the smaller cake on top, making sure that the complete display looks balanced.

6 Attach a clump of florists' staysoft on to each of the small perspex discs using a glue gun and place one at the back of each cake. Start to position the main focal

flowers, inserting the end of each stem into the staysoft. You will soon reach the stage where you will have to dismantle the cakes before you can carry on and complete the arrangements. With this design it is important to tangle the flowers and buds as much as possible, and also use the stems as part of the finished design.

7 Re-assemble the cake. Stand back and then re-arrange anything that looks out of place.

ICELAND POPPY TABLE SETTING

It can be quite a fun idea to use sugar flowers to decorate various items for a wedding reception. The Iceland poppy with its long stems makes an ideal choice. Here I have used Iceland poppies to decorate a glass, napkin and plate. However, these pieces can be time-consuming, so they could be used for perhaps only the wedding couple or for the bride and groom's mothers, or if time and money are not an issue, then for everybody!

FLOWERS FOR THE PLATE, NAPKIN AND GLASS

4 Iceland poppies
(see page 107)
2 buds

EQUIPMENT

Nile green floristry tape
Pliers
Wire cutters
Plate
Napkin
Wine glass

PLATE AND NAPKIN DECORATION

1 Tape together 1 bud, 1 half open, 1 nearly open and 1 fully open Iceland poppy, using ½-width floristry tape. Tuck the stems behind the plate and then attractively bend part of their stems and heads on to the plate.

2 Curl and then wrap the stem of a poppy bud around a folded napkin. Place on top of the plate.

3 Bend the stem on the fully open poppy and curl the base of the wire round. Tuck underneath the napkin, making sure that the flower head is steady.

4 Wrap a fully open poppy stem attractively around the stem of the wine glass.

ICELAND POPPY

The original colour of the Iceland poppy (*Papaver nudicaule*) was yellow; there are now many cultivars in all shades of yellow, white, salmon pink, orange and red. There are no leaves on the stems themselves, only at the base of the plant and, because of this, the leaves are rarely used. They are available from the florist in April to August and once in water can last for up to nine days! In the past, I have used Iceland poppies with montbretia, roses and virginia creeper in a bridal bouquet to wonderful effect.

OVARY

1 Roll a small ball of green flower paste into a cone shape. Tape over a length of 20-gauge wire, moisten the end with egg white and insert into the fine end of the cone. Pinch the pointed base of the cone to secure it in place and flatten the top. Cover the cone with a plastic bag to stop the surface of the paste drying out before the next stage.

2 Roll out a small amount of white paste thinly and cut out a daisy shape using the small daisy cutter. You will find it easier if the paste sticks to the cutter, as you can then simply press the cutter (with the paste inside) on top of the ovary. As the paste is still soft, the daisy shape should be released from the cutter and adhered to the top of the cone. Using a pair of angled tweezers, re-emphasize the shape of the daisy if needed. Dust the green part of the ovary with moss green and the daisy shape with a mixture of primrose and lemon.

STAMENS

3 You will need to use approximately half a bunch of seed-head stamens for each flower. (I have tried other less expensive materials to create the stamens but the seed-head stamens give far more interest!) I also find that because of the amount of stamens required, it is better to use a non-toxic craft glue to stick the stamens around the ovary, otherwise too much bulk is created behind the flower with the use of

MATERIALS
Pale holly/ivy and white
flower paste
20 and 28-gauge wires
Small seed-head stamens
Moss green, primrose, lemon
and aubergine petal dust
(blossom tint)
Mimosa sugartex
Orange and scarlet craft dust

EQUIPMENT
Tiny eight-petal daisy cutter (OP)
Angled tweezers
Non-toxic craft glue
Glue gun and non-toxic
glue sticks
Petal templates (see page 158)
or poppy cutters (TT)
Sharp scalpel
Asi-es orchid veiner (CC)
Ceramic silk veining tool (HP)
Leaf texturing tool
Nile green floristry tape

floristry tape. (For competition work this is a method that could lose you marks or if the schedule stated no inedible materials other than wire, tape and stamens you would be disqualified. I always feel that for personal use, non-toxic craft glue is acceptable when you consider that both floristry tape and paper covered wire have a certain amount of glue in their makeup.) The ovary must be completely dry before any glue comes into contact with the sugar.

4 First of all, spread the stamens open a little and then apply some glue in a strip across the stamens at the length required. Squeeze the stamens together to make sure that they are all included and then place to one side to allow the glue to dry. Cut the stamens

using scissors, apply some glue to the base of the ovary, this time using the glue gun, and wrap the stamens around the ovary quickly before the glue has a chance to dry. Allow to dry thoroughly and then dust the length of each stamen with a mixture of moss green and primrose petal dust. Colour the tips with mixture of primrose and lemon petal dust. To make more mature stamens, paint the tips with egg white and dip into some mimosa sugartex. Using tweezers, bend the stamens open to produce a more realistic effect (if you are making a flower that is not quite fully open, leave the stamens tight around the ovary).

PETALS

5 Very thinly roll out a small amount of white flower paste on a grooved board. Place one of the petal templates on top of the paste and cut out the petal using a sharp scalpel; or use a petal cutter. Remove from the board and insert a moistened 28-gauge white wire into the central ridge.

6 Place the back of the petal on to the orchid veiner and press the surface of the paste with the side of your hand. Remove the petal, turn it over and vein on the upper side. Place the petal down against the board and thin out and frill the top edge using the ceramic silk veining tool and then with a cocktail stick (toothpick). (It does not matter too

much if the edges get torn slightly here and there as this happens to the real poppy petals.) Cup the centre of the petal and allow to dry slightly over some bubble foam. Repeat to make at least one more petal of that size.

7 Repeat this process again, but this time cut out at least two petals using the larger template or cutter. Once you have finished veining and frilling, pinch a ridge on the upper surface of each petal. Allow to dry as before.

COLOURING AND ASSEMBLY

8 It is important to dust the poppy petals while they are still very fresh, so that the vibrant colours can be achieved easily. Dust a patch at the base of each petal on both sides with a mixture of primrose and lemon, then add a small amount of moss green to the very base. The rest of the colouring of the petal is up to you. I am fond of the orange/red poppies and for that I would start by rubbing the orange craft dust into

the paste with a brush, leaving the back a touch paler, and then over-dust the edge with scarlet craft dust.

9 Tape the two small petals tightly behind the stamens, and then tape the two larger petals behind the small petals to fill in the gaps. As the petals are still soft, you can re-shape them to give a more realistic finish to the flower. Allow to dry. Steam the flower to remove the dry appearance left by the dusting process.

BUDS AND STEMS

10 Tape over a length of 20-gauge wire several times to thicken the stem. Bend a small open hook on the end, moisten with egg white and attach an egg shaped piece of flower paste in the required size (remember the bud size varies quite a lot). Allow to dry.

11 Roll out some white flower paste very thinly and cut out two or three petals. Vein and frill as for the flower. Apply a little egg white to each petal and arrange on to the dry base. Crumple the petals

as you go, as this will help to give it a realistic appearance. Dust the petals with your chosen colours.

BRACT

12 Roll out some green flower paste quite thickly and texture the surface with the texturing brush to give the characteristic hairy appearance. Using the small poppy cutter, cut out two bract shapes and hollow out the centre slightly. Apply a little egg white to the underside and attach the two bracts on to either side of the bud or semi-opened flower. Once the bracts are in position, add a little more texture to the surface using a small pair of sharp scissors. Mark a definite indent with a scalpel to divide the two bracts.

13 Dust with moss green, leaving the open edges paler, then over-dust gently with aubergine to accentuate the rough texture. Dust the stems gently with the same colours. Bend the stem into shape. (Real poppy stems are covered with tiny black hairs, fortunately this is not required for sugar work!)

WINTER SOLSTICE WEDDING

Sometimes an impressive centrepiece is requested for a small wedding reception; here is an excellent example of a single-tiered cake displayed to maximum effect with the help of a couple of props and a lavish selection of flowers and foliage – the end result is a dramatic and romantic cake.

MATERIALS

20cm (8 in) heart-shaped cake
Apricot glaze
750g (1 ½ lb) almond paste
(marzipan)
Clear alcohol (kirsch or vodka)
1kg (2lb) champagne sugarpaste
Fine green ribbon to trim cake
Green velvet ribbon to trim board
A small amount of flower paste
Holly/ivy, aubergine, plum, primrose
and gold petal dust (blossom tint)

EQUIPMENT

Sugarpaste smoothers
28cm (11 in) heart-shaped cake board
Curved leaf cutters (ECC)
Side design template (see page 158)
Quilting wheel (PME)
Fine paintbrush
Nile green floristry tape
Posy pick
Broad green paper ribbon
Long perspex tube stand
Tilting cake stand

FLOWERS

Winter Solstice Free-flowing Posy
(see page 113)
Winter Solstice Teardrop-shaped
Spray (see page 113)
5 stems of large dark ivy
(see page 114)

PREPARATION

1 Brush the cake with apricot glaze and cover with almond paste. Allow to dry overnight. Moisten the almond paste with clear alcohol and cover with champagne sugarpaste, using smoothers to achieve a smooth finish.

2 Cover the cake board with champagne sugarpaste and transfer the cake on top, making sure that you have a neat join between the cake and the board. Allow to dry.

3 Attach a band of fine green ribbon around the base of the cake. Glue a length of green velvet ribbon to the board edge using a glue stick.

SIDE DESIGN

4 Finely roll out some flower paste and cut out two large and four small curved leaves for each section of the design; you will need five sets to complete the cake design. Cover the leaves that you are not working on with a plastic bag to prevent drying . Moisten the back of each of the leaves with clear alcohol and attach to the cake starting with the point of the heart shape, following the template design on page 158.

5 Using the quilting wheel, run a line of stitch marks down the centre of each of the leaves. Dilute a small amount of holly/ivy petal dust with alcohol and, using a fine paintbrush and firm brush strokes, colour in the leaf shapes from the base fading towards the centre. Using the same brush and colour, paint in the trailing green leaf stem and add a

couple of small painted leaves to the design. Clean the brush. Dilute some aubergine and plum petal dust, and paint in the remainder of each of the paste leaves and also add the dotted flower arrangement to both sides of the main design. Allow to dry.

6 Mix a small amount of holly/ivy with a dash of primrose and dust in the heart of the design to soften the whole appearance. Apply a little gold petal dust over the top of the paint work on the paste leaves.

ASSEMBLY

7 Wire up the flowers for the sprays (see page 113), taping together with floristry tape, creating a handle. Insert the handle of the teardrop-shaped spray into a posy pick and then into the top left hand corner of the cake.

8 Insert the green paper ribbon through the centre of the long perspex tube stand. Wrap the remainder around the outside using a small piece of double-sided sticky tape at the base to hold it in place. Insert the free-flowing posy into the top of the tube. Adjust the stems a little if needed. Place the cake on to the tilting cake stand using double-sided carpet tape to secure. Place the cake next to the tall floral display and then arrange the extra ivy around the base of the cake and arrangement.

WINTER SOLSTICE SPRAYS

The flowers used in the free-flowing spray have been taped together to form a very unstructured and natural display. It is based on a tussie-mussie shape to begin with, but has a few stems that trail beyond the basic posy shape (there are no strict rules to this type of bouquet). The smaller spray has been formed into a teardrop shape to fit in with the curve of the heart-shaped cake.

FREE-FLOWING POSY (TOP)

3 stems of small eucalyptus and
3 stems of large eucalyptus
(see page 120)
2 stems of ivy (see page 114)
1 full apricot-tinged rose, 1 half rose
and 4 rosebuds (see page 136)
2 cream half roses (see page 136)
2 sets of rose leaves (see page 138)
1 stem of cream dendrobium
orchids, plus one extra flower
(see page 116)
5 burgundy hellebores,
3 hellebore buds and 2 sets of
hellebore foliage (see page 115)

TEARDROP-SHAPED SPRAY

1 stem of cream dendrobium orchids
2 pieces of small eucalyptus and
1 piece of large eucalyptus
2 stems of ivy
1 full apricot-tinged rose, 1 half rose
and 1 rosebud
2 sets of rose leaves
2 hellebores and 2 hellebore buds

EQUIPMENT

20-gauge wires
Nile green floristry tape
Pliers and wire cutters

PREPARATION

1 Strengthen any of the stems that need extra support or length, taping in 20-gauge wires using ½-width nile green floristry tape.

FREE-FLOWING POSY

2 Tape together the foliage first of all, forming a loose posy shape (with a few extra long pieces), bending each of the stems to an angle of 90 degrees. Tape them together using ½-width floristry tape. This will form the handle to the spray.

3 Add the full rose in the centre of the spray – this will form the focal point. It should be slightly higher than any of the other flowers. Continue to add the other half roses and rosebuds (usually these would be placed fairly evenly around the posy, but in this case make them irregular).

4 Add and tape in the dendrobium orchids and hellebores to complete the spray. Cut off any excess wire from the handle to cut down on the bulk and then tape over with full-width floristry tape to neaten.

TEARDROP-SHAPED SPRAY

5 For the teardrop-shaped spray, start the spray with a single stem of dendrobium orchids, a stem of eucalyptus and a stem of trailing ivy.

6 Next, for the basic outline, use the various types of foliage. Tape the stems together at one point to form a handle as described in Step 2.

7 Tape in the roses, positioning the full rose at the focal point of the spray. Fill in the gaps with the hellebore flowers and any extra foliage.

IVY

Ivy (*hedera*) is the most useful form of foliage for the sugar flower maker, as there are many different shapes, shades of green and sizes. It is sometimes thought however to be unlucky for brides to carry ivy in their bouquets – a theory that is totally unfounded, as it is used to symbolize fidelity.

LEAVES

1 Roll out some green flower paste on to a grooved board. The thickness of the paste will depend upon the size of the leaf you are making. Cut out as many leaves as possible from one strip of paste. Cover the leaves that you are not working on to stop the paste drying out.

2 Insert a 24 or 26-gauge wire into the central ridge. Try to insert the wire into at least half the length of the leaf.

3 Vein the leaf using your chosen veiner; the large one pictured has been veined with the large nasturtium leaf veiners.

4 Soften the edges of the leaf using the rounded end of a large celstick. Allow to dry a little before dusting. Tape over each stem with nile green floristry tape.

COLOURING

5 Dust with holly/ivy petal dust on both sides of the leaf, making the back slightly paler. Over dust the upper surface with the dark green

mixture. For variation, dust the edges with aubergine or plum petal dust or a mixture of the two. Allow to dry overnight.

6 Dip into ½ glaze, shake off the excess and allow to dry. To create the paler veins, support the leaf from behind with a finger and, using a scalpel, etch off the colour and part of the sugar to show up the paler base colour. Start with the main veins, and then work on the finer ones to complete the leaf.

ASSEMBLY

7 Tape over the end of a 24-gauge wire with ½-width beige floristry tape. Curl the end around a celstick to form a start to the stem (this part would usually be made up from young leaves beginning to form). It usually looks best in bouquets if you start with the smaller leaves and gradually work down to the larger ones. (In nature this is not always the case.) You will need to add an 18-gauge wire quite early on to strengthen the stem.

MATERIALS

Pale green flower paste
18, 24, 26 and 28-gauge wires
Holly/ivy, dark green, aubergine
and plum petal dust
(blossom tint)
½ glaze (see page 151)

EQUIPMENT

Large ivy cutters (J)
Large ivy or large nasturtium
leaf veiners
Nile green and beige floristry tape

HELLEBORE

The hellebore (*helleborus*) was described in detail in my last book. I wanted to use them in this book, but instead of repeating all the text again the instructions below give a brief reminder.

MATERIALS

20, 24, 26 and 28-gauge wires
Small white seed-head stamens
Lemon, spring green, plum, aubergine, dark and moss green petal dust (blossom tint)
Pale and mid-green flower paste
½ glaze (see page 151)

EQUIPMENT

Large Christmas rose cutter (282)
Christmas rose veiner (GI)
Small hellebore leaf veiner (GI)

PISTIL AND STAMENS

1 The pistil is made with five pieces of twisted green floristry tape. Tape them together on a 24-gauge wire. Tape a reasonable quantity of stamens around the pistil so that the pistil is higher in the centre. Dust the tips of the stamens with lemon petal dust, then dust some spring green in at the base. Colour the pistil tips with plum petal dust.

NECTARY (PETALS)

2 Roll small balls of pale green flower paste into cone shapes. Hollow out the broad end and then thin the edges with the broad end of the dresden tool. Make ten. Attach to the base of the stamens with egg white or softened flower paste. Dust with spring green petal dust.

SEPALS

3 Roll out pale green flower paste on to a grooved board. Cut out five sepals. Insert a 28-gauge wire in at the base, then vein using the Christmas rose veiner. Soften the edges and firm up on a slight curve.

4 Dust while the paste is at the leather hard stage with plum and aubergine petal dust. Steam, then re-dust to a very dark colour.

5 Tape the sepals around the dried centre using ½-width tape. Tape in two 24-gauge wires to lengthen and strengthen the stem.

BRACTS

6 Form a slender teardrop of mid-green flower paste on the end of a 28-gauge wire. Flatten the paste, using the flat side of a veiner, to make it finer.

Vein using the hellebore leaf veiner. Soften the edges, then place the bract on the board and create a serrated edge using the fine end of the dresden tool. Make two or three bracts to add to each bud and flower. Dust with dark green and moss. Dust the edge with a little plum and aubergine mixed. Glaze using a ½ glaze and leave to dry. Tape the bracts behind the flower.

BUDS

7 Attach a cone of pale green paste on to a taped, hooked 20-gauge wire. Form five indents on the bud using a cage with five 24-gauge wires. Pinch the paste out from between the wires to thin the paste and represent tepals. Remove the cage, then twist the sections of the bud together to form a neat shape. Dust to match the flower. Add the bracts, then bend and curve the stem. Dust the stem of the flower and bud with aubergine and plum.

LEAVES

8 Using mid-green paste, cut out leaves. Vein using the hellebore or large briar rose leaf veiner. Make the leaf in the usual way, creating a serrated edge with the fine end of the dresden tool.

DENDROBIUM ORCHID

Often called Singapore orchid, this is the most commonly used orchid in bridal bouquets. White and cream are the most popular colours, although they are available in various shades of pink, magenta, purple and green as there are over a 1,000 species of dendrobium orchid. Sometimes this orchid is dyed to a peach, turquoise or bright yellow – the result is a very artificial-looking flower.

COLUMN

1 Roll a small piece of white or pale melon flower paste into a ball and then into a teardrop shape. This teardrop shape should be no longer than the section between the two side sections and the base of the labellum (lip) cutter. Hollow out the inside of the column using the rounded end of a small celstick. Curve slightly.

2 Tape over a ½-length of 22-gauge wire and bend a hook at one end. Hold the hook with pliers and bend to form a ski stick shape. Moisten the end and pull through the centre of the column to embed the hook into the paste. Pinch the outer part of the column between your finger and thumb to form a subtle ridge. Allow to dry.

3 Attach a tiny ball of paste to the front of the column, tucked on to the inner part. Indent the ball in half using a sharp scalpel. This forms the pollinia.

LABELLUM (LIP PETAL)

4 Roll out a piece of paste quite thinly. Cut out one petal using the labellum cutter/veiner. Press the paste firmly against the veins in the cutter, clean off the edges and then

MATERIALS
White or very pale melon flower paste
18, 22 and 24-gauge white wires
White, primrose and moss green petal dust (blossom tint), plus your chosen colour if you are making a coloured variety

EQUIPMENT
Dendrobium orchid cutters (HH)
White and nile green floristry tape
Sharp scalpel
Thin sponge

remove gently from the mould. Place against the board and frill the bottom section of the lip using the double frilling technique and the broad end of the dresden tool.

5 Place the petal on to a pad and soften the edges of the two side sections, using the rounded end of a small celstick. Hollow out and cup these two side sections using the same tool. Turn the petal over and draw down a central vein on the back of the petal to form a ridge on the upper side.

6 Moisten the base and part of the side sections of the petal and attach to the column. Curl the edges back a little and curl the lip to form an attractive shape. The two side sections should not overlap each other (you should be able to see the central part on the back of the column). Allow to dry.

LATERAL PETALS (WING PETALS)

7 Roll out some more paste and cut out two lateral petals. Press into the mould to get the strongest veining possible. Remove from the

mould and place on a pad. Soften the edges of the petals (do not frill). Place to one side to allow to dry slightly.

SEPALS

8 The three sepals are cut out as one complete piece, as this is how they are formed on the flower. Roll out the paste, cut out the sepal shape and press firmly into the mould. Remove and place on to a pad. Soften the edges of the sepals using the rounded end of a celstick.

9 Using the fine end of the dresden tool, draw a strong central vein on the two base sepals (the 'legs'). Pinch the tips of the three sepals between your finger and thumb.

ASSEMBLY

10 To attach the petals to the sepals you can use either egg white or softened flower paste. Position the petals in between the dorsal and lateral sepals (they do not overlap at the centre – see photograph).

11 Moisten the central section below the petals, in between the lateral sepals. Thread the dried column and labellum through the sepals in the centre of the junction between the dorsal sepal and lateral petals. Press the dorsal sepal firmly against the back of the column. Pinch the section in between the two lateral sepals around the base of the labellum (you might need to use a little more egg white at this stage). Cut off the excess paste from the base of the sepals.

12 Curve the dorsal sepal back and the two lateral sepals up

towards the labellum and then curl their tips back.

13 Cut a small square of thin sponge and cut a slit down the centre. Place over the back of the orchid to support the sepals and petals. You might also need to cut two small pieces of sponge to sit behind and support the petals until they are dry.

BUDS

14 The dendrobium orchid bud is quite a difficult shape to replicate. However they always look fine when they are dusted and taped together. They vary between 1-3cm (½ -1¼ in) in length. Roll a ball of flower paste into a teardrop shape. Pinch the tip to a sharp point and curve the teardrop, stroking it at the same time to flatten out one side slightly.

15 Pinch a small spur at the base of the bud and shape between your fingers until it looks complete. The smaller buds often look like small slippers and the larger ones in profile like birds! I suggest that you have to hand a fresh sample as they are not easy to produce without one and even then they are not the simplest of shapes to make. Hook and moisten the end of a 24-gauge wire and insert it into the back of the bud, towards the base. Pinch the paste on to the wire to secure the bud on to the wire. Divide the surface of the bud into three sections using a sharp scalpel to represent the three outer sepals.

COLOURING AND ASSEMBLY

16 Tape over the stem of the flowers and buds with ½-width white tape to thicken each of them. Mix together white, moss and primrose petal dust. Aim the colour at the centre of the flower (the column and centre of the labellum). If the colour is too strong, clean the brush with cornflour (cornstarch), then dust on to the paste. Dust the tips of the sepals and the back of the flower a little stronger.

17 It is best to tape the buds on to the stem and then dust them – this gives more graduation of colour on the stem. Tape a small bud on to the end of an 18-gauge wire. Continue to add the buds down the stem, leaving a little more of each of the short stems a little longer the larger the buds get. Add the flowers, again leaving a reasonable length to each. Dust the main stem and part of each of the shorter stems with the primrose and moss green mixture. Dust the buds with this mixture making the smaller buds much stronger in depth. Steam the whole stem to give a clean, slightly waxy appearance and to seal the colour on to the flowers and buds.

PHOTINIA

It is the new growth of photinia (*Photinia fraseri*) that provides the attractive glossy red leaves over quite a long period of time. Although the plant produces small white flowers in large groups during the spring, it is however usually only the decorative quality of the foliage that is used. I have used some artistic licence with this leaf, reducing the size slightly.

MATERIALS

Pale green flower paste
18, 22 and 26-gauge wires
Plum, aubergine, red, dark green and moss petal dust
(blossom tint)
½ and ¾ glaze (see page 151)

EQUIPMENT

Rose leaf cutters (J)
Extra large rose leaf cutter (J)
Large briar rose leaf veiner (GI)
Nile green floristry tape

LEAVES

1 Although these leaves are very red, it is best to start off with a pale green flower paste, then dust them afterwards. Roll out some pale green flower paste on to a grooved board.

2 Cut out leaves of various sizes using the rose leaf cutters. You will need more large leaves to complete a stem. Cut lengths of 26-gauge wire into three lengths. Moisten the end of the wire and insert it into the ridge down the centre of the leaf.

3 Place the leaf between the double-sided briar rose leaf veiner and press firmly. Remove the leaf and place on a pad. Soften the edges of the leaf, working half on the paste and half on the pad, using the rounded end of a large celstick.

COLOURING

4 Dust the leaves while they are still damp. Dust in layers with plum, aubergine, red and add a touch of the greens to the larger leaves. Dip them into either a ½ or ¾ glaze (depending on your own taste), shake off the excess and allow to dry. It is at this stage that the leaves can be reshaped a little before they are allowed to dry.

5 Tape over each stem with ½ width floristry tape, then tape them on to a stronger wire to form a main stem. Tape several stems together to form larger stems of photinia. The leaves also look good when used as individual items in formal sprays, perhaps as an alternative to rose leaves in sprays where roses are dominant. Dust the stems with plum, red and aubergine petal dust.

EUCALYPTUS

Eucalyptus is an ideal foliage for a bride who wants a very soft colour combination. There are many species of eucalyptus available from the florist in different seasons. I prefer the large-leafed forms, as they fill more space and give much more impact.

MATERIALS

Very pale holly/ivy flower paste
20, 26 and 28-gauge wires
Dark green, holly/ivy, white, aubergine, plum and black petal dust (blossom tint)
¼ glaze (see page 151) (optional)

EQUIPMENT

Circle cutters (TT)
Rose petal cutters (TT)
Australian rose petal cutters (TT)
Eucalyptus templates
(see page 158)
Fresh eucalyptus leaves or fine large rose leaf veiner
Nile green floristry tape

LEAVES

1 Roll out some pale green flower paste, leaving a thick ridge down the centre. The leaves should not be made too fine. Cut out the shape using your chosen cutter or with a scalpel and the leaf templates on page 158.

2 Cut a length of 26-gauge or 28-gauge wire into five. Moisten one end of a piece of wire and insert it into the central ridge of the leaf. The

wire should be inserted into at least half the length of the leaf. Elongate the leaf if required, simply by stretching the paste between your fingers.

3 Place the leaves on a pad and soften the edges with a large celstick. Vein the leaf using either the double-sided rose leaf veiner or preferably with a fresh (or dried) eucalyptus leaf. These leaves tend to be very flat, but I find that drying some with a little curve makes a more attractive finish. You will need to repeat the above process to make a variety of sizes for each stem, remembering that the leaves grow in pairs down the stem.

COLOURING

4 Start colouring the leaves using a flat-headed brush and a little dark green petal dust to add depth to the leaf. Over-dust gently with holly/ivy and a little white petal dust. Dust the edges and the base with aubergine and plum petal dust mixed together. Over-dust with white petal dust heavily. Add a little black petal dust to parts of the leaves if they require more depth. One of the lustre dusts can also be used as an alternative, especially for silver, pearl or Christmas wedding displays.

ASSEMBLY

5 At the top of each eucalyptus stem there are some fine stems, occasionally with tiny leaves attached. The florist usually trims these off. If you would like to add them, simply twist pieces of ¼-width floristry tape back on to itself to form fine strands.

6 Start to tape the stem together by taping a few strands on to the end of a 20-gauge wire using ½-width floristry tape. Start adding the small leaves in pairs and, as you work down the stem, add the medium and then the larger leaves. If you are making a very long stem, you might find that you will need to add an extra 20-gauge wire for strength and to give the overall appearance of more bulk. Smaller stems can be added on to the longer ones to give variation.

7 Dust the main stems with a touch of dark green and a lot of aubergine and plum petal dust. At this final stage you might need to add more white or aubergine on some of the leaves. Bend the whole stem and leaves to give movement to the whole piece.

PEONY WEDDING CAKE

The peony (*Paeonia*) has long been a popular flower for weddings. Here I have used only three flowers to create impact on a very stylish yet simple wedding cake. I have supplied a brush embroidery design on page 157 if a cake side design is preferred.

MATERIALS

20cm (8 in) and 30cm (12 in)
long octagonal cakes
Apricot glaze
2kg (4lb) almond paste (marzipan)
Clear alcohol (kirsch or vodka)
3kg (6lb) pale green sugarpaste,
using mint and holly/ivy paste
food colouring
Fine dusky pink ribbon to trim cakes
Broad dusky pink ribbon
to trim boards

EQUIPMENT

Sugarpaste smoothers
20cm (8 in), 28cm (11 in) and 40cm
(16 in) long octagonal cake boards
Medium tube stand
2 posy picks

FLOWERS

3 peonies (see page 124)
4 buds
25-35 sets of leaves

PREPARATION

1 Brush both the cakes with apricot glaze and cover with almond paste. Allow to dry overnight. Moisten the almond paste with clear alcohol and cover with pale green sugarpaste, using sugarpaste smoothers to achieve a good finish.

2 Cover the two larger cake boards with pale green sugarpaste. Transfer the cakes on top, making sure you have a neat join between the cake and board.

3 Attach a band of fine dusky pink ribbon around the base of the cakes. Glue a length of broad dusky pink ribbon to the board edges using a non-toxic glue stick.

ASSEMBLY

4 Place the base tier on top of the smallest cake board to lift it up from the table slightly. Place the tube stand directly behind the large cake, then position the smaller cake at a slight angle pointing away from the base tier.

5 Wire up the flowers, bud and foliage, making the larger spray with two flowers, three buds and leaves. Make the other spray with just one peony. Insert a posy pick into each cake and insert the main stem of each of the sprays into them. Place a bud and some foliage towards the back of the base tier on the board to add a little more interest and balance the design.

6 If required, pipe the brush embroidery design on to the sides of the cakes following the template on page 157.

7 The single tier cake shown provides an alternative using only the larger base tier. The three peonies have been used to create a slightly different, more compact design.

PEONY

The peony (*Paeonia*) originates from China where it has been cultivated for over 1000 years. The colour variation is vast, including white, cream, yellow, pink, magenta and burgundy varieties. They are available from the florist from May to July which, being the height of the wedding season, makes them a popular choice. As this is a large, showy flower you won't need to use many to make an amazing impact. The peony described here is based on one of the tree peony varieties.

MATERIALS
Pale green, pale ruby, white and mid-green flower paste
18, 20, 22, 24, 26 and 30-gauge wires
Vine green, aubergine, plum, lemon, primrose, dark green and holly/ivy petal dust (blossom tint)
Deep magenta craft dust
White or lemon small hammer-head stamens
½ glaze (see page 151)

EQUIPMENT
Nile green floristry tape
Large rose petal cutters (TT549,550,551) or templates (see page 157)
Small rose petals (TT276,278,279,280)
Ceramic silk veining tool (HP)
Apple tray or other suitable cupped former
Peony leaf templates (see page 157) or cutters (TT)
Peony leaf veiners (GI)

PISTIL
The pistil is made up in three or five sections; it depends how mature the flower is as to the size of the sections. A mature flower can have very large sections forming the

fruit: it is in this form that I prefer to make them. Cut three or five short lengths of 26-gauge wire. Hook and moisten the end. Roll a ball of pale green flower paste into a teardrop shape and insert the wire into the base. Pinch a ridge on one side of the teardrop, and then curl the tip on to the side with the ridge. Repeat this process to make three or five sections. Tape the sections together before they dry, using ½-width nile green tape. Press the separate sections together to form a tight, attractive centre. Allow to dry, then dust with vine green petal dust. Dust the tips with a little deep magenta and aubergine (this varies between the different varieties).

Stamens

2 The stamens vary a little between the different varieties and also at the various stages of maturity. The anthers are very large to begin with and, as the flower matures, they become very fine. They can be represented with thread or with commercially prepared stamens. I use small hammer-head stamens, as the peony is a large flower and I feel it gives a stronger centre to the flower. Tape approximately 80 (¼–⅓ of a bunch) lemon or white stamens around the fruit, using ½-width tape. Trim off the excess stamens from the base and tape down over the wire.

3 Dust the tips of the stamens with a mixture of lemon and primrose petal dust. Dust the length of each of the stamens with deep magenta craft dust. Using tweezers, bend and curl the stamens to open them slightly. In a flower that has only just opened, the stamens will be very tight together and the ovary not visible. Place to one side.

Petals

4 Roll out some ruby coloured flower paste, leaving a thick ridge at the centre. The paste should not be too fine or too thick. Squash the three large rose petal cutters into the shape to match the design on page 157 or cut out three templates.

5 Insert a moistened 26-gauge wire in at the base of each of the petals. Place the petal back on to the board and vein both sides using the silk veining tool. Roll the tool across the petal in a fan formation, trying not to alter the shape of the petal too much. Next frill the upper edge of the petal using the silk veining tool. Soften the frill by re-frilling with a cocktail stick (toothpick).

6 Hollow out the centre of each petal, by stretching and stroking the paste between your fingers and thumbs. Place on an apple tray to dry the petals into shape. You will need to cut out at least six medium and nine large petals to complete a flower – more petals will produce a more flamboyant flower.

COLOURING AND ASSEMBLY

7 As there are many different types of peony, the colouring will be very individual. If you want to copy the one pictured, then dust each of the petals from the base with deep magenta craft dust, fading the colour out towards the top edge. Dust a patch of aubergine petal dust at the base.

8 Tape the six smaller petals around the stamens using ½ – width nile green floristry tape. Add the larger petals, in between each of the first layer and then add the remaining petals wherever they are needed. If the petals are still damp, re-shape them to form a more relaxed, realistic effect. Tape an 18-gauge wire alongside the main stem if it needs extra support.

CALYX

9 The calyx is made up from three rounded sepals and two longer narrow sepals. Roll out a strip of pale green paste on to a grooved board and cut out three sizes of rose petal shapes (278, 279, 280). Insert a moistened 30-gauge wire into the thick ridge of each sepal. Place them on a pad and soften the edges. Cup and hollow out the ridged side of each sepal. Pinch a tiny point at the rounded end of the sepal. Allow to firm up a little.

10 To make the two narrow sepals, you can either cut them out with a scalpel or use the quicker method of rolling a sausage of paste on to a 30-gauge wire. Thin the sausage between your fingers and palms and form a neat point at the tip. Place on a board and flatten with the flat side of a veiner. You need to make one sepal slightly longer than the other. Pinch a vein down the centre and allow to firm up. Dust all of the sepals with some vine green petal dust and catch the tips with a mixture of aubergine and plum.

11 Tape the three rounded sepals on to the back of the flower first of all and then add the two narrow sepals so that they are quite evenly spaced.

BUDS

12 Tape over a ½ length of 18-gauge wire using ½-width nile green tape. Bend a large open hook at one end of the wire using pliers. Roll a medium to large sized ball of white paste, moisten the hooked wire and insert into the ball of paste. Pinch the paste on to the wire to secure it in place. Allow to dry completely.

13 Roll out some ruby paste thinly and cut out five or six petals using either rose petal cutter 551 or 276 (this will depend how big the central ball is). Vein and frill as for the flower. Moisten the base of each of the petals and attach them to the dried ball. Start by placing the petals on opposite each other, creasing and pressing down each of the petals as you put them on to create a tight bud.

14 Dust the petals to match the flower. Attach a calyx as for the flower, but this time do not wire the three rounded sepals – they are simply stuck to the base of the bud. Wire the two long sepals and wire them on to the stem. Thicken the stem with some shredded absorbent kitchen paper taped over with ½-width tape. Dust the stem with vine green and then over-dust with aubergine petal dust. Steam the buds and flowers to remove the dry appearance left by the dusting process.

LEAVES

15 The leaves grow in sets of three. There are a number of leaf templates on page 157. Some of the shapes are interchangeable and you will need a lot of foliage to complete a flower stem. Roll out some mid-green flower paste, leaving a thick ridge down the centre. Place a leaf template on top of the paste and cut out the leaf using a sharp scalpel. Insert a moistened 26-gauge or 24-gauge wire, depending on the size of the leaf, into the thick ridge so that it supports at least half the length of the leaf.

16 Vein the leaf using the peony leaf veiners. Place on a pad and soften the edges to take away the harsh cut edge. Pinch down the central veins (if the leaf is tri-lobed, then pinch each of the sections). Allow the leaves to firm up fairly flat but with a slight curve at the ends. Repeat to make a complete set of leaves.

COLOURING AND ASSEMBLY

17 Dust the leaves with vine green, dark green and holly/ivy petal dust. Dust the edges of the leaves with plum and aubergine. Dip into a ½ glaze. Dry. Tape the leaves together into sets of three. If the leaves are large, tape a 22-gauge or 20-gauge wire on to the stem.

18 Tape two or three sets of leaves on to each of the flower and bud stems. Join two bud stems together and add another set of leaves at the axil. Add the flowers and leaves, adding a set of leaves at the join between the two stems. Dust the stems with aubergine.

Autumn Haze

Autumn provides the sugarcrafter with the ideal opportunity to use some of nature's very rich colouring. This one-tier cake includes a vibrant selection of warm colours using the ever popular rose with some of the more unusual flowers, such as Guernsey lily or nerine and shining euphorbia, to make a stunning centrepiece.

EQUIPMENT

Sugarpaste smoothers
36cm (14 in) pointed oval
cake board
Florists' staysoft
Small perspex disc (HP)

MATERIALS

25cm (10 in) pointed oval cake
Apricot glaze
1kg (2lb) almond paste (marzipan)
Clear alcohol (kirsch or vodka)
1.5kg (3lb) sugarpaste
Nasturtium and poppy paste
food colouring
Orange ribbon and 'S' scroll
gold braiding to trim cake
Broad burnt orange ribbon
to trim board

FLOWERS

Autumn Haze Curved Arrangement
(see page 131)
1 Ranunculus (see page 72)

PREPARATION

1 Colour the sugarpaste with nasturtium and poppy paste colouring and allow to rest before handling again.

2 Brush the cake with apricot glaze and cover with almond paste. Leave to dry overnight. Moisten the surface of the almond paste with clear alcohol and cover with the pale orange sugarpaste, using sugarpaste smoothers and the pad technique (see page 94) to achieve a good finish. Cover the board with the pale orange sugarpaste. Transfer the cake on to it, in a slightly off-set position. Make sure there is a neat join between the base of the cake and the board. Allow to dry.

3 Attach two bands of orange ribbon (or one slightly broader ribbon) around the base of the cake. Position a band of the gold braiding over the top of the orange ribbon. Place a length of broad burnt orange ribbon around the cake board edge, attaching with non-toxic glue stick.

ASSEMBLY

4 Place a clump of florists' staysoft on to the small perspex disc. Arrange the flowers and foliage for the Autumn Haze Curved Arrangement into the staysoft as instructed on page 131. Place the arrangement on top of the cake. Add one single ranunculus at the base of the cake slightly underneath the arrangement.

Autumn Haze Curved Arrangement

You will find that with this type of arrangement it is better to arrange the flowers directly on to the cake; however you will need to be careful not to mark the sugarpaste as you do so, otherwise the arrangement will have to be re-designed to cover the error! This is often the way new floral designs are created.

FLOWERS

1 long stem of shining euphorbia with foliage and 2 short stems without foliage (see page 134)

1 full rose, 3 half roses and 1 rosebud (see page 136)

1 stem of red Guernsey lily with three flowers (see page 132)

3 sets of rose leaves (see page 139)

3 stems of hypericum berries (see page 78)

5 ranunculus, various sizes (see page 72)

5 photinia leaves (see page 119)

EQUIPMENT

Florists' staysoft
1 small oval acrylic base (HP)
Fine pliers
Wire cutters

PREPARATION

1 Attach a clump of staysoft to the acrylic base (as this arrangement is not too large there is no need to glue the two together). Hook the ends of each of the flower stems in turn, once they have been cut to the required size.

ASSEMBLY

2 Insert the three stems of shining euphorbia into the staysoft to form the first basic curves to the arrangement.

3 Add the large rose at the centre of the arrangement to form the focal point. Add the other roses around the main flower. Position the Guernsey lilies at the back of the arrangement, to the right hand side of the large rose. Insert the two sets of rose leaves opposite one another, either side of the large rose.

4 Next insert the three stems of hypericum, evenly spaced around the arrangement. Fill in the gaps with the various sizes of ranunculus. To add depth to the display, insert the five photinia leaves.

5 Finally, stand back from the cake and the arrangement to take another look to check to see if any of the flowers need re-positioning or relaxing.

GUERNSEY LILY

Originally from South Africa, the Guernsey lily (*Nerine sarniensis*) is a descendant of bulbs from a South African ship stranded on Guernsey. The flower that I have made is one of the red-flowering hybrids. There are also, on a limited scale, orange, salmon, pink and cerise flowers. Other varieties have provided the more popular bright pink flowers.

MATERIALS

18, 24, 28 and 33-gauge
white wires
Poppy and green flower paste
Aubergine, deep purple, white,
vine green, moss green, cream
and nutkin brown petal dust
(blossom tint)
Scarlet craft dust

EQUIPMENT

Cattleya orchid sepal cutter
(TT8) or template (see page 156)
Nile green floristry tape

STAMENS

1 Cut six short lengths of 33-gauge white wire. Bend a closed hook in one end of each wire. Hold the hook at its centre with pliers and bend it into a 'T' bar shape.

2 Attach a tiny sausage of paste on to each 'T' bar shape (without egg white) to form the anther, which should be a neat shape. Dust the filament with scarlet craft dust and the anthers with aubergine and deep purple petal dust. If making a mature flower, dot the anther with white petal dust to represent pollen.

3 Tape the six stamens together, leaving three of them longer in length. (The pistil is shorter than the stamens and is not essential to include.) However if you choose to do so, simply add an extra 33-gauge scarlet dusted wire. It is only in a very mature flower that the pistil is very prominent and the tip divided into three curled sections (this would then be made with floristry tape). Curl the group of stamens slightly.

PETALS

4 Roll out poppy coloured flower paste on to a fine grooved board. Squash the cattleya sepal cutter to make a slimmer petal shape. With a sharp scalpel, cut out six petals using the template or orchid cutter. Insert a moistened 28-gauge wire into the central ridge of each petal.

5 Place each petal in turn on to the board and frill the sides of the

petal, using the broad end of the dresden tool to double frill the edge. Place each petal on to a pad and, using the fine end of the tool, draw down a central vein on the upper surface. Curl into shape and allow to firm up a little, drying on their sides.

6 Dust each petal with scarlet craft dust, leaving the central part pale to allow the base colour to show through. If necessary, dust the centre with a little white petal dust. Tape three of the petals around the stamens and then tape the remaining three in between each of the first layer, slightly recessed. If the petals are still wet, you should now be able to re-curl the edges if needed.

OVARY

7 Attach a ball of green flower paste at the base of the flower. Divide the ovary into three sections using a scalpel. Dust with vine green petal dust and a touch of moss.

BUDS

8 The buds are long and slender in shape. Using poppy coloured flower paste, insert a 24-gauge wire, hooked in at the base. Divide the length of each into three sections using a cage made from three 28-gauge wires. Add the ovary as for the flower. Dust with scarlet craft dust. The number of buds vary from stem to stem, so the choice is entirely up to the individual.

ASSEMBLY

9 Tape together a group of buds and two to three flowers on to an 18-gauge wire using ½-width floristry tape. Add a couple more wires to strengthen the stem if the flowers are to be used in an arrangement. Thicken the stem with shredded absorbent kitchen paper and then tape over the top. Dust the stem with vine and moss green.

10 Where the flowers and buds join the main stem, there are some stringy bits and two bracts. The stringy bits can be made with either some thread dusted with a touch of cream or with the stringy bits at the base of a fresh corn on the cob husk. Simply tape them on to the stem and curl some of them back slightly. To form the bracts, either cut out two shapes using white flower paste or floristry tape. Try to give these pieces a distressed, crumpled appearance. Dust with cream and nutkin brown petal dust and tape on the stem. Re-dust the stem if needed.

NOTE

To make the more popular pink variety of nerine, colour the flower paste with a small amount of ruby paste colour. Dust with fuchsia, plum and deep purple petal dust. The anthers are coloured only for the red variety, but the filaments should be dusted to a strong pink instead of red. These flowers tend to be larger that the red type, although there are some varieties with very small, fine flowers.

Shining Euphorbia

Shining euphorbia (*Euphorbia fulgens*) is a shrub that originates from Mexico and is part of the family of plants that includes the ever popular poinsettia (*Euphorbia pulcherrima*). Like the poinsettia, shining euphorbia is used for the ornamental quality of the brightly coloured bracts (its flowers look very much like stamens at the centre of the flower-like bracts). The original colour was orange, but there are now many hybrid forms in white, cream, yellow, salmon pink and a deep orange/red. The long stems that are characteristic of this plant look wonderful in bridal bouquets. The leaves have a tendency to drop naturally (this does not indicate that the plant is past its best), and sometimes the florist will remove the leaves to form a neater stem for use in bridal work.

Flowers (stamens)

1 Cut a length of 33-gauge white wire into five. Bend each section in half and place to one side. Wrap some fine white thread around two slightly parted fingers several times, remembering that this is to form a fairly insignificant part to the finished piece. Remove from your fingers and twist it into a figure of eight shape. Bend the whole shape in half to form a smaller loop.

2 Bend the prepared wire through the centre of the thread and tape over the base of the thread and down the wire with ¼-width floristry tape. Repeat this process using the same loop of thread to form several short lengths. Cut the thread through at the required intervals to form separate central pieces.

3 Rub the tips of the thread against an emery board to give the tips more bulk. Dip each of the thread centres into red petal dust.

4 To add pollen to the flowers, paint a little fresh egg white on to your work board, rub the tips of the thread gently in the egg white and then dip the tips into some mimosa sugartex. Allow to dry.

Bracts

5 Roll a small ball of pale melon flower paste into a teardrop shape. Pinch out the broad end of the teardrop between your fingers and thumbs to form a pedestal. Place the shape, flat side down, on your board and roll out the paste finely using a small celstick. Place the small stephanotis cutter over the thick part of the pedestal and cut out the bract shape. Rub your thumb over the cutter before removing the paste

MATERIALS

20, 26, 28 and 33-gauge wires
Fine cotton lace-making thread
(Brock 120)
Red, tangerine, holly/ivy, dark
green and white petal dust
(blossom tint)
Mimosa sugartex
Pale melon or white and
mid-holly/ivy flower paste
Clear alcohol (kirsch or vodka)
¼ glaze (see page 151)

EQUIPMENT

Nile green floristry tape
Small stephanotis cutter (TT568)
Poinsettia cutters (J)
Poinsettia leaf veiners (GI)
Fine paintbrush

to make sure that you have clean cut edges to the shape.

6 Place the shape, flat side down, on to the board. Using the small celstick again, roll and broaden each of the five sections. Place the shape on to a pad and hollow out the back of each of the sections using the rounded end of the celstick.

7 Using the pointed end of the celstick, open up the centre of the bract shape. Moisten the base of the thread flower centre and pull through the centre of the bract shape. Allow to firm up a little before colouring. Repeat the process to make a large number of flowers.

BUDS

8 Bend a small hook on to the end of a very short piece of 33-gauge wire. Roll a small cone shaped piece of melon flower paste and insert the hooked wire into the fine end of the cone. Divide the rounded end into five sections using a cage made with five pieces of 33-gauge wire.

LEAVES

9 Roll out mid holly/ivy flower paste on to a grooved board. Cut out several leaves using the various sizes of poinsettia cutters (use the plainer cutters in the set). Insert a moistened 28-gauge or 26-gauge wire into the central ridge of each leaf.

10 Vein using the poinsettia leaf veiners. Place the leaves on to a pad and soften the edges. Pinch the central vein on the back of each leaf to emphasize the vein. Allow to firm up before dusting.

COLOURING AND ASSEMBLY

11 Dust each of the bracts with tangerine and over-dust with red petal dust. The back of the bracts should be paler and the tube should

be left cream. Dust the base of the tube with a touch of green. Dust the tips of the buds to match the flowers. Tape the flowers and buds into the mixed groups of three.

12 Dust the leaves with holly/ivy and dark green petal dust. Mix together a small amount of alcohol with white petal dust and a touch of green. Using a fine paintbrush, paint in the central vein fading out towards the tip, then paint in a few of the finer veins at the base of the leaf. Allow to dry. Dip into a ¼ glaze, shake off the excess and dry.

13 To form a stem, tape a small leaf on to the end of a 20-gauge wire, leaving part of its stem showing. Continue to tape down the stem adding leaves, graduating in size and alternating from left to right. Start to add the bracts at intervals down the stem, adding a single leaf to each group until you have completed the length of stem required. Dust the main stem with dark green and holly/ivy green. Bend the complete stem into its arching shape. Steam the whole piece.

ROSE

Roses (*Rosa*) are still by far the most popular and most loved flower in the world. Commercial roses can be divided into four main groups – large, medium, small and spray roses.

into the base of the cone, making sure that the hook goes almost to the tip. Pinch the base of the cone firmly on to the wire to secure. Make as many as you need and dry overnight.

2 Colour a large amount of flower paste to the required colour. Here the base colour is a pale melon. Start with a paler base colour and then achieve the depth and realism with petal dust when the flower is completed. If you intend to make white roses, use either a touch of melon (for a warm glow) or bitterlemon (to give a green tinge).

FIRST AND SECOND LAYERS

3 Roll out some coloured flower paste thinly, and cut out four petals using the smaller rose petal cutter. Place the petals on a pad and soften the edges using the rounded end of a large celstick, working half on the paste and half on the pad. If you work with the tool too much on the inner edge, the petal will curl up and form an unattractive shape. Do not frill the edges of the petals, simply soften the harsh cut edge.

MATERIALS

Ivory and green flower paste
18, 24, 26 and 28-gauge wires
Primrose, lemon, white, apricot, plum, aubergine, dark green, moss and holly/ivy petal dust
(blossom tint)
½ glaze (see page 151)

EQUIPMENT

Rose petal cutters (TT)
Large rose petal veiner (GI) or ceramic silk veining tool (HP)
Rose calyx cutters (R11b, R11c)
Rose leaf cutters (J)
Extra large leaf cutter (J)
Large briar rose leaf veiner (GI)
Apple tray cupped former

4 Moisten the central part of one of the petals and place it against a dried cone, leaving at least 5mm (¼ in) of the petal above the tip of the cone. Tuck the left hand side of the petal in towards the cone (to hide the tip of the cone completely). Wrap the other side of the petal around to form a tight spiral, leaving the end slightly open. Do not worry about the base of the cone at this stage, concentrate only on the formation of the petals from an overhead view.

5 Moisten the bases of the remaining three petals. Tuck the first of these underneath the open edge of the petal on the cone, the second underneath the first and the third underneath the second. The petals

PREPARATION

1 Roll a ball of white flower paste into a cone with a sharp point and a fairly broad base. (It should measure no longer than the small rose petal cutter you are planning to use; for a bud it should be quite a lot smaller.) Tape over a half length of 18-gauge wire and bend an open hook in the end using pliers. Moisten the wire with egg white and insert it

should now be fairly evenly spaced. Moisten the petals if needed and close them all tight, pulling the petals down at an angle rather than wrapping them straight around. There are now enough petals on the cone to make a small bud, but for a larger rose, open up one of the petals again.

THIRD AND FOURTH LAYERS

6 Roll out some more paste and cut out another three petals using the same size cutter as before. Soften the edges of each of the petals, then vein using either the double sided veiner or the silk veining tool or a combination of the two. If you are making smaller roses then you do not need to worry too much

about veining. Moisten the base of each of the petals again, tuck the first petal of the third layer underneath the last petal of the second layer. Continue to add the remaining petals as before, this time pinching a very gentle central vein on each of the petals between your finger and thumb as you add them to the rose.

7 Cut out another three petals and repeat Step 6, this time wrapping the petals less tightly.

FIFTH AND SIXTH LAYERS

8 Roll out more paste and cut another three petals using the slightly larger petal cutter. Vein and

soften each of the petals as before. Cup the centre of each petal using the rounded end of a large celstick.

9 Moisten the base of each petal and attach them as before, making sure that the centre of each covers a join in the previous layer. The rose should now be quite open; curl back the petal edges using your fingers or a cocktail stick (toothpick). This rose is termed a 'half rose'; I use more half roses than full ones in a spray or bouquet.

10 The sixth layer can either follow on as before or the petals can be wired individually. Roll out a small piece of paste leaving a thick ridge down the centre (this needs to be very subtle). Cut out the petal using same size cutter as before. Hook and moisten the end of

a 26-gauge wire. Insert into only the base of the thick ridge. Soften the edges and place into the veiner. Remove from the veiner and stroke the centre of the petal to stretch it and cup it slightly. Place into an apple tray former to firm up. Repeat to make eight to ten petals. Curl the edges back a little at this stage.

ASSEMBLY AND COLOURING

11 I usually tape the petals around the rose centre and then petal dust them as I find that I end up with a more balanced result. Mix together some primrose, lemon and white petal dust. Dust in at the base of each petal on the inside and slightly heavier on the back. Next, mix together the selected main colour; here I am using a mixture of apricot and plum petal dust. Start by dusting the centre of the rose, firmly and quite strong in colour. Gradually dust the outer petals starting at the edges and fading down to the base. Steam and re-dust if necessary.

CALYX

12 Roll a ball of mid-green flower paste into a cone and pinch out the base to form a hat shape. Using a small celstick, roll out the base to make it a little thinner, although the calyx should have quite a 'fleshy' appearance. Cut out the calyx, and elongate each sepal by rolling with the celstick.

13 Place the calyx cutter on a pad and cup the inner part of each of the sepals. Dust the inner calyx with a mixture of white and moss green to make it paler. If wished, make some fine cuts in the edges of each sepal with a pair of fine scissors, to give them a 'hairy' appearance. The number of cuts on a florists' rose vary and some have no cuts at all; only a wild rose has an exact number of hairs/cuts on each sepal.

14 Moisten the centre of the calyx and attach it to the back of the rose or bud, positioning each sepal so that it covers a join between two outer petals. On a full-blown rose, the calyx would curl right back and on a rosebud it would be tight around the bud. For a competition, where the sepals should curl right back, then attach the calyx just before you wire them into a spray. This will enable the sepals to move around comfortably, and dry in position. Dust the outer part of the calyx with dark green and moss. Keep the very edges of each sepal much paler. Some roses benefit from a touch of plum, red or aubergine to the tips of the sepals. Dry; paint the sepals with a ¼ or ½ glaze (optional).

LEAVES

15 Rose leaves are not used as a main foliage in bridal bouquets and sprays. They are however essential in arrangements and if you

are making roses to display in a vase. I occasionally incorporate a few stems into a spray or bouquet, especially if I am running short of other foliage and have rose leaves spare. Rose leaves on commercial florists' roses can grow in sets of three or five, depending upon the variety. Roll out some mid-green paste, leaving a thick ridge down the centre (a grooved board may be used for this). Cut out a selection of sizes using rose leaf cutters; the quality of rose leaf cutters varies a lot – avoid at all costs any metal rose leaf cutters. You will need one large, two medium and two small leaves per stem.

16 Choose lengths of 26-gauge or 28-gauge wire (depending on the size of the leaf), and cut into four. Moisten one end of each wire and insert into the thick ridge of a leaf. The wire should be inserted into at least half the length of the leaf. Vein the leaf using the briar rose leaf veiner. Place the leaf on a pad and soften the edges using a large celstick. Pinch a vein down the centre of the leaf and shape the leaf between your finger and thumb to give a little more movement.

17 Using a flat brush, dust the back of each leaf with white and a touch of moss green petal dust. Over-dust with plum and aubergine on the edges and bring a little of the colour down on to the veins (not all roses have this

colouring). Turn the leaf over and dust the edges and one side heavier with the aubergine and plum mixture. Dust the upper side of the leaf with dark green and then over-dust with either holly/ivy or moss green. Dip into a ½ glaze, shake off the excess and allow to dry.

ASSEMBLY

18 Tape the leaves together into groups of three or five, starting with a large leaf, then the medium leaves, and finishing with the two small leaves.

NOTE

If you have to make a few roses in a hurry and do not have any pre-dried centres, then try this alternative method. Hook an uncovered 18-gauge wire, make the cone as before and then, using a cigarette lighter or gas hob, heat the hook until it is red hot. Quickly insert the hook into the rose cone, neaten the base and allow to firm a little. The sugar caramelizes, cools quickly and gives a secure base (if you use moisture it tends to slide around during the making of a rose).

Groom's Cake

A groom's cake is an excellent choice for a wedding where the groom, or the bride (and perhaps some of the guests) does not like fruit cake. This cake would perhaps be a chocolate, carrot, Madeira or orange sponge cake in place of the traditional fruit cake. The decoration can be novelty or a floral combination of more masculine flowers to tie in with the main colour scheme.

MATERIALS

25cm (10 in) kidney-shaped cake
Apricot glaze
1kg (2lb) almond paste (marzipan)
Clear alcohol (kirsch or vodka)
1.5kg (3lb) white sugarpaste
Yellow and willow green ribbon
Green velvet ribbon to trim board
Lemon, primrose and tangerine petal
dust (blossom tint)

EQUIPMENT

36cm (14 in) oval cake board
Flat paintbrush
Flat or tilted cake stand
Posy pick

FLOWERS

1 stem of fragrant evening primrose
(see page 142)
1 stem of hypericum berries
(see page 78)
5 stems of large dark ivy
(see page 114)
5 photinia leaves (see page 119)
1 sprig of rosemary (see page 65)

Preparation

1 Brush the cake with apricot glaze and cover with almond paste. Moisten the surface of the almond paste with alcohol and cover with white sugarpaste.

2 Cover the board with white sugarpaste and transfer the cake on top, making a neat join between the cake base and board. Allow to dry.

3 Mix together some lemon and primrose petal dust. Using a flat brush, dust the sides of the cake with colour starting at the base and fading the colour out at about half the depth of the cake. Add some colour to the top of the cake where the spray is to be positioned. Intensify the colour on the sides and the top by adding some tangerine petal dust.

4 Attach a band of willow green ribbon and yellow ribbon to the sides of the cake. Using the yellow and tangerine petal dust, colour half of the yellow ribbon simply by dusting on top. Glue the green velvet ribbon to the board edge, using a non-toxic glue stick.

Assembly

5 Tape together the flowers, berries and foliage for the evening primrose spray into an informal tied bunch. If you are displaying the cake flat, then simply rest the spray on top of the cake.

6 If you are using a tilted cake stand as I have used here, then you will need to attach the spray to the cake. Therefore insert a small posy pick into the cake and fill with a sausage of sugarpaste. Position the spray on to the top of the cake and over the posy pick. Bend a piece of wire to form a staple; place over the handle of the spray and insert the two ends of the staple into the sugar-paste in the posy pick. Place the cake on the tilting cake stand.

FRAGRANT EVENING PRIMROSE

Evening primroses (*Oenothera stricta*) were introduced to Great Britain and now they have naturalized themselves. There are almost 100 species, including some white and pink forms, with varying sizes of flower. Most of the species have a fragrant perfume but this form, as it name implies, is very fragrant. Flowering from June to September, evening primroses open in the late afternoon to early evening and remain open, even during dull weather. A fading flower turns a rich orange/red colour.

MATERIALS

20, 26, 28 and 30-gauge wires
Small seed-head stamens or small hammer-head stamens (optional)
Lemon, vine green, primrose, red, apricot, tangerine, dark green, moss green and aubergine petal dust (blossom tint)
Pale melon, pale green and mid-holly/ivy flower paste
½ glaze (see page 151)

EQUIPMENT

White and nile green floristry tape
Heart cutter (TT333)
Ceramic silk veining tool
Fuchsia sepal cutter (TT309)
Leaf template (see page 156)

PISTIL AND STAMENS

1 To make the pistil, tape over the end of a 30-gauge wire with ½-width white floristry tape, leaving a flap at the end. Using a fine pair of scissors, cut the flap into four. Twist each section between your finger and thumb to make fine strands. Curl the tips back slightly.

2 The stamens can either be made by cutting the ends off eight seed-head stamens and attaching a tiny strand of paste to form a 'T' bar, or use eight small hammer-heads.

Tape the eight stamens around the pistil so they are a bit shorter. Dust the tips of the stamens with lemon. Tinge the tip of the pistil with vine green.

PETALS

3 Thinly roll out melon paste leaving the centre slightly thicker. Cut out a petal using the heart cutter. Insert a moistened 28-gauge white wire into the ridge to at least half the length.

4 Vein the petal using a silk veining tool. Frill the upper edge of the petal using the same tool, then soften the edge by re-frilling with a cocktail stick.

5 Pinch the upper surface to form a ridge. Repeat to make four petals. Dry with a gentle curve.

COLOURING AND ASSEMBLY

6 Before the petals have completely dried, dust them with primrose and a little lemon petal dust on the back and the front. Dust a patch of red at the very base of each petal. To make a fading flower, dust with apricot, tangerine and red.

7 Tape the petals around the stamens and pistil using ½-width floristry tape. Re-shape the petals to form a more relaxed natural finish. For a fading flower, scrunch the petals around the stamens.

CALYX

8 The calyx is very slender, so you will need to squash each of the sepals on the fuchsia sepal cutter with pliers. Form a teardrop-shaped piece of pale green paste. Pinch out the base to form a pedestal and thin out the base against the board using a celstick. Cut out the calyx shape using the re-designed fuchsia cutter. If the pedestal is too broad to fit the cutter over, place the paste on top of the cutter and rub your finger or thumb over the paste against the cutter to cut out the shape.

9 Elongate the sepals, rolling them on the board with a celstick. Hollow out and draw down a central vein on each sepal using the dresden tool. Moisten the back of the flower at the base and thread the calyx on to the back. Thin down the paste on the back of the calyx and remove excess. The sepals should lie straight down away from the petals. Dust the calyx with primrose and moss green mixed. Dust the edge with red.

BUDS

10 Roll a ball of paste into a cone shape and insert a hooked, moistened 26-gauge wire into the base. Work the paste down the wire, then thin out half of its length by rolling firmly between your fingers and thumb. Cut off excess paste. Flatten the sides of the upper half of the bud. Divide the surface of the bud into four using a scalpel. Cut the tip of the bud into four and pinch each of the sections to form four points at the tip. Pinch a ridge in between each of the indents. Dust with moss and primrose and then catch each of the pinched ridges with some red. Make buds of various sizes.

LEAVES

11 Roll out a strip of mid-green paste on to a grooved board and cut out the leaf shape. Insert a moistened 28-gauge wire into at least half the length of the leaf. Place on a pad and draw three veins on the leaf, using the fine end of the dresden tool. Soften the edges and allow to firm.

12 Dust with dark green and a touch of moss green petal dust. Dust the tip with a little red. Dip into a ½ glaze. This leaf has pale veins – etch off the glaze and colour on the leaf to reveal them if liked.

ASSEMBLY

13 Start the stem by taping a small leaf at the end of a 20-gauge wire with ½-width tape. Add a few more leaves around the stem at intervals. Introduce a small bud and where its stem joins the main stem, tape a leaf tight to the main stem. Continue to add buds and leaves, then introduce the flowers again adding a leaf at the axil. Finish with a fading flower. Dust the main stem with a little aubergine and red.

MIDSUMMER NIGHT'S DREAM

A beautiful wedding cake featuring the popular floral combination of roses, honeysuckle, ivy and hypericum berries – typical of a midsummer wedding. The sprays have been complemented with a delicate piped antique lace side design.

MATERIALS

18cm (6 in) and 25cm (10 in) oval cakes
Apricot glaze
1.75kg (3½ lb) almond paste (marzipan)
Clear alcohol (kirsch or vodka)
2.5kg (5lb) Champagne sugarpaste
Ivory coloured royal icing
Broad peach ribbon to trim boards

EQUIPMENT

20cm (8in) and 38cm (15in) oval cake boards
Nos. 0 and 2 piping tubes (tips)
Lace templates (see page 157)
A4 plastic file pocket
Firm foam
Nile green floristry tape
Pliers
Wire cutters
2 posy picks
Shallow perspex separator

FLOWERS

Small spray
1 large rose, 1 half rose, 1 rosebud and 1 set of rose leaves
(see page 136-9)
3 sets of honeysuckle buds with foliage (see page 62)
3 small sets of hypericum berries with foliage (see page 78)
5 stems of ivy (see page 114)
1 sprig of rosemary
(see page 65)

Large spray
5 stems of ivy
1 large rose, 1 half rose, 3 rosebuds and 2 sets of rose leaves

3 sets of honeysuckle buds with foliage
3 sets of hypericum berries with foliage
2 sprigs of rosemary

PREPARATION

1 Brush the cakes with apricot glaze and cover with almond paste. Allow to dry. Moisten the almond paste with clear alcohol and cover with champagne sugarpaste.

2 Cover the cake boards with champagne sugarpaste. Place the cakes on top, making sure they are central and that there is a neat join between the cake bases and boards. Allow to dry.

3 Using ivory coloured royal icing and a piping bag fitted with a no. 2 piping tube, pipe a snailtrail around the base of the cakes.

LACE

4 Trace the three sizes of lace design from page 157 on to a piece of tracing paper. Cut a piece of thick card to a size that will slide into an A4 plastic file pocket. Insert the card along with the tracing paper into the pocket so that the design shows through the plastic.

5 Pipe over the lace design using ivory coloured royal icing and a piping bag fitted with a no. 0 piping tube. It helps to shake a little as you pipe to create the antique quality to the lace. Pipe one large piece, 4 medium pieces and 4 small pieces for each scallop.

6 Scribe a fine line on to the cake, either freehand or using a template, to help position the lace. Using a no. 1 or 0 tube and ivory royal icing, attach the lace pieces to the cake, piping two dots. Support the lace until it has dried, using small cubes of firm foam. When dry, carefully remove the foam. Pipe a single dot in between the lace pieces.

SPRAYS

7 To form the basic outline of the large spray, bend the ends of several pieces of ivy at an angle of 90 degrees.

8 Tape the large rose into the centre of the spray to form the focal point. Tape in the three sets of honeysuckle buds, curving where required. Add and tape in the rosebuds and half rose, curving them to follow the basic shape.

9 Fill in the gaps with the hypericum berries, rose leaves, rosemary and extra pieces of ivy. Cut away any excess wires and tape over to neaten the handle of the spray. Repeat to make a slightly smaller spray for the top tier.

ASSEMBLY

10 Insert the posy picks into the cakes, then position the sprays, inserting the handles into the picks.

11 Place the divider on to the base tier and place the small cake on top. Adjust the flowers and leaves to create a balanced arrangement.

FLORAL ROMANCE

This beautiful wedding cake has the exquisite combination of gerberas and roses with delicate embroidery, lace and extension work. It was designed and decorated by Norma Laver, and was displayed on the Table of Honour at the International British Sugarcraft Guild Exhibition 1997.

MATERIALS

20cm (8 in) and 30cm (12 in) scalloped oval cakes
Apricot glaze
2kg (4lb) almond paste (marzipan)
Clear alcohol (kirsch or vodka)
3kg (6lb) white sugarpaste
White royal icing (see page 152)
Green velvet ribbon to trim boards

EQUIPMENT

25cm (10 in) and 40cm (16 in) scalloped oval cake boards
Nos. 0 and 1 piping tubes (tips)
Embroidery and lace design template (see page 158)
A4 plastic file pocket
Fine pins
2 posy picks
Perspex plinth cake stand

FLOWERS

8 stems of ivy (see page 114)
5 gerberas (see page 30)
12 roses (see page 136)
Assorted foliage
Several small filler flowers and buds, such as jasmine (see page 38)

PREPARATION

1 Brush the cakes with apricot glaze and cover with almond paste. Allow to dry for one week. Moisten the surface of the almond paste with clear alcohol and cover with white sugarpaste. Cover the cake boards with white sugarpaste and place the cakes on top. Allow to dry for a few days. Pipe a snail trail around the base of both of the cakes using white royal icing and a piping bag fitted with a no. 1 piping tube.

SIDE DECORATION

2 Trace the lace design on page 158 and a freestyle daisy shape on to a piece of tracing paper. Cut a piece of card to fit into an A4 plastic file pocket. Insert the card with the tracing paper into the pocket so that the design shows through.

3 Pipe over the designs using white royal icing and a no. 0 piping tube. Allow to dry.

4 Make a greaseproof (parchment) paper pattern for the embroidery design and the extension work. Scribe the design on to the sides of the cakes. Using a no. 0 tube and white royal icing, pipe the embroidery design on to the cakes. Allow to dry completely.

5 Insert sterile pins into the icing evenly spaced around the cake.

Brush a tiny amount of melted fat on to the pins. Using a no. 0 tube and fresh royal icing, pipe dropped lines from pin to pin, making the lines even in length – this forms the bridge. Allow to dry.

6 Next, pipe the threads of extension work from the cake on to the dropped line bridge. As you work around the cake and the icing dries, you can remove each of the pins in turn. Allow to dry.

7 Pipe another dropped line in between each of the scallops. Allow to dry. Remove a piece of lace from the plastic file and attach into the small scallop with a few dots of royal icing. Repeat to complete both of the cakes.

8 Pipe tiny scallops over the dropped scalloped bridge. Dry, then attach the daisy lace pieces.

9 Attach the lace on to the cake just above the extension work. Attach the green velvet ribbon to the board edges using a non-toxic glue stick, taking care not to damage the extension work and lace.

ASSEMBLY

10 You will need to make two sprays for this cake. Bend the end of two stems of ivy to a 90 degree angle, taping them together to form a semi-crescent shape and a handle at the centre of the spray. Tape in some extra ivy stems in the same way to form the basic outline of the spray.

11 Tape in the gerberas using one of the flowers as a focal point.

Add the roses to fill in the gaps in the spray. Add depth and fill in the backs of the sprays with assorted plain and variegated foliage and a few jasmine flowers and buds.

12 Insert a posy pick into each cake. Position the handle of each spray in them.

13 Place the small cake on top of the perspex plinth stand and position the larger cake in front of the stand.

EQUIPMENT AND TECHNIQUES

This basic list of equipment is required to make the sugar flowers and foliage used in the book. Any special pieces of equipment needed to make specific cakes or flowers is listed with each set of instructions. Most of the equipment is available from specialist cake decorating suppliers.

EQUIPMENT

Board and Rolling Pin

A non-stick board and rolling pin are essential for rolling out flower paste thinly. I prefer to work on a dark green non-stick board, as a white board strains your eyes if you are working for long periods of time. If you are making a lot of flowers and foliage, then you might prefer to use a grooved board or rolling pin to create thick central ridges on petals and leaves to allow the wires to be inserted, rather than using the other method as described in Techniques. These are available commercially, but you can also make grooves yourself in the back of a non-stick board. To do this, heat a metal skewer until it turns red hot, then brand the back of the board several times until you have achieved a groove of the required depth and width. I find that one long groove across the board is most useful, plus a smaller finer groove at one side of the board. Scrape off any excess plastic, and then smooth the board with some fine glass paper.

Foam Pads

These are used to hold paste while you soften or vein a petal or leaf. There are several pads that are commercially available. If you are planning to buy a pad for the first time, it must be firm and have a fine texture – there are several brands that are too rough and can easily tear the edges of the paste.

Dresden/Veining Tool

My personal favourite is the black dresden/veining tool made by Jem. The fine end of the tool is used for drawing veins down the centre of petals, sepals and leaves. The broad end is used to draw veins and to hollow out the edges and centres of petals and leaves. The broad end is also used to create an effect known as 'double frilling'. This gives a 'ridged look' and, if worked to a certain degree, is ideal for creating jagged or ragged edges to leaves and petals.

Celsticks

These are available in four sizes: small, medium, large and extra large. One end of each tool is pointed; the other is rounded. The pointed end is used to open up the centres of flowers and can also be used for veining. The rounded end is used like the bone-end tool, but with the advantage of a range of different sized tools for the various sizes of flowers and leaves. The central part of each of the celsticks can also be used as a rolling pin for flowers formed from a

pedestal shape. They are also regularly used for rolling thick ridges on paste needed for wired petals and leaves.

Pliers and Wire Cutters

Small fine-nosed pliers are essential, but a good pair will cost you between £25–£30! They are a delight to use and when you buy a pair you often wonder how you managed without them! They can be purchased from specialist electrical supply shops. Wire cutters are also very useful; either electrical cutters or a pair of heavy duty florist's scissors.

Floristry Tape

Paper floristry tape is available in many colours but I use mainly nile green, white, beige and twig. The tape has a glue in it that is released when the paper is stretched, so it is important to stretch the tape firmly as you tape over a wire.

Florists' Staysoft

This is basically plasticine, but it is sold by florists' suppliers and some cake-decorating shops in long blocks. It is easier to arrange flowers into this medium, as they can be removed and re-arranged if a mistake is made (as the name implies - it stays soft). Blocks of green can also be obtained from good art shops. If you are planning to use this medium, it must be arranged on to a container or disc so that it does not come into immediate contact with the cake.

Tape Shredder

This is used to cut lengths of floristry tape into various widths. If you remove one of the blades, you will have a shredder that will cut one half and two quarter width lengths at the same time. The blades are actually razor blades and will need to be replaced from time to time.

Wires

The quality of the wires available varies; it is best to buy A-grade wire, which can be identified by a red spot on the packet. Although it is more expensive I advise you to use only this wire. I personally now only buy white wire in gauges from 33-gauge (fine) to 24-gauge (thicker), preferring to tape over the wire with nile green tape during the assembly of the flower. There are also stronger wires available from 22-gauge to 14-gauge wire (the higher the number the finer the wire). These can be covered or uncovered, it does not matter which you use. You can also buy very fine silk-covered 36-gauge wire on a reel, which is ideal for very small flowers.

Great Impressions (GI) Veiners

These are double-sided rubber veiners moulded from real flowers and foliage. They add a great deal of realism to flower work. Once you have cut out the leaf or petal and inserted a wire (see right), place the shape into the veiner (the ridge on the paste should fit into the back piece of the veiner). Press the two sides together firmly and then remove the leaf, now veined on both sides to natural perfection. You will need to assess the thickness of paste required for some of the more heavily veined petals and leaves – if you make the paste too fine the veiner might cut the paste!

Ceramic Silk Veining Tool (HP)

This tool has veins on the surface; when rolled over the paste it gives a delicate texture. It can also frill the edges of petals, veining them at the same time.

Cutters

There are many different types of cutters available. Cutters speed up the flower-making process and help to add consistency and accuracy easily to your work. I use mainly metal cutters as there are

more shapes available, plus if I need to alter the shape of a cutter I can adjust the shape using pliers. I also have a large range of plastic cutters. For many forms of foliage I prefer to use these as they can often be more intricate in shape. The majority of the cutters used in this book are readily available from most good cake decorating shops. Some cutters however can be difficult to buy and you will need to order these. See page 160 for suppliers.

Thread

Fine white lace-making cotton thread (Brock 120) is best used for stamens, although some thicker cotton threads can also be useful.

Stamens

There is a vast range of stamens available to the flower maker. I use mainly white stamens, preferring to colour them to the required colour as I need them. I always keep a supply of small white seed-head stamens and some finer white stamens.

Paintbrushes

Good brushes are essential, although they don't necessarily have to be very expensive. They are one of the most important items in a flower-maker's kit. Remember that the final control and accuracy with colouring can make or break your work. Flat brushes are the most useful for dusting flowers and foliage (round brushes are not firm enough to colour accurately with petal dust/blossom tint). Recently I have been using brushes by Robert Simmons called Craft Painters nos. 6 and 8. You will need a good selection of finer brushes for painting fine details on flowers and foliage.

Low Heat Glue Gun

This is an item of equipment that can be very useful for gluing florists' staysoft or oasis to boards and stands. The glue sticks are fed into the gun and, when the glue is hot, it can be eased through the gun on to the object you need gluing. Although it operates at a lower temperature, you still need to be careful not to burn your fingers. This can also be used for gluing stamens on to wires for flowers with very neat shallow or fine backs. Do not use for competition work.

Hi-tack Glue

This is a non-toxic glue that can also be used to glue stamens on to wire and glue florists' staysoft on to boards etc. It should not come into immediate contact with the surface of the cakes but is quite safe to use on flowers with wires in them. Do not use for competition work.

𝒯ECHNIQUES

Wiring Leaves and Petals

Roll out some flower paste to the required thickness leaving a thick ridge down the centre – this can either be achieved by rolling a piece of well kneaded paste with a large celstick, leaving the centre thicker or by rolling out the paste on a grooved board. I prefer to use the first method if I have time, as the finished result is often neater and stronger. Cut out the petal or leaf shape using a cutter or template. You will need to position the cutter so that the ridge of paste runs from the tip to the base of the leaf or petal. Press the cutter down firmly, then release the paste from the cutter. (I often find that I end up with cleaner cut edges if I scrub the cutter and paste against the board.) Moisten the end of a wire and insert it into the thick ridge, holding the paste firmly between your finger and thumb to prevent the end of the wire coming through. Insert the wire into at least half the length of the ridge to give support.

Colouring

I use a small selection of paste food colourings to colour flower paste, preferring to alter and colour the flowers and foliage with petal dusts (blossom tints) after shaping. Petal dusts can also be mixed into flower paste to colour it, but if used in large proportions they can alter the consistency too much. I usually colour the paste a paler shade of the colour that I want the finished flower to be, then dust on top to achieve more depth and realistic effects. It is important to have a good selection of petal dust colours and to experiment with different colour combinations to obtain the effect you want. I rarely use only one colour on a flower or leaf. The colours can either be mixed together or simply brushed on to the paste in layers. The instructions for each of the flowers in this book include a list of colours used. I am very fond of green and so most of my cakes have a lot of foliage on them. In the instructions I often mention a dark green mixture which adds a lot of depth to foliage. To achieve the depth of green required, mix together equal proportions of moss green and jade, and then darken with nutkin brown and a little black. I usually mix up a large pot of colour in advance, rather than mixing up small amounts of dust at a time as this wastes both time and dust!

If you want to make a colour a paler shade, it will need to mixed with white petal dust. Sometimes a little cornflour

(cornstarch) is added, but this is usually to clean the colour out of a brush to give a very, very subtle tinge of colour to the tips of petals (usually it involves green and primrose petal dust). I use only a few liquid colours, the main one being cyclamen, to paint detail spots and lines on to petals.

Glazing

There are several ways to add a glaze to flowers and leaves; I use only two. The steaming method is used not to give a high gloss, more to create a 'waxy' finish or, more often, to remove the dry dusted appearance left by petal dust. It is also used when trying to create a velvety finish or darken the depth of colour of a flower or a leaf, since the surface of the paste is still slightly damp after steaming. Hold each flower or leaf in the steam from a boiling kettle for a few seconds, or until the surface turns shiny. Take great care as too much steam can soften and dissolve the sugar. For a more permanent and shiny glaze, use confectioners' varnish. Used neat (full glaze), this

gives a high gloss, which is ideal for berries and glossy leaves. However, for most foliage this looks too artificial, so it is better to dilute the varnish with iso-propyl alcohol (available from chemists). Confectioners' varnish is actually made from a base of iso-propyl alcohol and shellac. Mix the varnish and alcohol in a lidded container and shake to mix – not too much as this will form tiny air bubbles. The glaze may be used straight away. Simply dip the leaf, petal or a group of pieces into the glaze, shake off the excess and dry on absorbent kitchen paper. The glaze may be applied with a paintbrush, but I find the brush strokes tend to remove the colour in streaks. The following glazes are those most often used.

¼ glaze

Three-quarters alcohol to a quarter part varnish. This is used for leaves that don't have much shine; the glaze just takes away the flat, dusty look of a leaf or petal.

½ glaze

Equal proportions of alcohol and varnish. This gives a natural shine that is ideal for many foliages, including ivy and rose leaves.

¾ glaze

Quarter part alcohol to three-quarters varnish. This gives a semi-gloss without the 'plastic' appearance of a full glaze.

Using a 'Cage'

A wire 'cage' is used to mark the impression of unopened petals on a bud. The 'cage' is made from wire, the gauge depending on the size of the bud. If you are making the bud of a five-petalled flower, you will need five pieces of wire for the 'cage'. Tape the pieces of wire together at one end with ½-width floristry tape and open up the cage, trying not to cross the wires at the base. Insert the modelled bud, tip or base first, depending on the effect required. Close the wires on to its surface, keeping them as evenly spaced as possible. For some buds, a more realistic effect is achieved if the paste between the wires is pinched out and thinned with your finger and thumb to form a ridge that gives the appearance of larger petals. After removing from the 'cage', twist to give a spiral effect.

Flower Paste

The type of flower paste you use is a matter of personal preference. I prefer a paste that stretches well and does not dry out on the surface too fast, allowing me to wire petals together whilst they are still damp (a factor that most pastes fall down on). I now always buy ready-made flower paste (by mail order) because it is more consistent than home-made paste, and it saves me a lot of time and trouble. Make your own from the following recipe if you wish.

25ml (5 teaspoons) cold water
10ml (2 teaspoons) powdered gelatine
500g (1lb/3 cups) icing (confectioners') sugar, sifted
15ml (3 teaspoons) gum tragacanth
10ml (2 teaspoons) liquid glucose
15ml (3 teaspoons) white vegetable fat (shortening)
1 medium egg white (preferably free-range)

1 Mix the water and gelatine together in a small heatproof bowl and leave to stand for 30 minutes. Sift the icing sugar and gum tragacanth into the bowl of a heavy-duty mixer and fit the bowl to the machine.

2 Place the bowl with the gelatine mixture over a saucepan of hot water and stir until the gelatine has dissolved. Warm a teaspoon in hot water, then measure out the liquid glucose (the heat should help to ease the glucose off the spoon). Add the glucose and white fat to the gelatine mixture, and continue to heat until all of the ingredients have melted and are thoroughly mixed together.

3 Add the dissolved gelatine mixture to the icing sugar, along with the egg white. Fit the beater to the machine and

turn it on at its lowest speed. Beat until mixed, then increase the speed to maximum until the paste is white and stringy.

4 Remove the paste from the bowl and rub a thin layer of white fat over it to prevent the outer part drying out. Place in a plastic bag and store in an airtight container. Allow the paste to rest and mature for at least 12 hours before using it.

Working with Flower Paste

You will need a pot of fresh egg white, a pot of cornflour (cornstarch) and white vegetable fat. There has been a trend over recent years to use gum arabic solution, gum glues, water and alcohol as replacements for egg white (because of the salmonella scares). I have continued to use fresh egg white as it is far superior to any of the alternatives.

1 The paste should be kneaded well before it is modelled into a flower or rolled out on a board, otherwise it has a tendency to dry out and crack around the edges. If the paste is dry or tough, then soften it using fresh egg white (not gum arabic etc) – do not add white fat in large quantities as this will make the paste short, difficult to work with and it will take longer to dry.

2 If the paste is sticky then a small amount of white fat may be used on the fingers while you knead it – but do not add too much! For many people the temptation when the paste is sticky is to

add cornflour (cornstarch); while corn-flour can be used on the surface of the paste quite happily, if it is added to flower paste it seems to aggravate the stickiness.

3 Always grease the board with white fat, then remove almost completely with absorbent kitchen paper. This will form a very thin layer of fat on the board and stop the paste gripping to the board. If you use too much fat it will show up on the finished petal or leaf when you petal dust as a darker patch.

4 Although the commercial paste that I use does not dry out very quickly, it is advisable if you are cutting out a large number of petals to cover them with a celflap or a plastic bag to stop the surface crusting over.

Royal Icing with dried albumen

This royal icing recipe is suitable for coating, piping a snail trail, and shells, runouts, brush embroidery etc. It makes about 2kg (4lb) of icing.

45g (3 tablespoons) pure dried albumen powder
315ml (10floz/1¼ cups) water
1.75kg (3¼lb/10½ cups) icing (confectioners') sugar, sifted

1 Wash the mixer bowl, a small bowl and the beater with a concentrated detergent and scald to remove any grease and leftover detergent.

2 Reconstitute the dried albumen with the water in a small bowl or other container. It will become very lumpy, but do not worry about it, just stir it and leave it to dissolve for about 20 minutes. Strain the mixture into the mixer bowl.

3 Add the sifted icing sugar gradually and mix it into the albumen. Fix the bowl and beater to the electric mixer and beat on the slowest speed for 4 minutes (soft peak) or 5 minutes (full peak).

Royal Icing (with fresh egg white)

This recipe is intended for fine lace work and long extension work, although I have been known to use it for embroidery, snail trail, shells and brush embroidery, omitting the tartaric and acetic acids. These are added to the egg white to alter the PH balance of the egg whites.

1 medium egg white (preferably free-range and at room temperature)
Pinch of tartaric acid (for fine lace work)
or 2 drops of acetic acid (for long dropped lines of extension work)
225g (8oz/1¼ cups) icing (confectioners') sugar, sifted

1 Wash and scald the bowl and beater as described before. Place the egg white into the bowl with the pinch of tartaric acid. Add the majority of the icing sugar and mix the two together.

2 Fix the bowl and beater to the machine and beat on the slowest speed until it has reached full peak, this takes about 8 minutes. You might need to mix in some more sugar if the mixture is too soft.

Coating with Sugarpaste

1 Knead the sugarpaste to make it smooth: try not to knead too many air bubbles into it. Lightly dust the work surface with icing (confectioners') sugar. Roll out the sugarpaste to an even thick-

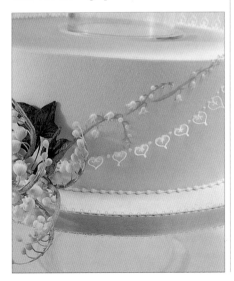

ness, about 1cm (½ in). Moisten the surface of the almond paste with clear alcohol (vodka, kirsch, cointreau etc). Form an even coating of alcohol – if you have dry areas then these are prone to form air bubbles with the sugarpaste.

2 Lift the sugarpaste over the cake and ease into position, smoothing out the top to remove air bubbles before working on the sides. Trim the sugarpaste from around the base of the cake. Polish the top and the sides of the cake using sugarpaste smoothers. I also use a pad of sugarpaste pressed into the palm of my hand to smooth the edges and corners of the cake. If you catch the paste and make an indent, try smoothing over with the pad of paste as it often disguises the fault quickly.

Covering a Cake Board with Sugarpaste

Moisten the cake board with a small amount of boiled water or clear alcohol. Roll out sufficient sugarpaste to cover the board. Trim the edge. Soften the cut edge using the sugarpaste smoother.

NOTE

If you are concerned about the cake and the sugarpaste on the board becoming sticky in between being decorated and the cake-cutting ceremony, you have several options. Firstly, you can cut out the sugarpaste from the board the same shape and size of the cake, then position the cake on top. Alternatively, place the cake on a thin board of the same size and shape before it is almond-pasted and sugarpasted, then position it on to the larger sugarpasted board.

The Parts of a Flower

Throughout this book, reference is made to the various parts of a flower. The illustration and following notes will help you identify them.

Pistil

This is the female part of a flower and is made up of a stigma, style and ovary. The pistil varies in its formation between the

various different flowers. In some flowers, such as a lily, the pistil can be large.

Stamens

The stamens provide the male part of a flower and are made up of a filament and a pollen-covered anther.

Petals

These are usually the most attractive, coloured parts of a flower, their main purpose being to attract insects to the flower.

Tepals

These look like petals and appear in flowers that have no calyx, such as anemone, hellebore or lily.

Calyx and Sepals

The calyx is made up of several individual sepals. It is the outer layer of a bud that protects the flower while it is forming inside.

Bract

This is located where the flower stem joins the main stem. It is a small, modified leaf (intermediate between the sepals and the leaves).

Spadix

This is a fleshy axis that carries both male and female flowers, such as the centre of an arum lily or anthurium.

Spathe

This is a large petal-like bract that is usually wrapped around or positioned below the spadix of the arum lily and anthurium.

TEMPLATES

TUBEROSE
leaves and bracts
page 12

HEAVENLY SCENT
embroidery side design
page 8

GOOD-LUCK PALM
leaves
page 21

PHAIUS ORCHID
page 18

dorsal

lateral petals

lateral sepals

bract

throat

PURE ELEGANCE
brush embroidery designs
page 31

LILY-OF-THE-VALLEY
CAKE

embroidery design
page 50

LILY-OF-THE-VALLEY
WEDDING CAKE

lace design
page 50

LILY-OF-THE-
VALLEY

leaves
page 54

ARUM LILY

spathe
page 36

ARUM LILY

spadix
page 36

FLORAL WEDDING CAKES

SWEET PEA

petals
page 46

*standard
petal*

*standard
petal*

wing petals

*wing
petals*

make 3

AMARYLLIS

petals
page 80

**GUERNSEY
LILY**

petal
page 132

**FRAGRANT EVENING
PRIMROSE**

leaf
page 144

**FLORAL
RHAPSODY**

embroidery side design
page 66

RANUNCULUS

leaves
page 72

PEONY
leaves
page 124

MIDSUMMER
NIGHT'S DREAM
lace page 144

PEONY
petals
page 124

PEONY
calyx
page 124

PEONY
WEDDING
CAKE
brush
embroidery
page 122

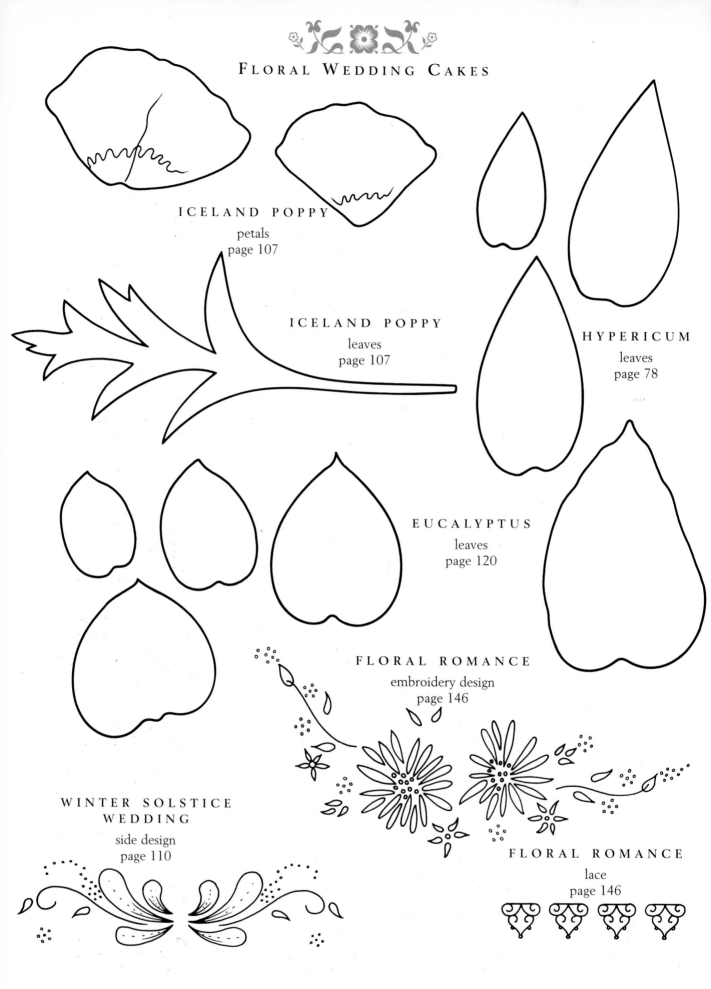

FLORAL WEDDING CAKES

ICELAND POPPY

petals
page 107

ICELAND POPPY

leaves
page 107

HYPERICUM

leaves
page 78

EUCALYPTUS

leaves
page 120

FLORAL ROMANCE

embroidery design
page 146

**WINTER SOLSTICE
WEDDING**

side design
page 110

FLORAL ROMANCE

lace
page 146

INDEX

FLORAL WEDDING CAKES

ACKNOWLEDGEMENTS

This book would not have been finished when it was, without the help, support, faith and tolerance of my friends listed below.

My most humble and grateful thanks go to them all. I appreciate their help and am indebted to them all.

Thank you to Alice Christie who has been a constant help throughout the writing of this book (and the previous two)!! And to Tombi Peck for her help and sense of humour during the last crucial and exhausting week of photography – it has been proven once again that we work well together under extreme last-minute pressure; to Norma Laver for the orange conversations and getting me out of a tight corner by allowing her Table of Honour cake (see page 146) to be included in this book, and also to Tony Warren for his 'you-can-do-it' phone calls, and for allowing me to use his Table of Honour cake (see page 84); to Peter Stott for his support over the years, and for flat icing (with his natural perfection) the royal iced cake.

Thank you to the following for supplying the various items used: to Renshaws Ltd for the Regalice used to cover all of the sugarpaste cakes in this book; to Margaret and David Ford of Celcakes for the perspex tube cake stands; to Beverley Dutton of Squires Kitchen for the almost never ending supply of holly/ivy petal dust and the use of the cake knife; to Paula Stock for allowing me to use her cutwork cutters on the Orchid Inspiration cake (see page 14); to June Twelves of Holly Products for the silk veining tool; to Joan Mooney of Great Impressions for the veiners; to Sally Harris of Tinkertech for the metal cutters; to John Quai Hoi for the perspex flower stand used with the cake on page 110; to Brenda Munger for sharing her tip with the Iceland poppy ovary (see page 107); to Wendy Mabbot and the gang at Cooks Corner. Thanks to Jenny, Norma and Co. at A Piece of Cake for their excellent service and friendly banter. Also thanks to

Peggie Green for her very kind hospitality.

Once again my thanks to Sue Atkinson for her patience, kindness and superb photography (working miracles when required) which is equally important to this book as it was to the previous two collaborations.

Thanks also to Barbara Croxford, my editor, for her help in turning my sometimes chaotic ramblings into an organized text; and to Anita Ruddell for her design work and support for the Iceland Poppy Cake campaign.

And finally thank you once again to my long suffering parents, Allen and Avril, and my sister, Sue, for their continuing support.

The author and publishers would like to thank the following suppliers:

Anniversary House
(Cake Decorations) Ltd
Unit 5a
Roundways
Elliott Road
Bournemouth BH11 8JJ
Tel: 01202 590222

A Piece of Cake
(Mail order flowerpaste, etc)
18 Upper High Street
Thame
Oxon OX9 3EX
Tel & fax: 0184 421 3428

Cake Art Ltd
Venture Way
Crown Estate
Priorswood
Taunton
Somerset TA2 8DE
Tel: 01823 321532

Cakes, Classes and Cutters
23 Princes Road
Brunton Park
Gosforth
Newcastle-Upon-Tyne
NE3 5TT
Tel & Fax:0191 217 0538

Celcakes and Celcrafts
(Cel products, perspex stands and Asi-es products)
Springfield House

Gate Helmsley
York, Yorkshire YO4 1NF
Tel: 01759 371 447

Cooks Corner
35 Percy Street
Newcastle-Upon-Tyne
Tyne & Wear
Tel: 0191 261 5481

Country Cutters
Lower Tresaldu
Dingestow
Monmouth, Gwent NP5 4BQ
Tel: 01600 740448

Creating Cakes
The Cake Decorating Centre
63 East Street
Sittingbourne
Kent ME10 4BQ
Tel: 01795 426358

Elegant Cutwork Collection
1007 Lochmoor Blvd
Grosse Ptd Woods
NJ 48236, USA

Fleurtatious (Flower shop)
58 Acorn Road
Jesmond
Newcastle-upon-Tyne
Tel: 0191 281 3127

Great Impressions
(veiners and moulds)
14 Studley Drive
Swarland, Morpeth
Northumberland NE65 9JT
Tel & Fax:01670 787 061

Guy, Paul and Co. Ltd
Unit B4, Foundry Way
Little End Road
Eaton Socon
Cambs PE19 3SH
Tel: 01480 472545

Holly Products
(Silk veining tools etc)
Holly Cottage
Hassall Green
Cheshire CW11 4YA
Tel & Fax:01270 761 403

JF Renshaw Ltd
Crown Street
Liverpool L8 7RF
Tel: 0151 706 8200

W Robertson
The Brambles
Ryton
Tyne & Wear NE40 3AN
Tel: 0191 413 8144

Squires Kitchen
Squires House
3 Waverley Lane
Farnham
Surrey GU9 8BB
Tel: 01252 711749

Sugar Celebrations
80 Westgate Street
Gloucester GL1 2NZ
Tel: 01452 308848

The British Sugarcraft Guild
National Office
Wellington House
Messeter Place
Eltham
London SE9 5DP
Tel: 0181 859 6943
Fax: 0181 859 6117

The Flower Basket
10 High Street
Much Wenlock
Shropshire
Tel: 01952 728 101

The Old Bakery
Kingston St Mary
Taunton
Somerset TA2 8HW
Tel: 01823 451205

The Secret Garden
(Flower shop)
17 Clayton Road
Jesmond
Tyne & Wear
Tel: 0191 281 7753

The Stencil Library
Stocksfield Hall
Stocksfield
Northumberland

Tinkertech Two
(Metal cutters)
40 Langdon Road
Parkstone
Poole
Dorset BH14 9EH
Tel: 01202 738 049

Sugar Flowers

For All Seasons

Sugar Flowers

For All Seasons

Alan Dunn

Dedicated with love to my parents, Allen and Avril; to my sister, Susan; and to my part-time partner in sugar-crime, Tombi.

ACKNOWLEDGEMENTS

I would like to thank the following people, some for their direct help with this book, and others for their indirect help, support and, most importantly, their friendship before, during and after the writing of this book:
Alice Christie, Peggy Green, Maria Harrison, Margaret Morland, Sandra Robertson, Stephanie Scott, Viv Soulsby, Peter Stott and Tony Warren; Joan Mooney of Great Impressions, Sally Harris of Tinkertech Two, Norma Laver and Jenny Walker of A Piece of Cake, David and Margaret Ford of Celcakes, everyone at Cooks Corner, and Beverley Dutton of Squires Kitchen. Thank you also to Annemieke Mein for allow-ing me to use the Frog Down Under design, and to Rosemary Macdonald for the witch hazel and Caroline Goodrick for the silk.

An extra special thanks must go to Tombi Peck, without whose help this book would not have been finished in time, and I certainly would not have had so much fun during one very hot summer!

The author and publishers would also like to thank the following suppliers:
Anniversary House (Cake Decorations) Ltd., Unit 5a, Roundways, Elliott Road, Bournemouth BH11 8JJ; A Piece of Cake, 18 Upper High Street, Thame, Oxon OX9 3EX; Cake Art Ltd., Venture Way, Crown Estate, Priorswood, Taunton TA2 8DE; Celcakes and Celcrafts, Springfield House, Gate Helmsley, York, North Yorkshire YO4 3EX; Cooks Corner, 35 Percy Street, Newcastle-upon-Tyne, Tyne & Wear; Creating Cakes, 63 East Street, Sittingbourne, Kent ME10 4BQ; Great Impressions, Greenlea, 14 Studley Drive, Swarland, Morpeth, Northumberland NE65 9JT; Guy, Paul and Co. Ltd., Unit B4, Foundry Way, Little End Road, Eaton Socon, Cambs. PE19 3JH; W. Robertson, The Brambles, Ryton, Tyne & Wear NE40 3AN; Squires Kitchen, Squires House, 3 Waverley Lane, Farnham, Surrey GU9 8BB; Tinkertech Two, 40 langdon Road, Parkstone, Poole, Dorset BH14 9EH.

Contents

Introduction

When I first started decorating cakes, at the age of four-teen, flowers formed only part of the cakes' decorations, and my early floral efforts, made from sugarpaste, bore little resemblance to the real thing. After I was introduced to fine wired flowers, however, my ideas changed and flowers are now the main feature of my work.

Although I have had an interest in fresh flowers from an early age (I can remember quite clearly picking and col-lecting flowers, only to turn around and find that my two-year-old sister had plucked their heads off!), my love, fascina-tion and appreciation for them has grown enormously in recent years. Now I am constantly in search of new and unusual flowers and foliage to copy in sugar, but sometimes I get so carried away with my admiration for the real thing that I don't get a sugar version finished! However, this all adds to the pleasure I get from my work. If I find an unusual flower to copy, I always make notes and templates in case I want to make the flower again at a later date and cannot find another specimen.

The flowers and foliage featured in this book are arranged into four sections – Florists' Flowers, Exotic Flowers, Garden Flowers and Wild Flowers – and each section includes some of my favourites from each season of the year. Although the flowers might appear very realistic, some of them only resemble the real thing and are not intended to be exact copies. In some cases, this is because the flowers were not in season at the time I needed to make them for the book (May to August 1995), and were therefore not available to copy. In any case, I feel it is more important to create the character of a plant or flower in a decorative display, rather than to strive for botanical correctness. It is also important to give your work soul; if a flower has been copied too closely and is too neat in form, the result can often look very sterile and lifeless. Most of all, it is important to enjoy what you are doing and to have fun when making sugar flowers!

Many of the cake designs in this book feature quite large bouquets and arrangements. I am very much inspired by the work of flower arrangers and florists, whose work tends to be on a large scale. Moreover, wedding cakes can often go unnoticed at a reception if the floral displays are small, especially if the reception is held in a large hall or room, so I tend to favour large displays. However, the instructions can easily be adapted to smaller arrangements, and I hope that this book will inspire you to develop your own ideas, making use of a selection of the flowers featured to suit your own personal taste and style.

Alan Dunn

Equipment & Techniques

Equipment

To make the sugar flowers and foliage in this book you will need the basic equipment listed here. Details of other items needed to make specific flowers are given with each set of instructions. Most of the equipment is available from specialist cake decorating suppliers.

BOARD AND ROLLING PIN

A non-stick board and rolling pin are essential for rolling out paste without it sticking. Grooved boards and rolling pins are very useful for creating thick central ridges on petals and leaves to allow wires to be inserted (see page 10). These are available commercially, but you can also make grooves yourself in the back of a non-stick board. To do this, heat a metal skewer until it turns red hot, and then brand the back of the board several times until you have achieved a groove of the required depth and width. (Several grooves of varied lengths and depths are useful.) Scrape off the excess plastic, and then smooth the board with some fine glass paper.

MEXICAN HAT BOARD

This board has holes in it of various sizes and depths and can be used for rolling out paste when a thicker central area is required. Start by rolling out some paste quite thickly, and then roll it out over the required hole until the surface paste is thin enough. Remove the paste from the board and you will be left with a thick area in the centre. This forms the back of a flower or the ovary on a calyx.

DRESDEN TOOL

This modelling tool can be used to create several different effects. The fine end of the tool is excellent for drawing veins down the centre of petals, calyx sepals and leaves, while the broad end can be used to draw veins on large pieces and to hollow out the inner edges and the centres of petals, sepals and leaves. The broad end is also used to create an effect known as 'double frilling'. This technique can give a 'ridged look' and, if worked to a certain degree, is ideal for creating jagged or ragged edges to leaves and petals. To create double frilling, press the broad end of the tool on to the paste and then drag it down against the board. Repeat the process many times until you have frilled the required area.

BONE-END TOOL

This is used to soften and gently frill the edges of petals and leaves. To use this tool place the petal or leaf on a pad and place the required end of the tool half on the paste and half on the pad. (For larger pieces, choose the larger end of the tool, saving the finer end for smaller pieces.) Use long, strong strokes on the edge, repeating until you have the desired effect. This tool can also be used for cupping and hollowing out petals.

CELSTICKS

These are available in four sizes: small, medium, large and extra large. One end of each tool is pointed; the other is rounded. The pointed end is used to open up the centres of flowers and can be used for veining. The rounded end can be used like the bone-end tool, but with celsticks you have the advantage of a range of different-sized tools for various-sized flowers and leaves. The central part of a celstick is also regularly used as a miniature rolling pin.

PLIERS AND WIRE CUTTERS

Small fine-nosed pliers are essential, but they are expensive and an item to be treasured! I bought mine from an electrical supply shop. Wire cutters are also very useful; although scissors can be used, wire can ruin them.

FLORISTRY TAPE

Paper floristry tape is available in many colours but I use mainly pale green, white, beige and brown. The tape has a glue in it that is released when the paper is stretched, so it is important to stretch the tape firmly as you tape over a wire.

TAPE SHREDDER

This is used to cut lengths of floristry tape into various widths. If you remove one of the blades you will have a shredder that will cut one half- and two quarter-width lengths at the same time. The blades will need to be replaced from time to time.

WIRES

Various coloured wires are available in many thicknesses, from 14-gauge (thick) to 33-gauge (very fine). The quality of the wires available also varies; although expensive, it is best to buy A-grade wire. I use mainly white wires, preferring to tape over the stems when the flower is complete.

GREAT IMPRESSIONS (GI) VEINERS

These are double-sided rubber veiners moulded from real flowers and foliage. They add a great deal of realism to flower work. Once you have cut out your leaf or petal and inserted a wire (see page 10), place the shape into the veiner (the ridge on the paste should fit into the central vein on the back piece of the veiner). Press the two sides together firmly and then remove the leaf, now veined on both sides to natural perfection.

CERAMIC SILK VEINING TOOL

This tool has veins on the surface; when rolled over the paste it gives a delicate texture.

CUTTERS

There are many different types of cutters available on the market. I use mainly metal cutters as there are more shapes available, although I also have a large collection of plastic cutters. Cutters speed up the flower-making process and help to add consistency and accuracy to your work.

THREAD

Fine white lace-making thread (brock 120) is best used for stamens, although some thicker cotton threads can also be useful. Silk is used to make the Old man's beard seed-heads (see page 131). It is available from specialist lace-making shops.

PADS

These are firm pieces of foam-like material and are commercially available. They are used to hold paste while you soften or vein a petal or leaf.

PAINTBRUSHES

Good brushes are essential. They are one of the most important items in a flower-maker's tool kit. Remember that the final control and accuracy with colouring can make or break your work! Flat brushes are most useful for dusting flowers and foliage (round brushes are not firm enough to colour accurately with petal dust/blossom tint). I use mainly ¼-inch and ½-inch sable/synthetic flat brushes (such as Windsor and Newton series 606). You will also need a good selection of finer brushes for painting details on to petals and foliage.

Techniques

WIRING LEAVES AND PETALS

Roll out some flower paste to the required thickness using a grooved board or rolling pin. Remove the paste from the board and turn it over, if necessary, so that the ridge in the paste is on top. Cut out the shape, positioning the cutter so that the ridge of paste runs from tip to base of the leaf or petal. Press firmly, then release the paste from the cutter. Moisten the end of a wire and insert it into the thick ridge, holding the paste firmly between your finger and thumb to prevent the end of the wire coming through. Insert the wire into at least half the length of the ridge.

COLOURING

I use a small selection of paste food colourings to colour flower paste, preferring to alter and colour the flowers and foliage with petal dusts (blossom tints) after shaping. Petal dusts can also be mixed into flower paste to colour it, but if used in large proportions they can alter the consistency too much. I usually colour the paste a paler shade than I want the finished flower to be, and then dust on top to obtain more depth and realistic effects. It is important to have a good selection of petal dust colours and to experiment with different combinations to achieve the effect you want. I very rarely use one colour by itself. The instructions for each of the flowers in this book include a list of the colours used. One of the colours I use frequently is a dark green mixture which adds a lot of depth to foliage. To achieve the depth of green required, mix equal proportions of moss green and jade together, and then darken with nutkin and a little black.

GLAZING

In this book I have used two methods for glazing flowers and leaves. The steaming method is used to give a flower a slightly 'waxy' finish or simply to remove its dusty appearance. It is also used when you want to darken the colour of a flower or leaf, since the surface of the piece will accept more colour if redusted when it is still slightly damp after steaming. Hold each flower or leaf in the steam from a boiling kettle for a few seconds, until the surface turns shiny. Take great care as too much steam can soften and dissolve the sugar.

For a more permanent and shiny glaze, use confectioners' varnish. Used neat (full glaze), this gives a very high gloss, which is ideal for berries and glossy leaves. However, for most foliage this looks too severe, so it is better to dilute the varnish with iso-propyl alcohol (available from chemists; although vodka or other high-proof alcohols can be used, sometimes there is a reaction and a jelly-like substance is formed, so it is easier and cheaper to use iso-propyl). Place the varnish and alcohol in a lidded container and shake to mix. The glaze can be used straight away. Simply dip the leaf or petal (or a group of pieces) into the glaze, shake off the excess and dry on absorbent kitchen paper. It is important to shake the glaze in its container from time to time to prevent separation. The glaze can be applied with a paintbrush, but I find the brush strokes tend to remove the colour. The following glazes are those that I use most often.

¼ glaze
Three-quarters alcohol to a quarter part varnish. This is used for leaves that don't have much shine; the glaze just takes away the flat, dusty look of a leaf or petal.

½ glaze
Equal proportions of alcohol and varnish. This gives a natural shine that is ideal for many foliages, including rose leaves.

¾ glaze
Quarter part alcohol to three-quarters varnish. This gives a semi-gloss without the 'plastic' appearance of a full glaze.

USING A 'CAGE'

A wire 'cage' is used to mark the impression of unopened petals on a bud. The 'cage' is made from wire, the gauge depending on the size of the bud. If you are making the bud of a five-petalled flower, you will need five pieces of wire for the 'cage'. Tape the pieces of wire together at one end with

½-width floristry tape and open up the 'cage', trying not to cross the wires at the base. Insert your modelled bud, tip or base first depending on the effect required, and close the wires on to its surface, keeping them as evenly spaced as possible. For some buds, a more realistic effect is achieved if the paste between the wires is pinched out and thinned with your finger and thumb to form a ridge that gives the appearance of larger petals. After removing the bud from the 'cage', twist the petals to give a spiral effect.

Making flower paste

The type of flower paste used is a matter of personal choice. I prefer a paste that stretches well and does not dry out too fast. I always buy (by mail order) ready-made-up flower paste because it is more consistent than home-made paste and it saves me a lot of time and trouble. You can make your own from the following if you wish.

5 teaspoons cold water
2 teaspoons powdered gelatine
500g (1lb/3 cups) icing (confectioners') sugar, sifted
3 teaspoons gum tragacanth
2 teaspoons liquid glucose
3 teaspoons white vegetable fat (shortening) or 2 teaspoons soya oil
1 egg white (size 2)

1 Mix the cold water and gelatine together in a small heat-proof bowl and leave to stand for 30 minutes. Sift the icing sugar and gum tragacanth into the bowl of a heavy-duty mixer and fit the bowl to the machine.

2 Place the bowl with the gelatine mixture over a saucepan of hot water and stir until the gelatine has dissolved. Warm a teaspoon in hot water and then measure out the liquid glucose (the heat should help to ease the glucose off the spoon). Add the glucose and white fat or soya oil to the gelatine mixture, and continue to heat until all the ingredients have dissolved and are thoroughly mixed together.

3 Add the dissolved mixture to the icing sugar with the egg white. Fit the beater to the machine and turn the mixture on at its lowest speed. Beat until all the ingredients are mixed, then increase the speed to maximum until the paste is white and stringy.

4 Remove the paste from the bowl and rub a thin layer of white fat over it (to prevent the outer part drying out). Place in a plastic bag and store in an airtight container. Allow the paste to rest and mature for at least 12 hours before using it.

Identifying the parts of a flower

Throughout this book, reference is made to the various parts of a flower. The illustration and following notes will help you identify them.

Pistil
The pistil is the female part of the flower and is made up of stigma, style and ovary. In many flowers, e.g. a lily, this piece can be quite large.

Stamens
The stamens are the male part of the flower and are made up of a filament and a pollen-covered anther. In order for a flower to be pollinated, the pollen must be transferred to the stigma on the pistil. Once a flower has been pollinated the ovary will start to grow and, in some cases, fruit will form.

Petals
These are the most attractive, coloured parts of a flower, their main purpose being to attract insects to the flower.

Tepals
These look like petals and appear in flowers that have no calyx, e.g. lily, anemone or Christmas rose.

Calyx and sepals
The calyx is made up of separate sepals. It is the outer layer of a bud that protects the flower while it is forming inside.

Bract
This is located where the flower stem joins the main stem. It is a small, modified leaf (intermediate between the sepals and the leaves).

The parts of a flower

Petal — Stamen { Anther, Filament — Bract — Leaf

Stigma } Style } Pistil, Ovary } — Sepals (together forming the calyx)

Florists' Flowers

THIS SECTION IS PROBABLY the
most useful for sugarcrafters, as these are
the flowers most frequently given as gifts
for birthdays, anniversaries, mother's day,
etc., and, most importantly, are those used
in bridal bouquets and arrangements. I
visit flower shops on a regular basis, in the
hope of finding something unusual and
exciting to inspire me.

Rose

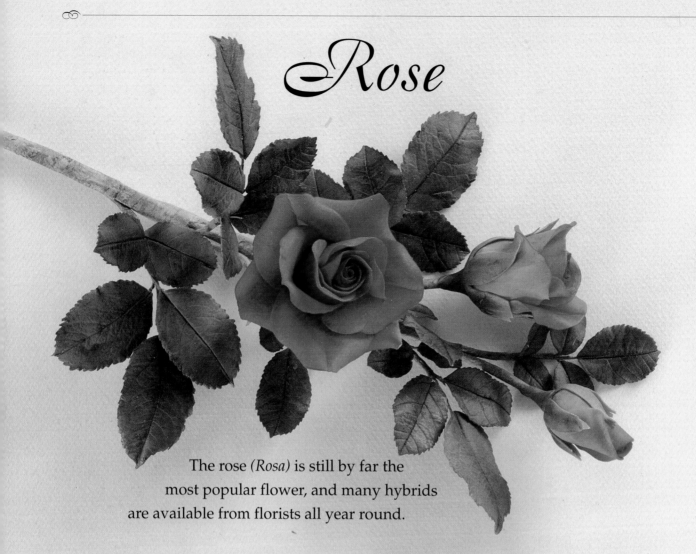

The rose *(Rosa)* is still by far the most popular flower, and many hybrids are available from florists all year round.

Materials

White and mid-green flower paste
18, 26 and 28-gauge wires
Selected paste food colourings
Primrose, lemon, white, aubergine, plum, dark green, moss, holly/ivy and selected colours of petal dust (blossom tint)
½ glaze (see page 10)

Equipment

Pale green floristry tape
Rose petal cutters (551, 550)
Rose petal veiner (GI) or ceramic silk veining tool (HP)
Rose calyx cutters (R11b, R11c)
Rose leaf cutters
Large rose leaf veiner (GI)

PREPARATION

1 Roll a ball of white flower paste into a cone with a sharp point and a fairly broad base (it should be no larger than the small petal cutter you are planning to use; for a bud it should be quite a lot smaller). Tape over an 18-gauge wire and bend an open hook in the end. Moisten the wire and insert it into the base of the cone, making sure that the hook goes almost to the tip. Pinch the base of the cone firmly on to the wire to secure. Make as many as you need and allow to dry overnight.

2 Colour some flower paste as required. I have used ruby paste colouring and, although I wanted the finished flower to be quite dark, I started with a paler base. For white roses, add a tiny amount of melon or bitter lemon colouring to give the finished flowers their characteristic warm glow or green tinge.

FIRST AND SECOND LAYERS

3 Roll out some coloured flower paste fairly thinly, and cut out four petals using the smaller cutter (551). Place the petals on a pad and soften the edges with the rounded end of a large celstick, working half on the paste and half on the pad.

4 Moisten the central part of a petal and place it on a dried cone, leaving about 5mm (¼ in) of the petal above the tip of the cone. Tuck one side of the petal in towards the cone (you are aiming to hide the tip of the cone completely), and wrap the other side of the petal around to form a tight spiral, leaving the end slightly open. (Do not worry about the base of the cone at this stage.)

5 Moisten the bases of the remaining three petals. Tuck the first of these underneath the edge of the petal on the cone, the second underneath the first and the third underneath the second. The petals should now be fairly evenly spaced. Moisten the petals a little more if needed and close them all tight, pulling the petals down at an angle rather than wrapping them straight around. There are now enough petals on to make a small bud, but if you are planning to make a larger rose, open up one of the petals again.

THIRD AND FOURTH LAYERS

6 Roll out some more paste and cut out another three petals with the same cutter (551). Vein the petals, if you wish, using either the ceramic tool or the double-sided veiner (some roses have a texture, others do not; decide which you prefer). Soften the

edges as before. Start again by tucking the first petal of the third layer underneath the last petal of the second layer. Continue to add the remaining petals as before, this time pinching a very gentle central vein on each of the petals between your finger and thumb as you add them to the rose.

7 Cut out another three petals and repeat step 6, this time wrapping the petals less tightly to give a more open appearance.

FIFTH AND SIXTH LAYERS

8 Roll out some more paste and cut out another three petals using either the same size cutter as before or the next size (550), depending upon how large the rose has already become. Vein and soften as before. This time you will need to cup the centre of each petal, using a large celstick.

9 Moisten the base of each petal and attach them as before, making sure that the centre of each covers a join on the previous layer. The rose should now be quite open; curl back the edges of each petal using your fingers or a cocktail stick (toothpick). At this stage, the rose is termed a 'half rose'; I usually use more half roses than full ones in a spray or bouquet.

10 Roll out yet more paste and cut out five petals using the larger cutter (550). Vein, soften and cup each petal, and moisten the base edge. Place the first petal over a join on the previous layer, and place the second petal over another join on the opposite side of the rose. Place the third petal over the join (or gap) created by the previous two, and the last two next to each other, covering the large space on the other side of the rose. Curl back the edges of each petal as before, and, if you have damaged the cupped shape of the petals, place the broad end of a dresden tool down the centre of each to re-form. A few more smaller petals can be added if the rose looks unbalanced at this stage.

11 If you are working on a pale coloured or white rose, it looks attractive if you dust the inside of the base of each petal lightly with a mixture of primrose, lemon and white petal dust. It is easier to do this while the flower is still soft. Dust the outer petals of a bud, half rose or full rose at the base with the same colour. The roses illustrated have been dusted with fuchsia and plum petal dusts, and then over-dusted with aubergine.

Calyx

12 Roll a ball of mid-green flower paste into a cone and pinch out the base to form a hat shape. Using a small celstick, roll out the base to make it a little thinner, although the calyx should have quite a 'fleshy' appearance. Cut out the calyx, and elongate each of the sepals by rolling over with the celstick.

13 Place the calyx on a pad and cup each sepal on the inside. Dust the inside of the calyx with a mixture of white and moss green petal dust to make it paler. If you wish, you can make some fine cuts in the edges of each sepal with a pair of fine scissors, to give them a 'hairy' appearance.

14 Moisten the centre of the calyx and attach it to the back of the rose or bud, trying to position each sepal so that it covers a join between two outer petals. On a full-blown rose, the calyx would curl back, but position it tightly around a bud. Dust with moss and dark green.

Leaves

15 Rose leaves can grow in groups of three or five, depending upon the variety. Roll out some mid-green paste using a grooved rolling pin or board. Remove the paste from the groove and cut out a selection of sizes using rose leaf cutters. You will need one large, two medium and two small leaves per stem.

16 Choose lengths of 26-gauge or 28-gauge wire (depending on the size of leaf) and cut into four. Moisten one end of each wire and insert into

the thick ridge of a leaf. The wire should be inserted into at least half the length of the leaf. Vein the leaf using the double-sided veiner. Place the leaf on a pad and soften the edges using a large celstick. Pinch a vein down the centre, and shape the leaf between your finger and thumb to give a little movement.

17 Dust the back of each leaf with white and a little moss green petal dust. Overdust with aubergine/plum on the edges. Turn the leaf over and dust the edges with aubergine/plum, making the colour heavier on one side. Dust the main part of each leaf with dark green and then over-dust with holly/ivy. Glaze using ½ glaze.

Assembly

18 Tape the leaves together into groups of three or five, starting with a large leaf, then medium, and finishing with small leaves. Dust the stem with a little dark green, holly/ivy, aubergine and plum.

Stargazer Lily

There are many species of Oriental lily *(Lilium)* and most of those we buy from flower shops are hybrids. The 'Stargazer' hybrids are large, colourful flowers with an exquisite scent, making them ideal for bridal bouquets.

Materials

18, 24 and 26-gauge wires
Fuchsia, plum, red, moss, dark green, skintone, primrose, aubergine and deep purple petal dust (blossom tint)
Ivory, pale holly/ivy and mid-holly/ivy flower paste
Semolina
½ glaze (see page 10)
Cyclamen liquid colouring

Equipment

Fine pliers
White and pale green floristry tape
Lily cutters or templates
Casablanca lily veiners (GI)

STAMENS

1 Use a third of a length of 26-gauge wire for each stamen. Using fine pliers, bend a flat hook in one end of each, then hold the hook halfway down with the pliers and bend it again to form a 'T'-bar. The filaments are very fleshy in this lily so thicken them with several layers of ¼-width white floristry tape. Dust the tape with a mixture of primrose and moss green petal dust.

2 Attach a sausage of ivory flower paste over the 'T'-bar to form the anther, bending both ends down so that it resembles a moustache. To make pollen, mix a little semolina with some skintone petal dust. Moisten the anthers and dip into the pollen mixture. Allow to dry thoroughly. (Florists usually trim off the anthers as the pollen can stain fabric very badly, especially bridal gowns! Nevertheless, I still prefer to make the flower with them.)

PISTIL

3 Form a ball of pale holly/ivy flower paste and insert a moistened 24-gauge wire. Work the paste between your finger and thumb in a rubbing motion, and try to cover a good length of the wire. (The pistil should measure at least the length of one of the petals.) Smooth the pistil between the palms of your hands and trim away any excess paste. Flatten the top of the pistil with your finger, and then, using a pair of tweezers, pinch the end into three. Flatten the top again if needed, then divide the upper surface into three using a scalpel. Bend the whole pistil slightly. Attach another piece of green paste at the base of the pistil to represent the ovary. Divide this into six.

4 Colour the pistil with a mixture of moss and primrose petal dust, making the ovary a little darker. The tip of the pistil is coloured with a touch of deep purple and aubergine. Dip into a ½ glaze, shake off excess, and leave to dry.

5 Tape the stamens around the pistil, making the pistil slightly higher than the stamens. Bend the stamens into the required position. (The more mature the flower is, the more curl the stamens should have.)

PETALS

6 Roll out some ivory flower paste, leaving a thick ridge down the centre. (You can use a grooved board or rolling pin if you wish.) Using lily cutters (or a scalpel and templates made from the outlines on page 140), cut out three large and three smaller petals. Insert a moistened 24-gauge wire into each petal, making sure that it is at least halfway up the ridge in the petal.

7 Vein the large petals in the larger veiner and the smaller petals in the smaller veiner, pressing the two sides of the veiners firmly to give a good impression. Place the petals on a pad and use the rounded end of the largest celstick to soften the edges, working half on the paste and half on the pad. The petals of some lilies have very frilled edges, but I prefer to give them only a little movement. Pinch down the centre of the whole length of each petal, especially strongly at the tips.

8 The three large petals have a hairy area towards the base. Using a pair of fine scissors, cut several fine hairs, holding the blades very close to the surface. Curl the hairs back using your finger. Curl the whole length of each petal and dry over a curved surface until firm enough to handle.

COLOURING

9 Dust the base of each petal with primrose, and then over-dust half of this area with moss green. (The area to be coloured should be roughly the shape of a triangle.) The main colouring of the flower depends on your own personal taste as there are so many different variations. The petals illustrated are coloured using a mixture of plum, fuchsia and red. Dust the central area with this colour, then add a little depth using aubergine petal dust. Try to keep the colour away from the primrose at the base otherwise the results will be unattractive. The smaller petals tend to have less colour on them.

10 Using a fine paintbrush and a little cyclamen liquid colouring, paint on the spots; they should be stronger and slightly larger at the base. (It is always a good idea to have a photograph or the real flower to copy). Again, the smaller petals have fewer spots.

11 Dust the tip of each petal with the brush you used for the primrose and moss green. The colour should be very pale; cleaning your brush with a little cornflour will help to give a more subtle effect.

ASSEMBLY

12 Start by taping the larger petals around the base of the stamens using ½-width pale green tape. Add the smaller petals in between each of the larger ones, slightly recessed. If the petals are still slightly soft, you can now re-curl the petals if needed. Dust the back of the flower with a little moss green and primrose, making it darker towards the base.

Tape each flower on to an 18-gauge wire for strength.

BUDS

13 Tape over an 18-gauge wire several times with ½-width green floristry tape. Bend a large hook in one end, and moisten the end. Roll a large sausage of paste and insert the wire into one end, making sure that it is firmly fixed. (I usually push the wire in at least halfway.)

14 To mark the impression of petals, make a 'cage' using three 24-gauge wires (see page 10). Open the cage and insert the bud, tip first. Arrange the wires equally and close them together so that they press into the paste and mark it equally into three. Release the cage and move each of the wires a few millimetres to one side. Close the cage again to form three ridges down the length of the bud. Remove the cage, and then, using your finger and thumb, pinch a deep ridge on the paste between each pair of division lines.

15 Dust the surface of the bud with a little of the flower colour, and over-dust

with the primrose and moss green mixture. The base of the bud should be slightly darker so increase the moss green at the base. The smaller the buds are, the more green they should be.

16 Steam both the flowers and buds to give a waxy appearance (see page 10).

LEAVES

17 Roll out some mid-holly/ivy paste using a grooved rolling pin or board. Cut out the leaves using a scalpel and templates made from the outlines on page 140. Insert a moistened 24-gauge wire into at least half of the length of the ridge on each leaf. Place each leaf on a pad and soften the edges using the rounded end of the largest cel-stick. Vein either by marking on some veins with a dresden tool, by veining with a double-sided veiner, or by using a fresh leaf. Allow to dry for about 1 hour.

18 Dust the leaves with dark green, and then over-dust with moss. The smaller leaves should be more of a lime green in colour. Dip each leaf into a ½ glaze, shake off excess, and leave to dry.

Chinese Jasmine

There are some 300 species of jasmine. *Jasminium polyanthum* is native to China, hence its common name. This plant is regularly used in bridal bouquets, its delicate white or pink-tinged flowers and slender foliage adding elegance to any spray.

Materials

White and mid-holly/ivy flower paste
24, 28 and 33-gauge wires
Fine stamens (optional)
Plum, moss, pink, dark green and holly/ivy petal dust (blossom tint)
¼ glaze (see page 10)

Equipment

Small stephanotis cutter (568)
Simple leaf cutters (229-232)
Pale green floristry tape

FLOWER

1 Form a small ball of white flower paste into a teardrop shape. Pinch out the broad end of the teardrop between your fingers and thumbs to form a pedestal. Place the shape down on a board and roll out the paste very finely using a small cel-stick. Place the stephanotis cutter over the thick part of the pedestal and cut out the flower. Rub your thumb over the cutter before removing the flower to make sure you have clean-cut edges to the petals.

2 Place the flower on a pad and, using the rounded end of the small celstick, soften the back of each petal, working half on the paste and half on the pad. Using the pointed end of the tool, open up the throat of the flower. Moisten the end of a 28-gauge wire and pull it through the centre of the flower, until the end is just hidden.

3 If you wish you can insert a fine stamen in the centre of the flower. Move the petals around a little to add some movement. The flower has such a very fine calyx that it is usually unnecessary to add one; if anything, mix a little moss and dark green petal dust and dust at the base of the flower.

BUDS

4 I tend to use many more buds than flowers, as they have a softer appearance and, more importantly, they are quicker to make! Form a tiny

ball of white paste into a cone shape, and insert a dry 33-gauge wire into the broad end. (There is no need to use egg white with such a small piece.) Hold the base of the bud between your finger and thumb and gradually thin down the bud using a rubbing motion. Try to keep the tip of the bud very pointed.

LEAVES

5 The leaves can be cut freehand but I prefer to use cutters. I use simple leaf cutters, but before you use them for jasmine leaves you need to squeeze the sides inwards to make them very narrow. (I suggest that you buy a set for just this purpose.) Using a finely grooved board or rolling pin, roll out some mid-holly/ivy paste quite finely. Cut out the leaves using the prepared cutters. The leaves grow in groups of five, seven or nine, and the first leaf is always larger than the others.

6 Insert a moistened 33-gauge wire into the central ridge on each leaf, and then place them on a pad. Soften the edges with the rounded end of the small celstick. Draw down a central vein on each using the fine end of a dresden tool, and pinch down the centre of each leaf

with your finger and thumb. Allow to dry for about 30 minutes before dusting.

COLOURING AND ASSEMBLY

7 Group the buds and flowers into mixed clusters, taping them together with ¼-width green floristry tape.

8 Dust the upper surfaces of the buds with a touch of plum or pink petal dust. The flowers have even less colour on them, again only on the upper surface (it tends to be wherever the light catches them). Dust a little dark green and moss at the base of the buds.

9 Tape together the leaves using ¼-width tape again, starting with a large one and

then taping the others in pairs down the stem. Dust the upper surfaces heavily with dark green, and then over-dust with holly/ivy. Dip into a ¼ glaze, shake off excess, and leave to dry.

10 To form a climbing stem, tape over a 24-gauge wire with ½-width tape, and then tape the leaves on to it so that you have two groups coming out at the same point on either side of the stem. The flowers and buds always appear out of these leaf axils. Continue to build up the stem until it is the length you need.

Ivy

Ivy *(Hedera)* is probably one of the most useful forms of foliage, taking on many different shapes, colours and sizes. It is often used to symbolize fidelity, making it an ideal subject for a wedding cake! See pages 122–123 for instructions on how to make the Common Ivy.

Materials

Pale or mid-green flower paste
18, 24, 26 and 28-gauge wires
Holly/ivy, dark green, plum,
aubergine, blue, black and
white petal dust (blossom tint)
½ glaze (see page 10) or aerosol
confectioners' varnish
Clear alcohol (gin or vodka)

Equipment

Large ivy cutters
African ivy cutters
Pointed ivy cutters
Birdsfoot ivy, large ivy or large
nasturtium veiners (GI)
Pale green, beige and brown
floristry tape
Small piece of sponge

LEAVES

1 Roll out some green flower paste using a grooved rolling pin or board. The thickness of the paste will depend upon the size of leaf you are making – a larger leaf looks much better if it is slightly thicker. Cut out as many leaves as possible from one strip of paste, using your chosen shape of cutter. Cover the leaves that you are not working on with a sheet of plastic to stop them drying out too quickly.

2 Insert a suitable moistened wire into the central ridge on each leaf (the size of leaf determining the strength of wire required). Try to insert the wire into at least half the length of the leaf.

3 Vein all the leaves using double-sided veiners: the African and pointed ivy will both fit into the birdsfoot ivy veiners and either the large ivy or nasturtium veiner is ideal for the larger ivy leaves. (You can, if you wish, use the veiner as a template as well, simply cutting out the leaf shape using a scalpel or scissors.)

4 Soften the edges of the larger ivy leaves only as these tend to be thicker; softening the edges with a celstick helps to give a more realistic effect. For the smaller ivies, especially the pointed ivy, simply stretch the sections gently with your fingers. (If you soften these their shape becomes very distorted.) Allow to dry a little before taping over each stem with pale green floristry tape.

COLOURING

5 It is best to colour the leaves as soon as possible, as the dryer they are the more difficult it is to achieve dark effects. Dust first of all with holly/ivy on both sides of the leaf and add depth using dark green. Some ivies have plum or aubergine

ASSEMBLY

8 Tape over the end of a 24-gauge wire with ½-width beige or brown floristry tape. (Some varieties of ivy have darker stems than others.) Curl the end around a celstick to form a delicate start to the stem. (This part would usually be young leaves beginning to form.) It usually looks best in bouquets and arrangements if you start with smaller leaves and gradually work down to the larger ones. Work from one side of the stem to the other, adding leaves as singles or in pairs. For longer stems, it is advisable to strengthen the wire by adding an 18-gauge wire (or more for very long stems). When the required length has been achieved, bend the stem a little to give a more natural effect.

colouring to the edge of the leaf and this should be added at this stage. Allow to dry overnight and then either lay the leaves on greaseproof paper and spray with aerosol confectioners' varnish (which will give a high gloss) or dip into ½ glaze, shake off the excess, and allow to dry.

6 To create paler veins, support the leaf from behind with a finger, and use either a scalpel or a scriber to scratch off the colour and a little of the sugar until enough of the base colour is showing through. Start with the main veins, and then work on the finer ones to complete the leaf.

VARIEGATED LEAVES

7 Mix together various greens with a touch of blue, black and white petal dust. Add some clear alcohol and, using a small piece of sponge, dab on some colour, adding darker green to areas of the leaf. Allow to dry, and glaze with ½ glaze. Pale veins can be scratched in if you wish (see step 6).

Eucharis Lily

Originating from South America, these unusual flowers (*Eucharis grandiflora*) are readily available throughout the year from any good florist's shop, being used mainly for bridal work. The word 'eucharis' is Greek for graceful or pleasing, which I think describes these flowers perfectly.

Materials

White and pale green flower paste
18, 24 and 28-gauge wires
Primrose, moss, spring green, champagne, nutkin and dark green petal dust (blossom tint)
Clear alcohol (gin or vodka)
Fine white stamens
½ glaze (see page 10)

Equipment

Eucharis lily cutters (670, 671)
White and pale green floristry tape
Amaryllis or other fine veiner

CORONA

1 Take a medium-sized ball of white flower paste and form it into a teardrop. Pinch out the paste at the broad end to form a mexican hat shape. Place the 'hat' on a board and thin out the brim using a celstick. Using the eucharis throat cutter, cut out the corona.

2 Hollow out the centre of the corona using the pointed end of a medium celstick, pressing the sides against the stick with your thumb. (The sides of the corona should be as straight as possible.) Press the rounded end of the celstick into the corona to create a flatter base.

3 Hook and moisten the end of a 24-gauge wire. Pull through the centre of the corona, embedding the hook deep into the base. Allow to dry.

4 The corona has six green lines radiating from the centre corresponding with each of the spikes on the edge. Mix a little moss and spring green petal dust with clear alcohol, and paint the markings on to the paste using a fine paintbrush. (These lines do not extend to the very ends of each point.) Dust a patch of spring green and primrose on either side of each line. (The more mature the flower, the paler the corona should be.)

STAMENS AND PISTIL

5 The stamens grow at the end of each spike on the corona. To make these, cut six short strands of stamen and attach one to the end of each spike to form 'T'-bars. Secure with a little softened flower paste. Allow to dry. Moisten the tips with egg white and dip into a mixture of champagne and nutkin petal dust.

6 The pistil is made by twisting a short piece of ¼-width white floristry tape to form a fine strand. Flatten the end using the broad end of a dresden tool; this will form a flap which needs to be cut into three with scissors. Place in the centre of the corona, using softened flower paste.

PETALS

7 Roll out some white flower paste using a grooved board or rolling pin. Cut out three petals using the single cutter, and insert a moistened 28-gauge wire into the central ridge of paste on each petal. Vein both sides of each petal.

8 Place the petals on a pad and soften the edges with a celstick. The edges are not very frilled so be careful not to overwork them. Taking each petal between your finger and

thumb, pinch a vein down the centre. Allow to dry slightly over the edge of the pad.

9 Repeat the above instructions to make three more petals for the outer layer. The base of each of these outer petals needs to be pinched from the upper surface to curl the edges back slightly.

10 Once all of the petals are firm enough to handle, tape the first three petals around the corona using ½-width floristry tape. The three outer petals are then taped in between the previous three.

11 The next part of this flower is optional, depending upon how the flowers are going to be displayed and whether the backs are going to show or not. The back of the eucharis lily is formed into a long, fine tube. To make this, add an extra piece of paste to the stem, blending it into the backs of the petals using the broad end of the dresden tool. Work the paste until it is smooth and the tube is the required length. Bend the flowers gently into shape.

12 Roll a ball of green paste to form the ovary and attach this to the base of the fine tube. Work the ovary between your finger and thumb until it is slightly oval in shape. Using a scalpel, divide the ovary into three and pinch each section down the centre to form a ridge.

13 Dust the ovary and the base of the tube using a mixture of moss and spring green petal dust. Glaze using a ½ glaze.

BUDS

14 Form a cone of white flower paste and insert a moistened 24-gauge wire into the base. Work the base of the cone between your finger and thumb until you have formed a fine tube. Using a scalpel, divide the top of the bud into three to give the impression of unopened petals. Add an ovary as for the flower.

ASSEMBLY

15 Tape together a collection of buds and flowers. (There are usually four or six flowers and buds to each stem.) To form a thicker stem, add an 18-gauge wire and pad out the stem using strips of kitchen paper taped over with ½-width green floristry tape.

16 There are two bracts at the base of the clump and these are cut out of green flower paste. Vein the bracts with a sweetcorn husk, soften the edges and mark a central vein on each with the fine end of the dresden tool. Moisten the base of the paste and attach to the flower stem. Dust with the green mixture and add a touch of primrose. Steam the flowers to give a waxy appearance (see page 10).

Stephanotis

Originating from Madagascar, this plant *(Stephanotis floribunda)* is often called Madagascan jasmine. It is a climbing plant with large dark green foliage and clusters of highly scented flowers that are always in great demand for bridal work.

Materials

White and mid-green flower paste
18, 24 and 28-gauge wires
Primrose, moss, spring green, dark green and champagne petal dust (blossom tint)
½ and ¾ glazes (see page 10)

Equipment

Celpad
Nasturtium calyx cutter (448)
Small stephanotis cutter (568)
Zimbabwean miniature calyx cutter
Large rose petal cutters (optional)
Pale green floristry tape

FLOWER

1 Roll a ball of white flower paste into a sausage shape and pinch out one end to form a pedestal. Place the flat part of the pedestal on a board and roll out the paste using a small celstick, remembering that stephanotis produces a fairly thick, waxy flower. As the back of the flower is much wider than the centre of the nasturtium calyx cutter, it is easier to insert the back into one of the holes in a celpad, and to cut out the flower by pressing the cutter firmly against the soft pad.

2 Remove the flower and place the petals face down on the board. Using the small celstick again, broaden each petal, trying not to make the flower too fine. Each petal has an indent down the centre; to make this, place the flower back into the hole in the celpad and press the broad end of a dresden tool firmly on to each petal.

3 Open up the centre of the flower using the pointed end of a celstick, and insert a moistened 24-gauge wire. Holding the back of the flower directly behind the petals with your finger and thumb, work the paste to form a slender back that broadens towards the base. Trim off any excess paste. Dust the flower from the base with a mixture of spring green, moss and primrose. Add a small amount of this colour to the flower centre, along with a dash of champagne petal dust. Stephanotis can be either steamed (see page 10) or dipped in a ½ glaze to help give it its waxy appearance.

CALYX

4 Roll out some mid-green paste thinly and cut out the calyx using the small stephanotis cutter. The calyx does not have much shape

and I usually stick it straight on to the base of the flower. The calyx should be left flat; resist the temptation to stick the sepals on to the sides of the back of the flower.

BUD

5 Roll a ball of white paste into a cone shape. Hook and moisten a 24-gauge wire, and insert it into the base of the cone. Working the centre of the cone between your finger and thumb, elongate the bud to form its characteristic shape (it should be pointed at the top, narrow at the centre and broader towards the base which needs to be fairly flat).

6 Make a 'cage' (see page 10) with five 28-gauge wires. Insert the pointed end of the bud into the cage and close the cage over it to mark the impression of five unopened petals. Pinch each of the petals a little to make a ridge of paste between the wires before removing the cage.

7 Add a calyx as for the flower, using a smaller calyx cutter for the smaller buds. Dust with a mixture of spring green, moss and primrose from the base of each bud.

LEAVES

8 Roll out some mid-green paste using a grooved rolling board. Use a fresh leaf as a template and veiner, and cut around the edge with a scalpel. (For speed, you can use a set of large rose petal cutters and simply stretch each leaf after it has been cut.) Insert a suitable moistened wire into the central ridge in each leaf, making sure that you insert it to at least half the length of the leaf. Pinch down the centre and allow the leaves to dry fairly flat.

9 Dust the leaves heavily with dark green petal dust and

glaze using a ¾ glaze. Allow to dry and then remove the colour from the centre vein with a scalpel.

ASSEMBLY

10 Tape over the stems and tape flowers and buds into clusters of various sizes using ½-width pale green floristry tape. The main stem is an 18-gauge wire taped over with green tape. Add the smaller leaves in pairs, gradually working down to the larger ones. At any stage you can add the flower and bud clusters, starting usually with a cluster of buds, but every time you tape on a flower cluster you must add a pair of leaves at the same point. When you have made the required length, bend the whole stem to create an attractive display. Dust the stems with dark green petal dust.

Eustoma

This beautiful plant *(Lisianthus ressellianthus)* is a member of the Gentian family (it is often known as the prairie gentian). It gives a very delicate appearance to an arrangement, mainly due to its graceful twisted buds and fine stems.

Materials

White, pale melon and pale holly/ivy flower paste
20, 24, 26 and 33-gauge wires
Primrose, lemon, moss, deep purple, African violet, spring green, holly/ivy, white and dark green petal dust (blossom tint) ¼ glaze (page 10)

Equipment

Large rose petal cutters (550, 549)
Eustoma petal veiner (GI)
Ceramic silk veining tool (HP)
Fine pliers
Green floristry tape
Long-nosed tweezers
Cattleya orchid wing petal cutters (3, 6)

PETALS

1 Shape a ball of pale melon flower paste into a cone, and then roll it out thinly on a board, leaving a slightly raised area towards the pointed end. Cut out the petal using the chosen size of rose petal cutter.

2 Cut a length of 26-gauge wire into three. Moisten one end of a piece and insert it into the thick area of the petal. Because the flower is usually seen from the side, the wire is inserted only a little way into the base of the petal; a small hook can be made in the wire if you feel it needs some extra support. Pinch the base to make it slender.

3 Place the petal in a double-sided eustoma veiner, pressing firmly to give the full effect. Remove the petal and return it to the board.

4 Frill the upper edge of the petal with the ceramic veining tool or a cocktail stick (toothpick). Some flowers have more frills than others, so decide which you prefer. I find that quite a lot of frilling gives the flowers some movement.

5 Cup the centre of the petal gently using a large celstick. Make another four petals in exactly the same way. Allow to dry until firm enough to handle.

PISTIL

6 Cut a short length of 26-gauge wire, moisten the end and attach a small ball of pale holly/ivy paste to the end. Roll the paste between your finger and thumb until it covers a short piece of the wire very finely. Attach a larger piece of paste at the base, and form it into an oval shape to represent the ovary.

7 Roll a small sausage of paste and flatten both ends between your finger and thumb, so that it looks like a little bow-tie. Place the paste on a pad and hollow out both flattened ends using a small celstick. Pinch the centre slightly between your finger and thumb, giving the piece a heart-shaped appearance from the side.

8 Moisten the top of the wired pistil and position the heart shape on top, pressing firmly to make sure it is secure. In an immature flower this piece should be small and the two end sections squeezed closer together.

STAMENS

9 Cut five very short pieces of 33-gauge wire. Bend one end of each piece into a 'T'-bar shape. To do this, use pliers to bend the end at 90°, and then

bend this small piece at the centre to form a 'T' shape. Attach a tiny sausage-shaped piece of white paste to the end (with pieces as small as this you won't need any egg white).

10 Tape the five stamens around the base of the pistil, so that their tops are a little higher than the ovary. Dust the tip of each stamen with primrose and lemon. Dust the top of the pistil with primrose and a touch of moss petal dust. Colour the ovary a dull green.

COLOURING AND ASSEMBLY

11 Dust the petals using your chosen colours. The petals illustrated are dusted with deep purple and African violet. The edge of each petal should be dark and the base very pale.

12 Tape the petals around the pistil and stamens, so that they overlap each other. You will need to tuck the last petal in underneath the first. While the petals are still damp, move them around and bend them into shape. Squeeze in the base of the petals to form the tight base characteristic of the flower. You might find that you have to stick the petals together using egg white, or a little flower paste softened with egg

white, as they have a tendency to move around. Hang the flower upside-down until it is a little dryer, and then curl back the edges of each petal. Tape on a 20-gauge wire for strength. Steam the flower (see page 10) to give a gentle sheen.

CALYX

13 The eustoma calyx is very fine. Roll five fine strands of pale holly/ivy flower paste. Attach them to the base of the flower with egg white. Allow to the cage and twist the petals together from left to right.

16 Dust the bud with a little of the flower colour and a touch of pale spring green at the base. The smaller the bud, the less colour it should have. Add a calyx as for the flower.

LEAVES

17 Roll out some pale holly/ivy paste using a grooved rolling pin or board. (These leaves are quite fleshy.) Either cut the leaves freehand with a scalpel, or use orchid wing petal cutters. Insert a moistened 26-gauge wire into half the length of the leaf. Place on a pad and soften the edges with a celstick. Use the fine end of a dresden tool to draw down a central vein and a series of veins following the curved edge of each leaf.

18 Dust the leaves with a little dark green, and then over-dust with holly/ivy and white mixed together. Dip into a ¼ glaze, shake off excess, and leave to dry. Make as many leaves as you wish, remembering that they grow in pairs down the stem; each time you join buds or flowers together, there should be two leaves at the junction.

firm up, and then dust with a little dark green petal dust. (Alternatively, for general purposes, make the calyx from green floristry tape; this method avoids so many breakages!)

BUDS

14 Roll a ball of pale melon paste into a cone and insert a moistened 24-gauge wire. Work on the base of the cone to turn it into a more graceful shape.

15 To give the impression of petals, the easiest method is to make a 'cage' with five 26-gauge wires (see page 10). Place the bud, tip first, into the cage and close the wires around the bud as evenly as possible. While the wire is still in place, pinch out the paste from between the wires with your fingers or a pair of long-nosed tweezers. Release

Anemone

The anemone belongs to the *Ranunculaceae* family, which also includes buttercups. They are available from florists from November to May, making them an ideal choice for many occasions.

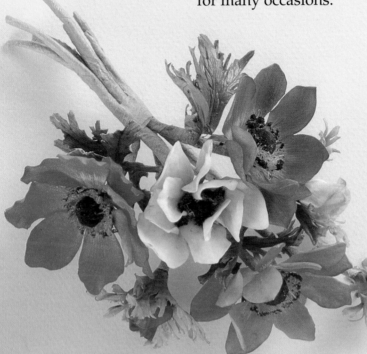

Materials

Pale melon, ivory and holly/ivy flower paste
20, 26 and 30-gauge wires
Violet, cornflower blue, plum, African violet, lavender, red, aubergine, dark green, spring green and moss petal dust (blossom tint)
Lace-making thread
Black pollen dust
¼ glaze (see page 10)

Equipment

Simple leaf cutters (228, 229, 230)
Round Christmas rose veiner (GI)
5mm (¼ in) flat-headed brush
Pale green floristry tape
Emery board
Daisy leaf cutter (J) or templates (see page 140)

PETALS

1 Roll out some pale melon paste thinly using a grooved rolling pin or board. Cut out the petals using the simple leaf cutters. Some anemones have more petals than others, and the size and shape can vary, even on one flower. I usually cut out 9–11 petals for each flower.

2 Cut lengths of white 30-gauge wire into four. Moisten the ends of the wires and insert one into the thick central ridge of each petal.

3 Vein each petal using a double-sided Christmas rose veiner, pressing firmly to give very definite veins. (Any other fine, fan-formation veiner could be used instead.)

4 Place the petals on a pad and frill the edges with a cocktail stick (toothpick) or with a cel-stick. Anemones vary so much that it is best to experiment to decide which you prefer. Cup the centre of each petal a little. Dry the petals for 15–30 minutes before you colour them; the strong colours are best achieved if the petals are dusted while they are still damp, as the petal dust adheres better.

COLOURING

5 Anemones are available in many different colours, ranging from strong, bold colours like purple, cerise and red, to paler, more delicate colours like mauve, pink and ivory. Some anemones are even bi-coloured. Using a 5mm (¼ in) flat-headed brush and your chosen colour, dust each petal with very firm strokes. The petals illustrated are coloured red, with a little aubergine on the edges. To achieve a very strong colour, steam each petal a little (see page 10), and then re-dust with your chosen colour. The backs of the petals should be slightly paler. Try to keep the base of each petal white, simply by avoiding this area when you dust. If you do dust over this

Note

The anemone has been cultivated since ancient times,
being native to the
Mediterranean countries and
parts of Asia. The red forms
would make a wonderful alternative to poinsettia in a
Christmas arrangement.

area, allow the petals to dry,
and then remove the colour
using a scalpel. (This actually
gives a slightly cleaner, more
realistic appearance.)

6 The purple flowers illustrated on page 31 are coloured
with a mixture of equal proportions of violet and cornflower
blue, and then over-dusted with
African violet. The paler flowers
are coloured with lavender and
a little of the violet mix. The
cerise flowers are dusted with
plum, with a little aubergine on
the edges. The ivory flowers can
be left plain or given a plum or
red tinge at the base.

STAMENS

7 Most anemone centres are
blackish-blue, although there
are some ivory forms that have
creamy-green stamens. The filaments of each stamen tend to be
the same colour as the flower.

8 Bend a length of 30-gauge
wire in half. Hold the bend
in the wire between your finger
and thumb, and twist it to form
a small loop. Set aside.

9 Wrap some fine white thread
around two parted fingers
many times. Remove from your
fingers and twist this large loop
into a figure-of-eight shape.
Bend this in half to form a
smaller loop.

10 Place the prepared wire
through the centre and
tape over the base of the thread
with floristry tape, down on to
the wire. (The small loop of wire
should still be visible in the centre of the thread.) You might
have enough thread for two sets
of stamens; if this is the case,
prepare another piece of wire as
before and place it through the
other side of the loop. Tape
over, and then cut the thread in
half. Trim the stamens a little,
trying to cut the thread into a
gentle curve.

11 Rub the tips of the stamens against an emery
board to give them a little more
bulk. Dust the thread with the
colour of the flower.

12 The centre of a real
anemone can be very
large; it is more attractive if kept

fairly small. Roll a ball of paste
and flatten the base. Place the
ball on a cocktail stick (toothpick), and use a pair of fine scissors to texture the surface. Paint
the surface with egg white and
dip it into some black pollen
dust mixed with violet and
cornflower blue petal dust.

13 Place the centre on the
hook in the middle of the
stamens. To add pollen to the
stamen tips, paint a little egg
white on your board, rub the
tips of the thread gently in the
egg white, and then quickly dip
the tips into the black pollen
mixture. Be very careful – if you
dip them in too far you will end
up with a very ugly centre; too
little and it will look patchy.
Allow to dry.

ASSEMBLY

14 Tape the stamens on to a
piece of 20-gauge wire
using ½-width tape. If you have
made any small petals, these
should be taped on first. I usually tape a few petals on at a
time, adding them opposite
each other. Gradually add the

larger petals, until you feel that the flower looks finished. Some flowers will look better with more petals than others.

15 Tape over the main stem several times with ½-width tape to create the characteristic fleshy stem.

BUD

16 Tape over a piece of 20-gauge wire and bend a large hook in the end. Attach a medium-sized ball of paste to the end. Allow to dry.

17 Roll out some ivory flower paste thinly, and cut out five or six petals using one of the simple leaf cutters. Vein both sides of each petal using the Christmas rose veiner. Frill or soften the edges of each petal and stick on to the prepared dried centre. Position the petals in a very informal way (if you make them too neat the bud will look like a badly made rose!). Flatten the tops of the petals to give a tighter appearance.

18 Dust the bud while the paste is still damp. Steam (see page 10), and dust again.

LEAVES

19 Anemones do not have a calyx, but they have a very interesting leaf formation behind each flower. Roll out some mid-holly/ivy paste fairly thickly using a grooved board or rolling pin. Cut out the leaves using the daisy leaf cutter, or use a scalpel and templates made from the outlines on page 140. Trim away the bottom piece of each shape, leaving three sections per leaf.

20 Insert a moistened 26-gauge wire into the central ridge of paste, so that it runs almost to the tip of the leaf. This leaf is very fragile and needs a lot of support. Broaden each of the sections by rolling them with a celstick. Using a scalpel, cut out some 'V' shapes from the edge of each leaf to give a 'frillier' effect. Flatten and thin the edges using the broad end of a dresden tool. Vein the leaf using the fine end of the tool (or use a fresh leaf). You will need a mixture of sizes.

21 Dust each leaf with some dark green petal dust, and give the edges a tinge of plum. Over-dust with either moss green or spring green (the depth can vary from stem to stem). Dip into a ¼ glaze, shake off excess and leave to dry.

22 Tape three or four leaves behind each bud and flower. The more mature the flower is, the further down the stem the leaves should be, but the leaves are taped tightly behind each bud.

Eucalyptus

Eucalyptus is a very versatile foliage, which can create a lovely soft feel with its silver-blue-green colouring. There are many types of eucalyptus; my favourite is this very large-leafed form. Another type has leaves with bronze-red edges, which are ideal for autumn arrangements.

Materials

Very pale holly/ivy flower paste
20, 26 and 28-gauge wires
Dark green, holly/ivy, white, aubergine and black petal dust (blossom tint)
¼ glaze (see page 10)

Equipment

Circle or rose petal cutters
Fine rose leaf veiner
Fresh eucalyptus leaves (optional)
Pale green floristry tape

Repeat with more wires and leaves. Elongate each leaf by stretching the paste with your fingers.

3 Place the leaves on a pad and soften the edges with a celstick, just enough to remove the cut edges. Vein the leaf using either a fresh leaf or a very fine rose leaf veiner. These leaves tend to be very flat, but I do dry some of them on a gentle curve. You will need to make a variety of sizes for each stem, remembering that the leaves grow in pairs down the stem.

LEAVES

1 Roll some flower paste out using a grooved rolling pin or board, remembering that the finished leaves should be slightly 'fleshy'. Cut out the leaves using the circle cutters, or use a scalpel and a fresh leaf as a template.

2 Cut a length of 26-gauge or 28-gauge wire into five. Moisten one end of a piece of wire and insert it into the thick central ridge of a leaf. The wire should be inserted into at least half the length of the leaf.

COLOURING

4 Start colouring the leaf using a flat-headed brush and a little dark green petal dust to add depth to the leaf. Over-dust gently with holly/ivy and a little white. Dust the edges and the base of each leaf with aubergine petal dust. Dip into a ¼ glaze, shake off excess, and allow to dry. As these leaves have a very dusty look their

appearance is improved if you over-dust with white petal dust (be very generous with this colour). Add a little black colour to parts of the leaf for more depth, if required. (One of the lustre colours can be used at this stage if you want to create a very soft effect.)

ASSEMBLY

5 At the top of each stem there are a few fine stems. The florist usually cuts these off, but, if time allows, I use them. They can be made from pieces of ¼-width tape, each twisted back on itself to make a fine strand.

6 Start to tape the stem up by taping two or three fine stems on to the end of a 20-gauge wire using ½-width tape. Start by adding the small leaves in pairs and, as you work down the stem, add the medium and then the larger leaves. If you are making a very long stem, you might find that you will need an extra 20-gauge wire for strength and to give the appearance of more bulk. Smaller stems can be taped on to longer ones to give variation.

7 Dust the main stem with a little dark green and a lot of aubergine petal dust. At this final stage you might find you have to dust some more white or aubergine on to the leaves. Bend the main stem and the leaves to add movement to the whole piece.

Ladder Fern

There are many cultivated forms of this attractively bold plant (*Nephrolepsis*). They are quite simple to make and, because of their size, you don't need many to fill in the gaps in a bouquet. This fern is, however, very fragile and it is advisable to wire them into the bouquet before they are fully dried.

FERN FROND

1 Roll out a large piece of green paste not too thinly. Cut out the shape using the sword fern cutter. (You might find that it is easier to place the paste on top of the cutter and then roll your rolling pin over the top to obtain a cleaner cut.)

2 Remove the paste from the cutter and place the shape on the board. Frill both edges of each 'leaf' using the broad end of a dresden tool. Place the frond on a pad and draw a central vein on each of the 'leaves' using the fine end of the dresden tool.

3 Tape over a length of 24-gauge wire with ¼-width pale green floristry tape. Paint egg white on to the wire, covering a length the same as the length of the fern. Place the moistened wire down the centre of the fern. Press the wire firmly on to the paste to make sure that it is secure. Quickly turn the fern over. You should now have a ridge on the back of the leaf. Pinch either side of this ridge from the tip to the base using a pair of tweezers (to make the wire more secure). Turn the fern

back over and pinch the tip of each section. Curl them in the required direction before you allow them to dry a little.

COLOURING

4 Dust the fern to various depths; the younger the fern is the lighter it should be. Start by dusting with dark green, then moss, and then over-dust with vine green. Dip into a ¼ glaze, shake off the excess, and leave to dry.

Materials

Mid-green flower paste
24-gauge wires
Vine green, moss and dark green petal dust (blossom tint)
¼ glaze (see page 10)

Equipment

Sword fern cutter (J)
Pale green floristry tape
Tweezers

Fern

Although this fern has features of many different species, it is purely the work of my imagination! I always feel it is important to create interesting foliage; it doesn't always have to be exactly correct. This fern is easier to wire into a bouquet because each section is wired separately.

Materials

Pale green flower paste
20, 24, 30 and 33-gauge wires
Moss, dark green, skintone, white (optional) and mother of pearl (optional) petal dust (blossom tint)
¼ glaze (see page 10)

Equipment

Australian fern cutters (three sizes)
Pale green floristry tape

'LEAVES'

1 Roll out the paste on a finely grooved board. (You will need to roll the paste very finely for this small fern.) Cut out the fern sections in various sizes, remembering that they grow in pairs down the stem. Insert a 33-gauge or 30-gauge wire, depending on the size of the piece.

2 Work on the edges of the pieces, using the broad end of a dresden tool to create a feathered effect. Mark a central vein on each piece with the fine end of the tool, then pinch down the centre of each piece and curve slightly if you wish.

COLOURING

3 Dust each piece with moss and dark green, with a little skintone on the edges. The backs can be dusted with mother of pearl if you wish. Glaze using a ¼ glaze. For a winter display, these ferns also look very good dusted all over with white petal dust to give a frosted appearance.

4 Tape a small piece of fern on the end of a 24-gauge wire to form the start of the frond, and then add some more small 'leaves' in pairs just below this. When you feel that the frond needs to be wider, start adding the medium and then the large 'leaves'. If you are making a very long piece of fern, you will need to add 20-gauge wire to support the weight. Bend the main stem into the desired shape and then dust with the green petal dusts.

Clivia

There are only four species of Clivia and they are all native to South Africa. They are mainly orange although there is a rare yellow form. The flower that I have copied *(Clivia gardenii)* is a variety that can be bought as a pot plant.

Materials

26 and 28-gauge wires
White, pale melon and mid-holly/ivy flower paste
Lemon, primrose, tangerine, red, coral and moss green petal dust (blossom tint)
¼ and ½ glazes (see page 10)

Equipment

Fine pliers
White and green floristry tape
Clivia petal cutters (610, 611)
Very large alstroemeria veiner (GI)

STAMENS AND PISTIL

1 Cut six short lengths of 28-gauge wire. Bend a closed hook in one end of each wire using pliers. Hold the hook at its centre and bend it into a 'T'-bar shape. Tape over the straight length of each wire with ¼-width white floristry tape.

2 Attach a tiny sausage of white paste to each 'T'-bar. (I usually find that I do not need any egg white for such a small piece.) Moisten the surface of the paste and dip it into lemon petal dust to form the pollen. Dust the length of the wire with a pale mixture of moss and primrose petal dust.

3 To form the pistil, tape over another piece of 28-gauge wire with white tape, leaving a flap of tape at the top. Cut this flap into three, using a scalpel or fine scissors, and then twist each piece between your finger and thumb to form three fine strands. Dust with the pale green mixture as for the stamens.

PETALS

4 Roll out some pale melon paste using a grooved board or rolling pin, and cut out three petals using the large clivia petal cutter.

5 Insert a moistened 26-gauge wire into the central ridge of each petal. Vein each of the petals using the double-sided alstroemeria veiner, then place on a pad and soften the edges a little with a celstick. Clivia have quite a stiff appearance so do not try to frill the paste. Pinch a ridge down the centre of each petal from the base to the tip, and allow to firm a little over a gentle curve.

6 Cut out three more petals with the smaller cutter, and repeat step 5.

COLOURING AND ASSEMBLY

7 Dust a patch of lemon and primrose from the base of each petal, tapering to a slight point approximately halfway up. Colour the remainder of each petal with tangerine and coral, and then over-dust with a little red. Dip each petal into a ¼

Note

Clivia can be used to great effect with cream roses, green helebores, berries and lots of foliage to make an unusual winter bridal bouquet.

glaze, shake off excess, and leave to dry.

8 Tape the stamens together around the pistil, which should be slightly taller. Bend the stamens into shape, with the anthers curving inwards.

9 Tape the three large petals around the stamens, and then tape the smaller ones in between using ½-width green floristry tape. As the paste is still soft, bend each petal back a little at the tip.

OVARY

10 Attach a ball of green paste at the base of the petals. Mark it into three using a scalpel, and then pinch each section down the centre between your finger and thumb to form a ridge. Dust with moss green and glaze using a ½ glaze.

BUD

11 Form a cone of paste and insert a 26-gauge or 28-gauge wire, depending on the size of the bud. Work the base of the cone between your finger and thumb to form a more slender shape. Divide the bud into three using a 'cage' made from three 26-gauge wires (see page 10). Insert the bud, tip first, into the cage and close the wires over it, keeping them as evenly spaced as possible. Open the cage and remove the bud. Pinch a ridge with your finger and thumb down the centre of each section now marked on the bud. Add an ovary as before. Dust with the same colours as the flower, then dip in ¼ glaze, shake off the excess, and leave to dry.

12 Tape the flowers and buds together. They all appear from the same point. At the base of the flower head there are some bracts which can be made with either tape or paste. The stems are flat on both sides. I usually use the flowers as single pieces rather than in a full flower head.

Oncidium Orchid

This is one of the larger hybrids of Oncidium orchid, although it is still a comparatively small flower, making it an ideal filler to use in an arrangement with larger flowers. I prefer the yellow varieties, but there are many other colours to choose from.

Materials

Pale melon flower paste
20, 24, 26 and 28-gauge wires
Lemon, primrose, red, skintone and nutkin petal dust
(blossom tint)
Clear alcohol (gin or vodka)

Equipment

Oncidium orchid throat
cutter (656)
Ceramic silk veining tool (HP)
Nasturtium petal cutter (446)
Medium stephanotis
cutter (566)
Pale green floristry tape

THROAT PETAL

1 Roll out some pale melon flower paste using a grooved rolling pin or board. Cut out the petal using the oncidium throat cutter. Insert a moistened 26-gauge wire into the whole length of the central ridge of paste.

2 Using the ceramic silk veining tool, frill the edges of the petal, leaving the two tiny pieces unfrilled. If you want the edge to be a little more jagged, use the broad end of a dresden tool to double frill the edge (see page 8).

3 Soften and cup the two tiny pieces of the petal, and then pinch down the length of the

whole petal to form a centra vein.

4 For smaller flowers, use the nasturtium petal cutter instead. Cut out a curved 'V' shape at the base and add two small pieces of paste at the top of the petal, where the paste joins the wire. Then work on the petal exactly as before.

OUTER PETALS

5 Roll out some more pale melon paste, leaving a raised area in the centre. (You could use a mexican hat board (see page 8) to achieve this.) Cut out the petal shape using the stephanotis cutter, making sure that the thick area of the paste is in the centre of the cutter. Before you remove the paste from the cutter, rub your thumb on the paste around the edge of the cutter to make sure you have cleanly cut edges.

6 Imagine the shape as a person, and then frill the edges of the two 'arms' using the broad end of a dresden tool. Place the piece on a pad and

often the other three petals using a bone-end tool. Cup the 'head' petal forward, turn the shape over and curl the 'legs' back.

7 Moisten the centre of the paste and pull through the throat petal so it fits securely. Curl the 'head' petal forwards again, if necessary, and the others slightly back.

8 Roll a tiny ball of paste into a teardrop shape and attach it to the top of the throat petal, between the two smaller sections. Blend into the surface using the broad end of the dresden tool. (This forms the column.) On a real flower, there is a raised piece on the petal below the column, but I prefer to leave this off as it can give a slightly ugly appearance. Allow to dry a little before colouring.

BUDS

9 Attach cone-shaped pieces of paste to 28-gauge wires. Divide the surface of each bud into five using a 'cage' made from five 28-gauge wires (see

Page 10). Make lots of buds of various sizes.

COLOURING AND ASSEMBLY

10 Dust the throat and the back petals with a mixture of primrose and lemon petal dust. Paint the back petals in very untidy stripes using nutkin and skintone petal dust mixed with a little alcohol. Paint some markings on the throat using red and skintone, forming a combination of stripes and spots.

11 Dust the buds with the yellow mixture, and then paint on horizontal stripes using the nutkin brown mixture.

12 Tape together a small group of buds and flowers on to a 24-gauge wire, alternating from one side of the stem to the other. Tape these small groups on to a 20-gauge wire to form a larger stem.

Winter Wedding Cake

Although the flowers on this wedding cake are available all year round, together they create a wintry feel. I'm very fond of combining white flowers with strong green foliage; here the two together make a very bold yet elegant design.

Materials

15cm (6 in), 23cm (9 in) and 30cm (12 in) round cakes
Apricot glaze
3kg (6lb) almond paste (marzipan)
Clear alcohol (kirsch or vodka)
5kg (10lb) white sugarpaste
Fine willow green ribbon to trim cakes
Green velvet ribbon to trim boards and stand
18-gauge wires

Equipment

23cm (9 in), 30cm (12 in) and 43cm (17 in) round cake boards
Sugarpaste smoothers
'E'-shaped chrome stand (CV)
Double-sided sticky tape
Beige floristry tape
Florists' staysoft
Small shallow plastic container

Flowers

6–7 ivy stems, various lengths (see page 22)
3–4 eucharis lilies (see page 24)
3–4 creamy-white half roses and 4–5 buds (see page 14)
2 full stems of stephanotis (see page 26)
5 caladium leaves, various sizes (see page 63)
Winter Wedding Arrangement (see page 45)

PREPARATION

1 Brush the cakes with apricot glaze and cover with almond paste. Leave to dry overnight. Brush the cakes with alcohol, and cover the cakes and boards separately with white sugarpaste, using sugarpaste smoothers to achieve a good finish. Position the cakes on the cake boards and allow to dry. Fasten fine willow green ribbon around the base of each cake, and velvet ribbon around the board edges.

2 Cover the long upright piece of the cake stand with green velvet ribbon, using a little double-sided sticky tape at the beginning and end. Place the cakes on the stand, positioning the upright piece of the stand to the left of the cakes.

FLORAL ARRANGEMENTS

3 Arrange some long stems of ivy on the middle tier to cover the top edge and right-hand side of the cake. You will need to add some extra 18-gauge wires to strengthen the stems, taping the whole piece together with full-width beige floristry tape. Curve the stems to follow the line of the cake, and simply place them on the cake's surface.

4 Follow the instructions on page 45 to make the large Winter Wedding Arrangement

that is displayed to the left of the cake. The base of the arrangement should sit on the cake board of the bottom tier, and the tallest piece of ivy should curl in front of the middle tier.

5 To make the smaller cake top arrangement, use the flowers and foliage listed above, arranging them in florists' staysoft in a small, shallow plastic container.

Note

As well as using smoothers, a good way to achieve a silky smooth finish on sugarpaste is to flatten a ball of sugarpaste in the palm of your hand and to smooth it over the paste. This is especially good for smoothing the top edges of cakes.

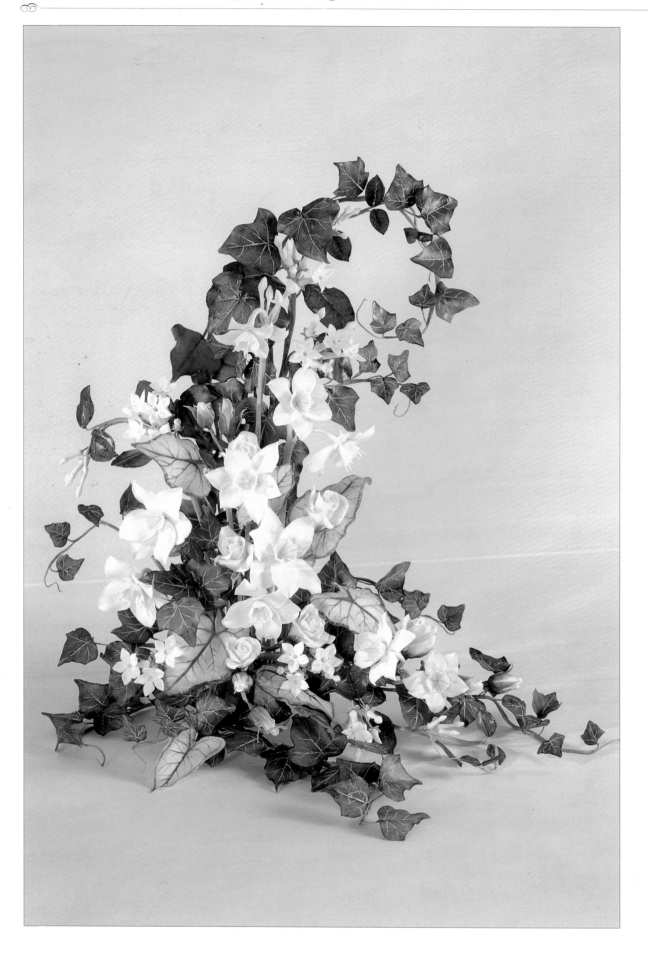

Winter Wedding Arrangement

This arrangement is quite an unusual shape, but it fits very well with the design of the cake on page 42. It could also be used with a single or two-tiered cake, with the top part of the arrangement curving over the cake.

see page 42

Flowers

7–9 ivy stems, various lengths (see page 22)

3 trailing stephanotis stems, plus one small piece (see page 26)

10–11 eucharis lilies (see page 24)

7 caladium leaves, various sizes (see page 63)

11–12 creamy white roses with foliage (see page 14)

Equipment

18-gauge wires
Pale green floristry tape
Pliers
Wire cutters
Florists' staysoft
Small shallow plastic container

1 As this is a large arrangement you will need to strengthen the stems of the taller flowers and foliage with 18-gauge wires, taping over using ½-width floristry tape.

2 Place a large clump of staysoft in a shallow plastic container. Start by arranging the ivy foliage, shaping it to look like a large ornate 'L' shape. Push in the stephanotis stems, positioning them alongside some of the ivy stems.

3 The eucharis lilies are the main flowers of the design, so place these in next. Push most of the stems in vertically and a few horizontally. The larger flowers should be placed at the centre of the arrangement to form the focal point. Fill in behind the eucharis lilies with the caladium leaves. (These will help add depth and detail at the same time with their interesting veining.)

4 Finally, tape up some of the roses into twos and threes, and push these in to fill in the gaps around the focal point, and to follow the lines of the ivy on the outer edges of the arrangement.

5 When you have everything in place, stand back and take a look at the arrangement from a distance. Sometimes you can spot mistakes that you are unable to see close up. If there are gaps or the whole shape needs defining, add some more foliage.

Mothering Sunday Cake

The glass plate on which this cake is displayed is hand-painted, making it the perfect gift. Once the cake has been eaten, both the anemone spray and the plate can be kept as reminders of the day!

Materials

20cm (8 in) round cake
Apricot glaze
750g (1½ lb) almond paste (marzipan)
Clear alcohol (kirsch or vodka)
750g (1½ lb) champagne sugarpaste
Fine pink and purple ribbon to trim cake

Equipment

Sugarpaste smoothers
38cm (15 in) perspex or glass plate
Selection of paintbrushes
Magenta, red, violet, black, light green, dark green, yellow and white glass paints
Posy pick
Green floristry tape

Flowers

5 anemones, assorted colours (see page 31)
5 anemone buds (see page 33)
5 rose buds and 4 half roses (see page 14)
5 fronds of ladder fern (see page 36)
35 large ivy leaves (see page 22)

PREPARATION

1 Brush the cake with apricot glaze and cover with almond paste. Leave to dry overnight. Moisten the almond paste with clear alcohol, and cover the cake with sugarpaste, using sugarpaste smoothers to achieve a good finish. Allow to dry.

GLASS PAINTING

2 This technique is very attractive when used to decorate base boards, perspex pillars, dividers and cake stands. The design will be permanent once it has been allowed to dry thoroughly. Before you carry out any work, make sure that the piece you are going to work on is clean and dry. The design was painted on to the plate freehand, but if you need guidance the pattern on page 140 should help you get started. You don't necessarily need to be neat or accurate with your design, as long as the colours are clean and balanced.

3 Using a broad, flat paintbrush, paint the flower petals on to the glass, cleaning the brush each time you change colours. (I used the colours neat, occasionally mixing them together to form slightly different tones.) Next, paint the leaves into the design using green and yellow colours, outlining here and there with a little magenta.

4 Once the flowers are dry, you can paint in the black anemone centres, this time using a smaller brush. Start by painting in the large round centre, then surround it with small dots to represent the stamens.

5 Outline areas of the design with diluted black paint, if needed. Allow the entire design to dry thoroughly.

ASSEMBLY

6 Position the cake on the painted glass plate. Attach a band of fine purple ribbon around the base of the cake and a pink ribbon slightly above it. Tie two small bows of ribbon, one of each colour, and position over the joins. Push a posy pick into the top of the cake.

7 Arrange the flowers and foliage in a suitably shaped spray, taping the wires together with floristry tape, and creating a handle. Insert the handle into the posy pick, and arrange the flowers as necessary.

Golden Days

This cake was designed to celebrate a golden wedding anniversary, but would be equally suitable as a 50th birthday cake. The large arrangement includes a variety of flowers from various parts of the world; together they create an autumnal feel, mainly due to the varied colours of the virginia creeper and cotinus foliage.

Materials

3kg (6lb) sugarpaste
Gold and dark green spray paints (optional)
30cm (12 in) teardrop cake
Apricot glaze
1.5kg (3lb) almond paste (marzipan)
Autumn leaf paste colouring
Clear alcohol (kirsch or vodka)
Fine brown ribbon to trim cake
Green ribbon to trim boards
Pale green flower paste
Moss, dark green, holly/ivy, aubergine, red, tangerine and white petal dust (blossom tint)
½ glaze (see page 10)
Royal icing

Equipment

43cm (17 in) round cake board
36cm (14 in) teardrop cake board
Virginia creeper templates (see page 143)
Hydrangea leaf veiners (GI)
Tilting cake stand

Flowers

Golden Days Arrangement
(see page 51)

PREPARATION

1 Cover the large round cake board with sugarpaste and allow to dry for at least 1 week as this will form the base for the whole piece. Colour the sugarpaste on the board with dark green spray paint, or if you prefer to use food colouring, paint with dark green and holly/ivy petal dust mixed together and diluted with clear alcohol. Overspray the green with a fine haze of gold. (When using spray paint, always work in a well-ventilated area.)

2 Brush the cake with apricot glaze and cover with almond paste. Leave to dry overnight. Colour 2kg (4lb) sugarpaste with autumn leaf paste colouring. Moisten the cake with alcohol, and cover the cake and teardrop board separately with sugarpaste. Transfer the cake on to the board, making sure you have a neat join between the cake and the board. Attach fine brown ribbon around the base of the cake and broader green ribbon around the board edge.

DECORATION

3 Roll out some pale green flower paste and use the virginia creeper templates (see page 143) to cut out some leaves with a scalpel. (You will need a good variation in size.) Vein each leaf using the hydrangea veiners, and then soften the edges with a large celstick. Pinch each leaf down the centre and allow to dry for 10–15 minutes.

4 Place the leaves on absorbent kitchen paper and dust with a variety of petal dusts, starting with the greens, and then adding red and aubergine to darken. Dip each leaf into a ½ glaze, shake off the excess, and allow to dry. Attach the leaves to the cake using a small amount of royal icing.

5 Paint some leaf stems and a main stem on to the cake to correspond with the paste leaves, using a mixture of dark green and holly/ivy petal dust diluted with a little clear alcohol. To create the paler veins on each leaf, use a fine paintbrush and some white and pale green petal dust mixed with a little alcohol, starting with the central vein and then painting in the finer veins.

6 To make the design easier on the eye, dust around the leaves with tangerine and holly/ivy. Dust the left-hand edge of the cake with a little tangerine petal dust, carrying the colour down on to the cake board. Add this colour very gently at first.

7 Place the cake on the display board using a tilting cake stand to prop the cake up at an angle. Position the flower arrangement in the gap created by the curve on the left-hand side of the cake.

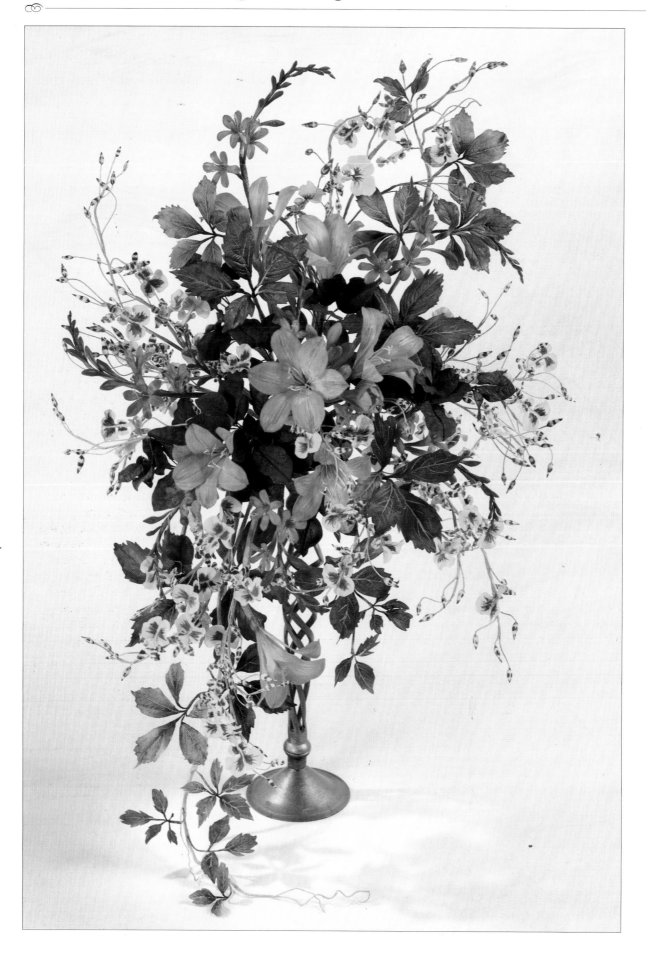

Golden Days Arrangement

Once the cake has been cut and the party is over, you can use this arrangement as a room decoration, and as a memento of a happy celebration.

Flowers

5 stems of Chinese virginia creeper (see page 92)
7 stems of clivia (see page 38)
5 large stems of oncidium orchid (see page 40)
Several pieces of cotinus foliage (see page 101)
7 stems of montbretia (see page 94)

Equipment

30cm (12 in) bronze candlestick
Gold spray paint
Glue gun and glue sticks
Florists' staysoft or oasis
18-gauge wires
Pale green floristry tape
Fine pliers
Wire cutters

PREPARATION

1 Spray the candlestick lightly with gold spray paint, leaving some of the base colour showing through. Allow to dry thoroughly.

2 Using the glue gun, stick a large ball of florists' staysoft to the candlestick. (If you prefer, dry oasis can be used instead.)

3 The long stems and heavier flowers will need extra support, so tape an extra 18-gauge wire to the main stem of each one. (The long stems of clivia will need two 18-gauge wires.)

4 Start by inserting the virginia creeper stems into the staysoft to form the outline of the arrangement. Add the pieces of clivia, positioning one clump as the focal point and spacing the others apart, working from one side of the arrangement to the other.

5 Add the oncidium orchids in the gaps between the virginia creeper and fill in the area around the focal point with the cotinus foliage. (This also adds a lot of depth to the arrangement.)

6 To complete the arrangement, thread in the montbretia stems, spacing the colour throughout. When you have finished, take a look at the arrangement from a distance, and then fill in any gaps with extra foliage, or correct errors that are not always obvious close up.

Floral Elegance

This spectacular two-tiered cake was made to celebrate my parents' pearl anniversary. The design could also be used to great effect as a wedding cake, with the ever-popular combination of lilies and roses.

Materials

20cm (8 in) and 30cm (12 in) elliptical cakes
Apricot glaze
2kg (4lb) almond paste (marzipan)
Clear alcohol (kirsch or vodka)
3kg (6lb) white sugarpaste
Royal icing
Fine magenta ('beauty') ribbon

Equipment

Sugarpaste smoothers
25cm (10 in) and 40cm (16 in) elliptical cake boards
Plain scalloped crimpers
No. 1 piping tube (tip)
Double tilting cake stand
Double-sided carpet tape
50cm (20 in) silver candlestick

Flowers

Floral Elegance Curved Bouquet (see page 55)
Small Floral Elegance Spray

PREPARATION

1 Brush both of the cakes with apricot glaze and cover with almond paste. Allow to dry overnight. Moisten the cakes with clear alcohol, and cover with white sugarpaste, using sugarpaste smoothers to achieve a good finish. Cover the cake boards with sugarpaste and crimp the edges using a pair of plain scalloped crimpers.

Transfer the cakes to the boards, making sure you have neat joins between the cakes and boards. Pipe a snail's trail border around the base of each cake with royal icing and a no. 1 piping tube. Allow the piping to dry overnight, then attach a band of ribbon and a small bow at the base of each cake.

2 Make the curved bouquet as described on page 55. The small bouquet is simply a smaller version of the large one.

ASSEMBLY

3 Position both cakes on the tilting cake stand, using double-sided carpet tape to hold them in place. Tie the large bouquet on to the candlestick with some fine ribbon. Position the candlestick behind the cake, trailing the long ivy stem on to the lower cake's surface. The smaller spray is positioned next to the base tier, again trailing some of the foliage on to the cake and board so that the whole cake is framed.

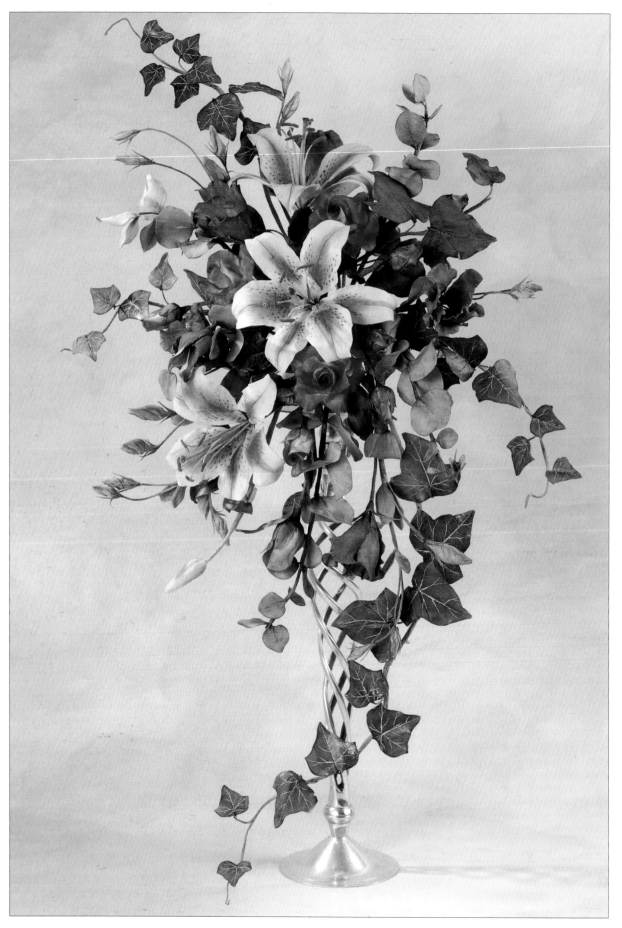

Floral Elegance Curved Bouquet

This style of bouquet is very popular with brides, and is a useful shape to use on cakes, although it does not have to be made on the same scale as the one pictured opposite.

Flowers

1 long stem and 4 shorter stems of large ivy (see page 22)
4–5 stems of eustoma (see page 28)
3 stargazer lilies (see page 17)
3 dark pink roses (see page 14)
6 dark pink rose buds with foliage (see page 14)
5 stems of eucalyptus (see page 34)

Equipment

18-gauge wires
Pale green floristry tape
Fine pliers
Wire cutters

PREPARATION

1 First of all, strengthen any of the flower stems that are to be very long or that are particularly heavy, by taping in additional 18-gauge wires.

ASSEMBLY

2 Decide how long you want the bouquet to be. The first long stem of ivy needs to measure approximately two thirds the length of the whole bouquet. Bend the stem to a 90° angle. Add the other ivy stems, bending each to the same angle and taping each piece in with ½-width floristry tape. (The aim is to form a handle to the bouquet.) Together the ivy stems should form the basic outline of the bouquet. This type of bouquet should be heavier towards one side, so you will need to use longer and more stems of foliage on the heavier side. If the shape is created symmetrically, you will form a 'shower' bouquet instead.

3 Start to tape in the eustoma flowers, then tape the lilies into the bouquet, following a diagonal line. Choose one lily for the focal point and position it a little higher than the others. Add any extra eustoma flowers and buds to fill in the gaps.

4 Tape in the roses, using the larger ones in the middle of the bouquet and the buds towards the edges, curving the stems to follow the lines of the ivy stems. Finally, fill in the remaining gaps using the eucalyptus and any other foliage. Neaten the handle of the bouquet using full-width tape.

5 To display a bouquet of this size on a cake you would need to use a Wilton-crystal-effect plastic pillar, as the normal size of posy pick is too small. For the cake on page 52, the flowers are displayed off the cake, tied to a large candlestick with a length of ribbon.

Exotic Flowers

EXOTIC FLOWERS make a very bold, colourful and unusual decoration for a cake. Although most originated in tropical and subtropical areas of the world, many have for so long been successfully grown locally or imported that they can hardly be considered 'exotic'. They can be used in numerous combinations to create new and interesting arrangements which automatically have a very modern and exciting appearance.

Bauhinia

This plant (*Bauhinia variegata*) originates from India, and is sometimes called 'camel's foot' because of the shape of its leaf! This large genus is very diverse in shape, size, colour and form. The first flowers appear before the leaves; it is only at the end of the flowering season that the two can be seen together.

Materials

24, 26 and 28-gauge wires
Cream, pink, deep purple, plum, fuchsia, aubergine, dark green, primrose, moss and holly/ivy petal dust (blossom tint)
White, pale pink, pale green and mid-green flower paste
Cyclamen liquid food colouring
½ glaze (see page 10)

Equipment

Fine pliers
Pale green floristry tape
Bauhinia cutters (460–462)
Amaryllis veiner (or similar)
Black bryony veiner (GI)

STAMENS

1 Cut five pieces of 28-gauge wire. Holding the end of a wire with pliers, bend approximately 5mm (¼ in) down close to the main section, then bend from the centre of this piece to form a 'T'-bar. Colour each wire with plum petal dust.

2 Attach a tiny sausage-shaped piece of white flower paste to each 'T'-bar (this forms the anther), paint with egg white and then dip into cream petal dust to form the pollen. Allow to dry. Bend each stamen into an 'S' shape, using the pliers and pinching at intervals to create a gentle curve.

PISTIL

3 Roll a pea-sized ball of mid-green paste. Moisten the end of a 24-gauge wire, and thread the ball on to it. Holding the

paste firmly between your finger and thumb, work the paste down the wire to cover approximately 5cm (2 in) of the wire. Tape the stamens around the pistil, positioning them so that the tip of the pistil is slightly above the stamens.

PETALS

4 Roll out some pale pink paste using a grooved board or rolling pin. Cut out one petal using the 'head' petal cutter (461). Moisten and insert a 26-gauge wire into at least half the length of the petal.

5 Vein the petal using the amaryllis veiner. Place the petal on a pad and soften the edges using a medium celstick. (Some of the bauhinias have petals with very frilled edges, while others don't – decide which you prefer!) Pinch the back of the petal from the base to the tip, using your finger and thumb, to create a central vein. Dry for about 30 minutes.

6 Cut out two more petals with the 'arms' cutter (460), and two with the 'legs' cutter (462). Repeat steps 4 and 5 with these four petals, and leave to dry for 30 minutes.

COLOURING AND ASSEMBLY

7 Dust each petal with pink and fuchsia using a 5mm (¼ in) flat-headed brush, and working from the edges down towards the base. Over-dust with a little plum, then, working with aubergine, dust the base of each petal, making the colour on the 'head' petal much stronger and extending it further down the petal.

8 Paint a series of lines in a fan formation on the 'head' petal only (some species have all plain petals) using cyclamen liquid colour and a fine paintbrush.

9 Tape the petals around the pistil and stamens, using ½-width floristry tape. Start with the 'head' petal, and attach the 'arms' on either side, slightly behind the 'head', and then attach the 'legs' at the base of the 'arms'. As the paste is still quite damp, you can now gently re-position any of the petals.

BRACT

10 Roll out some pale green paste and cut out an arrowhead shape with a scalpel. Place on a pad and soften the edges with a celstick. Using a dresden tool, draw a series of veins on the paste.

11 Moisten the bract and attach to the back of the flower, wrapping the base around the stem. Dust with a little primrose and moss mixed together.

LEAVES

12 Roll out some mid-green paste using a grooved board or rolling pin. Cut out the leaves freehand using a sharp scalpel; they are oval in shape with a deep rounded 'V' removed from the tip. Insert a moistened 26-gauge or 24-gauge wire into each leaf. Vein using the black bryony veiner, and soften the edges with a large celstick. Pinch down the centre to reinforce the central vein. Allow to dry until firm enough to handle.

13 Dust each leaf with dark green and holly/ivy. Glaze using a ½ glaze, allow to dry, and then remove the colour on each vein using a scalpel.

Chinese Hibiscus

There are many different colour variations of this very showy flower, including white, yellow, pink, orange and red. As the name implies, the plant originates from southern China.

Materials

Fine and small white stamens
20, 24 and 26-gauge wires
Watermelon, red, aubergine,
dark green and holly/ivy petal
dust (blossom tint)
Clear alcohol (gin or vodka)
White and mid-green flower
paste
Poppy paste colouring
Mimosa-coloured pollen dust
½ glaze (see page 10)

Equipment

Pale green and white floristry
tape
Hibiscus petal veiner (GI)
Jem plastic trumpet-shaped
former (optional)
Rose calyx cutter (R11b)
Daisy cutters (108, 109)
Hibiscus leaf veiners (GI)

STAMENS AND PISTIL

1 Tape five small white stamens on to a 24-gauge wire using ¼-width white floristry tape. Paint the stamens with red petal dust mixed with a little alcohol. This forms the pistil.

2 Colour some white flower paste with poppy paste colouring to a paler shade than you want the finished flower to be. Shape a little of this coloured paste into a small ball, and thread it on to the wire so that the ball is just below the stamens. Work the paste between your finger and thumb, gradually pulling the paste down the wire to form a very slender shape, the base of which, in a real flower, is sometimes slightly broader. The total length should measure at least the length of one of the petals (although it is more usual for it to be a little longer). Pinch off any excess paste. Bend the whole piece to form a gentle curved shape.

3 Before the paste has a chance to dry, cut lots of fine stamens into short lengths and insert into the top part of the paste, just below the pistil. Try to cover a short length of approximately 2cm (¾ in) with the stamens. Allow to dry just a little.

4 Dust the paste and stamens with watermelon and red to add depth to the flower. Moisten the tips of the stamens with egg white and dip them gently into some mimosa-coloured pollen dust. Try to avoid getting pollen on the pistil.

PETALS

5 Roll out some of the poppy-coloured paste using a grooved rolling pin or board, remembering that the petals should be fairly 'fleshy'. Using the flat back side of the top half of the petal veiner, press down on top of the paste to leave an indented outline on the surface. Using a sharp scalpel, cut around the shape.

6 Insert a moistened 26-gauge white wire into the thick central ridge, inserting it to approximately half the length of the petal.

7 Place the petal in the double-sided petal veiner. Press down firmly, but be careful as this veiner has very strong veining. Remove the petal and place it back on the board. Using a cocktail stick (toothpick) or a tiny celstick, frill the edges of the petal. Some flowers have very frilly edges; others do not, so decide which you prefer. Make four more petals in exactly the same way.

8 Pinch down the centre of the backs of the petals to reinforce the central vein. Allow to dry over a gentle curve or in a plastic trumpet-shaped former, until firm enough to handle.

COLOURING AND ASSEMBLY

9 Dust from the base of each petal, gradually fading the colour as you reach the outer edges. Start with watermelon, and then over-dust with a little red, especially at the base. The back of each petal should be paler than the front.

10 At the very base of the petals there is usually a dark red, shiny patch. Mix a little alcohol with some red and aubergine petal dust and paint

the very base of each petal. Dip the base in a ½ glaze if you wish to achieve the shiny finish. Shake off the excess, and leave to dry.

11 Tape the petals around the stamens with ½-width green floristry tape, overlapping them a little.

CALYX

12 The hibiscus has a double calyx. To make the first one, roll out some mid-green paste, leaving the centre slightly thicker. (You could use a mexican hat board for this.) Cut out the shape using a rose calyx cutter. Broaden each of the sepals a little, and then place the calyx on a pad. Soften the edges with a celstick and draw down a central vein on each sepal with a dresden tool.

13 Moisten the centre and each sepal with egg white, and thread on to the back of the flower, trying to position each sepal slightly over a join. (This calyx should fit quite tightly against the back of the flower.)

14 The second calyx is cut out with a daisy cutter (109), then treated in exactly the same way as the first calyx. Position on the base of the first calyx, curling the sepals back.

15 Dust both of the calyces with dark green and holly/ivy.

Buds

16 Larger buds are formed from a cone of flower paste coloured to match the petals. Insert a short length of taped 20-gauge wire into the broad end.

17 To give the impression of petals, the easiest method is to use a 'cage' made from five 24-gauge wires (see page 10). Open the wires up and insert the bud, tip first. Close the wires into the base, keeping them as evenly spaced as possible. Using your finger and thumb, pinch out some paste between the wires. Open up the cage and remove the bud. Twist the sections of the bud together in a clockwise movement to form a neat spiral effect. Dust the bud with watermelon and a little red petal dust.

18 Add a double calyx as described for the flower (see steps 12–15 above).

19 Smaller buds are made in the same way using green paste. Mark smaller buds with a 'cage' of wires, pinching a ridge on each section between the wires. Remove the cage but do not twist the bud as before. Instead, cut into the top of the bud using a pair of fine scissors, following the line of each of the sepals. Add only the second calyx as described above, but using a smaller daisy cutter (108). Dust with dark green and holly/ivy.

Leaves

20 Roll out some mid-green paste using a grooved rolling pin or board. Cut out a basic leaf shape using a sharp scalpel. Insert a moistened 26-gauge or 24-gauge wire, depending on the size of the leaf.

21 Vein the leaves using the hibiscus leaf veiners, pressing firmly to give the full leaf impression. After removing each leaf from the veiner, cut the edges using scissors to give a slightly jagged effect. Work a little more on these edges using the broad end of the dresden tool. Place on a pad and soften the edges a little more using a large celstick. Allow to dry just a little.

22 Dust with dark green petal dust, and then over-dust with holly/ivy. Use a touch of aubergine on the very edge of each leaf. Dip into a ½ glaze, shake off excess, and leave to dry.

Note

Some species of *Hibiscus* have variegated foliage, which can give an alternative, softer appearance to the plant.

Caladium

Although the caladiums are native to Central and South America, there are many cultivars, and it is widely available now as a pot plant. It is a useful foliage to use in arrangements because of its size and unusual markings.

Materials

Ivory flower paste
18, 20 and 22-gauge wires
Dark green, holly/ivy, primrose, moss, apricot, coral and red petal dust (blossom tint)
Clear alcohol (gin or vodka)
Cornflour
¼ glaze (see page 10)

Equipment

Caladium leaf cutters
Pale green floristry tape
Caladium veiners (GI)

1 Roll out some flower paste leaving a slightly thicker area down the centre. Cut out a leaf. Tape over a wire with ¼-width floristry tape. Moisten the end and insert it into the leaf.

2 Place the leaf between the double-sided veiners and press firmly. Remove the leaf and place it on a pad. Soften the edges with the rounded end of a large celstick, and pinch firmly down the centre of the leaf.

Allow to dry draped over the edge of the pad.

COLOURING

3 Mix together some holly/ivy and dark green petal dusts, and dilute with a little clear alcohol. Paint in the main markings following the veins on the leaf. Paint in the finer markings and a border around the inner edge.

4 Using a mixture of primrose, dark green, moss,

holly/ivy and a lot of cornflour, dust a little colour on to the leaf surface. Using the darker greens, dust from the edge of the leaf to the border line.

5 The leaf can be left green and white, or you can create some very strong colouring. The leaves illustrated are coloured with a mixture of coral and apricot, and then over-dusted with a touch of red. Glaze using a ¼ glaze.

Madagascar Flamboyant

Flamboyant by name, flamboyant by nature, *Delonix regia* is one of the most spectacular tropical flowering trees with its huge red flowers and lacy bright green foliage. Its size has been scaled down here to make it more suitable to use on cakes.

Materials

Tiny seed-head stamens
Red paste colouring
Clear alcohol (gin or vodka)
24, 28 and 30-gauge wires
White and holly/ivy flower paste
Red, white, spring green, lemon and moss petal dust (blossom tint)
¼ glaze (see page 10)

Equipment

Pale green floristry tape
Nasturtium petal cutter (447)
Orchid or other veiner with fan-formation markings
Ceramic silk veining tool
Small stencil brush (optional)
Nasturtium calyx cutter (448)

Stamens and Pistil

1 Paint the length of ten stamens with red paste colouring diluted with a little alcohol or water. The tips can be a dark burgundy (in new flowers) or white (in more mature specimens).

2 To make the pistil, tape over a short length of 30-gauge wire with ¼-width green floristry tape. Bend gently, and then tape the stamens around the pistil, making sure that the tips of the stamens are fractionally higher than the top of the pistil.

Flowers

3 Colour some flower paste a slightly paler red than you want the flower to be. Roll out the paste using a grooved board or rolling pin. Cut out four petals using the nasturtium petal cutter.

4 Insert a moistened 28-gauge wire into the central ridge of each petal, making sure the wire is inserted to at least half the length of the petal.

5 Roll the base of each petal between your finger and thumb to form a more slender shape. Place each petal on the orchid veiner and press very firmly to give a full impression. Remove from the veiner and place back on the board with the veined side facing you.

6 Using the broad end of a dresden tool, frill the edges of the petals to create a slightly jagged frilled effect. Frill over this area using the ceramic silk veining tool. Pinch each petal down the centre and curve very slightly. Allow to dry for approximately 30 minutes.

7 Make a fifth petal using white flower paste, following the above instructions. When you frill this petal, try to broaden the rounded part of the petal as this tends to be slightly larger.

Colouring and Assembly

8 Dust the red petals from the edges with red petal dust. If the petals have dried too much and the colour is not sticking very well, steam the petals (see page 10), and then re-dust.

9 Paint some darker markings on each petal using red paste colouring mixed with a little clear alcohol. The marking should be at the centre of each petal, following the direction of the veining. Dip into a ¼ glaze, shake off excess, and leave to dry.

10 The white petal has lots of markings which can either be painted on individually with a fine paintbrush, or sprayed on with a stencil brush (as for the flowers illustrated). Dab the brush in the darker red colouring that has been used for the other petals, then hold the brush above the petal and draw your finger over the bristles, spraying the colour on to the surface of the petal. (Be careful not to use too much liquid as this will give very large marks.)

11 As well as the small markings there are also some lines which should be painted on with a fine brush. Dust the base of the petal with lemon petal dust. Dip into a ¼ glaze, shake off excess, and dry.

12 Tape the white petal on to the stamens and pistil. Add the remaining four petals and, if the paste is still damp, curl the edges a little more if needed.

CALYX

13 Roll out some green paste fairly thickly and cut out a shape using the nasturtium calyx cutter, retaining the paste in the cutter after cutting. Roll out some red paste and, without removing the green paste, cut out another red calyx shape. The two pieces should hold together quite well. Remove the calyx from the cutter and if the two colours have not stuck together add a little egg white.

14 Place the calyx on a pad with the red side on top. Hollow out the sepals using the broad end of the dresden tool. It is important that the edges of each sepal curl inwards.

15 Moisten the centre of the calyx and position it on the back of the flower, making sure each sepal is positioned in between a petal.

16 Dust the inside of the calyx with a little red petal dust, and the back with spring green.

BUD

17 Roll a ball of green paste into a cone and insert a hooked, moistened 24-gauge wire into the pointed end. Pinch the paste down on to the wire a little. Divide the surface into five using a 'cage' made from five 24-gauge wires (see page 10). Remove the cage and pinch a sharp point at the tip of the bud.

18 Dust the bud with spring green and a touch of moss. Dip into a ¼ glaze, shake off any excess, and leave to dry, then tape over the stem with ½-width green floristry tape.

LEAVES

19 The leaves are very fine; here I have simply tried to represent them. The leaves tend to open when the tree has fairly mature flowers on each branch.

20 Cut lots of pieces of ¼-width green tape. Twist each piece of tape back on to itself to make fine strands.

21 Tape the first strand on to a 30-gauge wire. Continue to add more strands until you have created a reasonable length. Make several pieces and then tape these together on to a 24-gauge wire using ½-width tape. Dust with moss green and plenty of spring green.

Cape Leadwort

This plant *(Plumbago auriculata)* is a favourite choice for the tropical garden or conservatory. Occasionally white forms are seen, but most are pale to mid blue.

Equipment

Harebell cutter
Rose leaf veiner (GI)
Pale green floristry tape

Materials

White and pale green flower paste
28-gauge wires
Bluebell, lavender, deep purple, skintone, white, spring green and dark green petal dust (blossom tint)
Clear alcohol (gin or vodka)
¼ glaze (see page 10)

FLOWER

1 Roll a small ball of white paste into a fine teardrop shape. Pinch out the base to form a pedestal. Place the flat base down on a board and roll out the paste very finely using a small celstick.

2 Cut out the flower using the harebell cutter. Before you remove the paste from the cutter, rub your thumb across the edge to make sure you have cleanly cut edges to the petals.

3 Place the flower on a pad and soften the edges using the rounded end of the small celstick. Open up the centre of the flower using the point of a cocktail stick (toothpick). Vein the centre of each petal using a dresden tool. Insert a moistened 28-gauge wire. Work the back of the flower between your finger and thumb to form a very fine, slender tube.

4 To form the calyx, attach a piece of green paste to the base of the flower and snip several times with fine scissors.

BUD

5 Roll a small ball of white paste into a teardrop shape and insert a moistened 28-gauge wire. Work the paste between your finger and thumb to form a very slender bud. Add a calyx as described for the flower.

COLOURING

6 Dust the flowers and buds with a very pale mixture of bluebell, white and lavender, making the centre of each flower slightly darker. Mix a little of the flower colour with deep purple and a little clear alcohol. Using a very fine paintbrush, paint a line down the centre of each petal. Dust the calyx with skintone petal dust.

LEAVES

7 Roll a ball of green paste into a teardrop and insert a moistened 28-gauge wire into the pointed end. Flatten the teardrop and then place into the rose veiner, pressing firmly to thin the leaf out. Place the leaf on a pad and soften the back using the rounded end of the small celstick.

8 Dust with spring green and a touch of dark green. Glaze using a ¼ glaze.

9 Tape the buds and flowers into clumps, and then tape the leaves in twos and threes down the stem. Tape smaller stems together to form a larger one. Dust the stems with the greens and a little skintone.

Blue Gum Blossom

The gum blossom *(Eucalyptus globulus)* pictured below has been made with a lot of artistic licence! It is, however, great fun to make.

Materials

20, 24, 26 and 28-gauge wires
Lemon, maize and white cotton embroidery thread
White and pale holly/ivy flower paste
Lemon, cream, cornflower blue, white, dark green, spring green, holly/ivy, primrose, champagne, aubergine, nutkin and black petal dust (blossom tint)
Semolina
Couscous
¼ glaze (see page 10)

Equipment

Beige and pale green floristry tape
Emery board
Tweezers
Leaf templates (see page 141)

STAMENS

1 Bend a length of 28-gauge wire in half. Hold the bend between your finger and thumb and twist it to form a tiny loop.

2 Wrap some cotton thread many times around two parted fingers. Repeat this with the other colours of thread, and then place them all together to form one loop. Twist the loop into a figure-of-eight, and then bend it in half to form a smaller loop. Place the prepared wire through the centre and tape over with ½-width pale green floristry tape. You will have enough thread to make two sets of stamens, so form a loop in another wire, as before, and place this through the other side of the loop of thread. Tape over and cut the thread into two sets of stamens. Trim a little if needed, trying to cut on a gentle curve. Rub the tips of the stamens against an emery board to

create a little bulk. Attach a tiny piece of white flower paste over the loop of wire in the centre, and form into a point.

CALYX

3 Roll a ball of white paste into a cone shape and thin out the base into a tube. Open up and thin the rounded end using a celstick. Moisten the centre and thread the stamens through. Pinch the calyx firmly around the stamens. Using tweezers, pinch the calyx into four sections. Pinch the centre of each section with your finger and thumb to form a ridge.

4 Dust the calyx with a mixture of dark green, cornflower blue and white. Overdust with black and nutkin.

5 Dust the stamens to various depths using a mixture of primrose and lemon petal dust. The pollen on the stamens is made by mixing semolina and couscous with primrose, cream, champagne and lemon. Brush a little egg white on a board, dip the stamens in it, then dip in the 'pollen' mixture.

BUDS

6 Roll a small ball of paste into a cone shape and insert a moistened 26-gauge wire. Pinch a tiny point at the tip and then divide the cone into two using a scalpel to form the 'lid'. Pinch with tweezers as for the flower, this time continuing the indents on to the lid. Work the base of the cone down on to the wire. Dust as for the calyx.

7 To make a half-open bud, simply form a small bunch of thread on the end of a 28-gauge wire. Model the calyx as for the flower, and attach, and then model a separate piece to form the lid. Trim the stamens so that they are fairly short, and then attach the lid using egg white. Dust as before.

LEAVES

8 Roll out some pale green paste using a grooved board. Cut out the leaves using a scalpel and templates. Insert either a 26-gauge or 24-gauge wire. Soften the edges and draw down a central vein. Pinch the whole length of the leaf into shape and allow to firm up.

9 Dust with dark green, holly/ivy and white, adding a little aubergine on the very edges. Paint the central vein to make it paler. Glaze using a ¼ glaze. Make a variety of sizes, including some very small leaves to use at the base of each flower cluster. The smaller leaves are coloured to more of a fresh spring green. Tape pieces together on to 20-gauge wire using beige floristry tape.

Trumpet Vine

There are two species of Trumpet Vine *(Campsis)*, one from the eastern United States and the other from China and Japan. I have based my vine on both! The flowers and leaves are large; I have scaled them down to make them suitable to use on cakes.

Materials

20, 24, 26 and 33-gauge wires
White, peach and holly/ivy flower paste
Tangerine, red, coral, aubergine, lemon, dark green and moss petal dust (blossom tint)
½ glaze (see page 10)

Equipment

Fine pliers
Pale green floristry tape
Large blossom cutters (474, 475)
Ceramic silk veining tool (HP)
Rose calyx cutters (R11, R12)
Large and small hydrangea veiners (GI)

STAMENS AND PISTIL

1 Cut four short lengths of 33-gauge wire. Bend a small closed hook in one end of each. Holding the hook halfway along, bend it again to form a 'T'-bar. Attach a tiny sausage of white flower paste to the end and pinch slightly at the centre. Dust with lemon petal dust to form the pollen.

2 To make the pistil, attach a ball of white paste on the end of a 33-gauge wire, and work it between your finger and thumb until it covers the wire in a thin layer. Divide the top end into two. Dust with lemon and tangerine, leaving the end paler.

3 Tape the four stamens around the pistil using ½-width floristry tape. Tape a couple of lengths of 24-gauge wire on to the stamens to give a little more support.

FLOWER

4 Roll a large ball of peach-coloured paste into a cone shape. Pinch out the broad end of the cone, and then place it on a board. Roll out the broad end of the cone with a celstick, remembering that this flower is very 'fleshy' and it is important to work with the paste fairly thick.

5 Cut out the flower using a large blossom cutter. Cut out a 'V' shape from in between each petal using a scalpel.

6 Open up the centre of the flower using the pointed end of a small celstick. Work the sides of the flower against the stick, to thin it down a little.

7 Place the flower against your fingers with one petal over your index finger. Roll and frill the edges of each petal using the ceramic silk veining tool.

8 Moisten the base of the stamens and pull them through the centre of the flower. Pinch the base of the flower to secure it in place. Allow to dry a little before colouring.

9 Dust from the edges of each petal with tangerine, coral and then a little red. Dust aubergine deep in the flower centre. The back of the flower is dusted with lemon from the base, and then with the orange mixture from the edges of the petals, gradually blending into the lemon.

Calyx

10 Roll out a piece of green paste, leaving the centre slightly thicker. Cut out the calyx using the large rose calyx cutter. Broaden and elongate each of the sepals using a celstick. Place on a pad and draw down a central vein using the fine end of a dresden tool. Moisten the centre and position on the back of the flower, closing the sepals around tightly. Dust with a little moss green.

Buds

11 To make small buds, attach small cones of green paste on to 26-gauge wires. Divide the surface into five using a scalpel or a 'cage' (see page 10).

12 To make larger buds, attach a large cone of peach paste on to a 24-gauge wire, inserting the wire into the fine end. Pinch the broad end five times between your finger and thumb to form the petals.

Moisten the centre and then fold the petals back in over the top part of the cone. Add a calyx as described for the flower. Dust with the tangerine, coral and red petal dust. For smaller buds, use the smaller calyx cutter.

Leaves

13 Roll out some green flower paste using a grooved board or rolling pin. Cut out basic leaf shapes using a scalpel. Insert a moistened 26-gauge wire into at least half the length of each leaf.

14 Vein using the hydrangea veiners, pressing firmly together. After veining, cut into the edge of each leaf using a pair of fine scissors to give a jagged effect. Soften the edges a little and allow to firm up before colouring.

15 Dust with dark green and over-dust with moss. Dust the edges with aubergine and red mixed together. Dip into a ½ glaze, shake off the excess, and leave to dry.

16 Tape the leaves together in groups. On the real flower, the leaves usually grow in groups of five, seven or nine, but smaller groups of three can be made if needed.

Bauhinias in Rhapsody

This beautiful cake with its dramatic spray of exotic bauhinia would make an impressive centrepiece for a birthday or anniversary. The side design has been kept very simple in form to complement and not detract from the floral spray.

Materials

23cm (9 in) heart-shaped cake
Apricot glaze
1kg (2lb) almond paste (marzipan)
Clear alcohol (kirsch or vodka)
1.5kg (3lb) shell pink sugarpaste
White royal icing
Fine willow green ribbon to trim cake
Green velvet ribbon to trim board
Pale green flower paste
Dark green, white and pink petal dust (blossom tint)

Equipment

32cm (13 in) heart-shaped cake board
Sugarpaste smoothers
No. 1 piping tube (tip)
Simple leaf cutters (229–232)
Pale green floristry tape
Wire cutters
Posy pick

Flowers

7 stems of trailing ivy (see page 22)
about 5 stems of Chinese jasmine with foliage (see page 20)
3 bauhinia flowers (see page 58)
3 large ivy leaves (see page 22)

PREPARATION

1 Brush the cake with apricot glaze and cover with almond paste. Leave to dry overnight. Moisten the cake with alcohol, and cover the cake and board separately with sugarpaste, using sugarpaste smoothers to achieve a good finish. Position the cake on the cake board and allow to dry.

2 Pipe a snail's trail around the base of the cake using white royal icing and a no. 1 piping tube. Fasten willow green ribbon around the cake just above the snail's trail, and attach velvet ribbon to the board edge.

SIDE DECORATION

3 Roll out some pale green flower paste very finely and using squashed simple leaf cutters (see page 21), cut out jasmine leaves in various sizes. Place the leaves on a pad and soften the edges with a celstick. Draw down a central vein on each leaf with a dresden tool. Moisten the back of each leaf and position in groups on the cake board and sides of the cake. Use a template to mark the leaf positions first, if needed.

4 Mix some dark green petal dust with a little alcohol. Using a fine paintbrush, paint the main and smaller stems on the cake and board. Darken the leaves using a larger brush, and then, working with white petal dust and alcohol, paint some jasmine buds into the design. Add a little pink to areas of the design, especially on the buds.

SPRAY

5 Use the trailing ivy and jasmine stems to create the curved outline of the spray. Bend the stems at an angle of 90° to create a handle for the spray, and tape together with ½-width floristry tape. Trim away any excess wire.

6 Add the three bauhinia flowers, positioning them, if possible, so they each face in a different direction. Tape the best and largest flower in the centre, slightly higher than the other two, to form the focal point of the spray. Add the larger ivy leaves, and more stems of jasmine, if required, to fill in any gaps.

7 Insert a plastic posy pick into the cake, and then insert the handle of the spray into the posy pick. Gently bend and rearrange the flowers a little, if needed, to complete the display.

A Splash of the Exotic

This stunning two-tiered wedding cake is reminiscent of the Caribbean, making it the ideal centrepiece for any couple planning to honeymoon, or indeed marry, in such an exotic location.

Materials

15cm (6 in) and 20cm (8 in) heart-shaped cakes
Apricot glaze
1.5kg (3lb) almond paste (marzipan)
Clear alcohol (kirsch or vodka)
2.5kg (5lb) sugarpaste, coloured with a little poppy and mulberry paste colouring
Fine pale blue ribbon to trim cakes
Flesh-coloured ribbon to trim boards

Equipment

Sugarpaste smoothers
20cm (8 in) and 30cm (12 in) heart-shaped cake boards
Pale green floristry tape
Fine pliers
Wire cutters
Piece of conditioned drift-wood, 28cm (11 in) in height
2 posy picks
Double-sided carpet tape

Flowers

2 hibiscus flowers (see page 60)
14 hibiscus leaves, various sizes (see page 62)
5 small and 3 large hibiscus buds (see page 62)
12 caladium leaves, various sizes (see page 63)
3 bud clusters and 5 flower clusters of cape leadwort (see page 67)

PREPARATION

1 Brush the cakes with apricot glaze and cover with almond paste. Allow to dry overnight. Moisten the almond paste with clear alcohol and cover with sugarpaste, using smoothers to achieve a good finish. Cover the cake boards with sugarpaste and place the cakes on top, making sure you have a neat join between the base of each cake and its board. Attach a band of fine blue ribbon around the base of each cake. Attach flesh-coloured ribbon around the cake boards.

2 Tape the flowers and foliage into two modern-style sprays, using the leaves to form the basic shapes. Bend the stems at an angle of 90° to form handles to the sprays. Tape over with floristry tape and trim away excess wires.

CAKE STAND

3 The cake stand has been made using a piece of conditioned driftwood purchased from a florist's shop. The top of the wood needs to have a smooth surface to hold the cake, so cut it to the required angle. Push a posy pick into each cake, positioning one to the right of the top cake, and the other to the left of the bottom cake.

4 Position the smaller cake on the stand using double-sided carpet tape to hold it in place (see Note).

5 Place the bottom tier in front of the base of the driftwood. Once the two cakes are in position, insert the handles of the floral sprays into the posy picks, and gently bend and arrange the flowers decoratively on the cakes.

Note

If you are worried that the small cake will be too heavy to rest securely on top of the drift-wood stand, use a polystyrene dummy cake for the display and provide a separate cake for cutting.

Flamboyant Festive Cake

I love working with very strong, bold colours and Christmas provides the perfect opportunity. This cake, with its richly coloured flamboyant flowers, would make a stunning centrepiece for a Christmas table. The cake has a very unusual speckled surface which complements the flower sprays rather than detracts from them.

Materials

20cm (8 in) teardrop cake
Apricot glaze
750g (1½lb) almond paste (marzipan)
Clear alcohol (kirsch or vodka)
1kg (2lb) champagne sugarpaste
Fine red ribbon to trim cake
Green velvet ribbon to trim board
Dark green, red and gold petal dust (blossom tint)

Equipment

Sugarpaste smoothers
25cm (10 in) teardrop cake board
Stencil brush
Florists' staysoft
Glue gun and non-toxic glue stick
2 small round cake cards

Flowers

2 flamboyant sprays (see page 79)
25cm (10 in) twisted twig garland

PREPARATION

1 Brush the cake with apricot glaze, cover with almond paste and allow to dry overnight. Moisten the cake with clear alcohol and cover with champagne sugarpaste, using sugarpaste smoothers to achieve a good finish. Cover the cake board separately with sugarpaste, and place the cake on top, making sure that you have a neat join between the base of the cake and the board. Allow to dry. Attach fine red ribbon around the base of the cake, and green velvet ribbon around the board edge.

2 To create the speckled effect, mix some green petal dust with a little clear alcohol. Dab the bristles of a stencil brush in the colour, aim the brush at the cake and rub the bristles firmly, splashing the cake with colour. Cover the whole of the cake and the board, and then repeat the process using red and gold colour.

ASSEMBLY

3 Position the cake into the centre of the twisted twig garland, lifting the cake at the back so that it rests on the garland and tilts forwards. For more tilt (and to protect the garland), raise the back of the cake on a lump of staysoft, if preferred.

4 Using the glue gun, stick a clump of staysoft on each of the small round cake cards. Secure the floral sprays in the staysoft, and position them next to the cake. (The staysoft should not come into contact with the cake.)

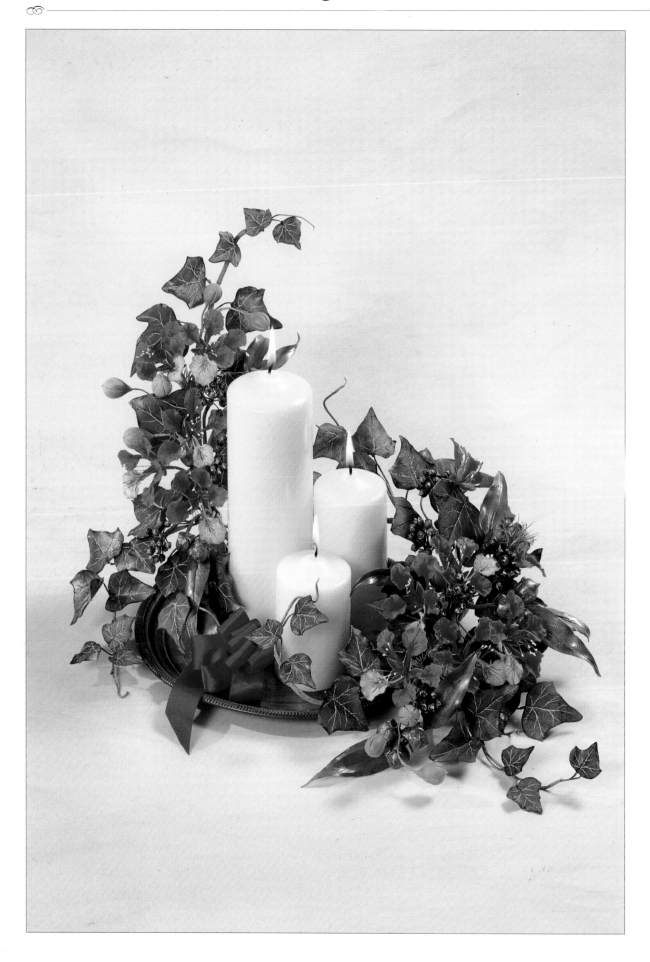

Flamboyant Candle Decoration

A Christmas cake has limited life, so using candles with the flower sprays before and after Christmas is a good idea. Simply remove the sprays and position them with the cake when needed!

Flowers

8 stems of large ivy (see page 22)
12 flamboyant flowers with buds and foliage (see page 64)
8 clumps of ivy berries, coloured gold (see Note), see page 123
6–8 clumps of long eucalyptus leaves with buds, coloured gold (see Note), see page 68

Equipment

18-gauge wires
Pale green floristry tape
Fine pliers
Wire cutters
25cm (10 in) pewter plate (or similar)
3 broad candles of various heights
Florists' staysoft
Broad red ribbon

FLORAL SPRAYS

1 Strengthen any of the flower stems, if necessary, by taping in 18-gauge wires. Start forming the outline of a large spray using five of the ivy stems. Bend each stem to an angle of 90° to form a handle before taping together with ½-width floristry tape. Introduce some full stems of flamboyant.

2 Add some more flamboyant (seven in all), spacing them to fill the main bulk of the spray. Try to use the largest and most attractive flower in the centre of the spray to form the focal point.

3 Add depth and interest to the spray by adding gold ivy berries and eucalyptus stems, slightly recessed in between the flamboyant flowers.

4 Wire up a similar spray with the remaining flowers to place on the other side of the arrangement.

ASSEMBLY

5 Group the candles together on a pewter plate and place a spray of flowers on either side, using florists' staysoft to hold them in place. Tie a bow of red ribbon and place it in front of the candles. (Before you light the candles, make sure the sugar flowers are not too close to the flames!)

Note

The easiest way to colour berries and buds gold is to spray them with gold spray paint.

Frog Down Under

This cake was inspired by a piece of work by the textile artist Annemieke Mein. I was so excited by her book, *The Art of Annemieke Mein* (Search Press/Schwartz), that I wrote to ask her permission to use the frog design on a cake. She agreed, and here it is. My version does little justice to the original, but this is still my favourite cake in this book.

Materials

25cm (10 in) long octagonal cake
Apricot glaze
1kg (2lb) almond paste (marzipan)
Clear alcohol (kirsch or vodka)
1.5kg (3lb), plus 125g (4oz), white sugarpaste
Fine willow green ribbon, to trim cake
Baby maize ribbon, to trim board
125g (4oz) flower paste
Lemon, moss, holly/ivy, aubergine, dark green, white, black, brown, nutkin, primrose and skintone petal dust (blossom tint)
Green, pearl and gold lustre colours
Black paste colouring

Equipment

Sugarpaste smoothers
36cm (14 in) long octagonal cake board
Posy pick

Flowers

Long stem of eucalyptus with flowers (see page 68)

PREPARATION

1 Brush the cake with apricot glaze and cover with almond paste. Leave to dry overnight. Moisten the almond paste with clear alcohol and cover with 1.5kg (3lb) white sugarpaste, using sugarpaste smoothers to achieve a good finish. Cover the board with sugarpaste and place the cake on top. Allow to dry thoroughly. Attach fine willow green ribbon around the base of the cake, and baby maize ribbon around the board edge.

BAS RELIEF FROG

2 Trace the frog design on page 142 on to tracing or greaseproof paper, then scribe the design on to the surface of the cake.

3 Mix together the remaining 125g (4oz) sugarpaste with the flower paste to form a modelling paste. Roll out the paste so that it is large enough to cut out the whole of the frog. Place the template on top of the paste, and scribe the design on to it. Using a scalpel, cut around the design.

4 Moisten the design on the cake surface with a little alcohol. Carefully lift the cut-out frog and place it on top of the cake so it fits into the scribed outline.

5 Certain areas of the design will need building up with more paste to give the frog a two-dimensional look. For example, the frog's stomach area, head, upper legs and calves will need to be built up. To do this, simply place extra

pieces of paste on to the surface and blend the edges into the piece beneath using your finger and a dresden tool.

6 To create the texture of the frog's body, roll tiny balls of paste and attach them all over the frog's torso up to its lips. Flatten and indent each ball to help give the appearance of scales.

7 Build up the branch so that it is slightly higher than most of the figure. Add an extension to the branch to hang over the edge of the cake. Again, simply blend the two pieces of paste together. Support the branch extension with a large piece of sponge until it is dry. Texture the whole branch with the fine end of the dresden tool, using long strokes.

8 Paint the branch with nutkin and brown petal dust mixed with a little alcohol. Shade in areas of the branch using a more concentrated mixture; add depth by mixing in a touch of black petal dust. Leave to dry.

9 Once the branch is dry you can start work on the frog's

hands and feet. Working with the modelling paste again, form each of the fingers and toes separately, joining them together when you put them in place. Indent the joint just above the rounded tip.

10 Build up the lips and indent down the centre using the fine end of the dresden tool. Roll a fine strip of paste to fit underneath each of the frog's eyes.

COLOURING

11 Paint the frog with a little holly/ivy, white and primrose mixed with alcohol, leaving the lips white. Shade in the edges of the frog heavier on one side than the other. At this stage you can also add finer detail. Paint over the base of the torso, inner parts of the legs and just underneath the lips with white.

12 Using lemon, white and a touch of skintone, paint in the eyes. Once they are dry, over-paint with some gold lustre colour. Paint in the pupils with a little black paste colouring.

13 Paint areas of the frog with some more of the gold lustre colour. The white areas are painted over with pearl lustre colour.

FLOWERS AND FOLIAGE

14 Using a very pale muted green, dust around the frog on the surface of the cake. Using a finer brush, paint in some fine movement lines with a mid-green mixture diluted with a touch of alcohol. Paint some leaves on the sides of the cake.

15 Position the eucalyptus stem on the cake's surface, inserting the end into a posy pick at the back of the cake. (You might find you have to stuff the pick with paste to help hold the stem in place.)

16 Finally, cut out some large leaves using a template made from the outline on page 141. I have made the base leaf much paler than the other two to help with the two-dimensional effect. Vein the leaves with the dresden tool, or use a tiny dressmakers' wheel to give the impression of stitch marks. Dust each leaf with various shades of dark green, holly/ivy and white. Catch the edge of each leaf with a touch of aubergine. Using a little clear alcohol and some dark green, paint over the stitch marks to emphasize the veins. Using fine scissors, cut some 'insect nibbles' out of some of the leaves.

17 Moisten the back of each leaf and position on the cake as shown in the main photograph (page 81).

Trumpet Vine Christening Cake

This delightful cake, with its bright colour and strong shape, makes a stunning alternative to a more traditional pastel-coloured cake. The trumpet vine flowers during the summer months, making it the perfect choice for a baby born at that time of year. The baby is represented by a blossom fairy, sleeping happily in a leaf hammock!

Materials

25cm (10 in) scalloped oval cake
Apricot glaze
1kg (2lb) almond paste (marzipan)
Clear alcohol (kirsch or vodka)
1.5kg (3lb) white sugarpaste
Fine bright orange ribbon to trim cake
Green velvet ribbon to trim board
18 and 33-gauge wires
White, green, peach and flesh-coloured flower paste
Tangerine, red, cream, nutkin, apricot, cornflower blue, lavender, dark green and white petal dust (blossom tint)
Blue and pearl lustre colours
½ glaze (see page 10)
Fine lace-making thread

Equipment

36cm (14 in) scalloped oval cake board
Pale green floristry tape
2 posy picks
Tiny baby mould
Tiny blossom cutter
Tropical and tiny butterfly cutters (HH)
Leaf template (see page 141)
Large hydrangea leaf veiner (GI)

Flowers

1 long and 1 short stem of trumpet vine (see page 70)

head using your chosen colour. (I have used a mixture of cream and nutkin brown.)

4 Colour the cheeks with a little apricot petal dust. Using a fine paintbrush, paint on the eyelashes (dark brown) and colour in the lips (apricot).

PREPARATION

1 Brush the cake with apricot glaze, cover with almond paste and allow to dry overnight. Moisten the almond paste with clear alcohol and cover with white sugarpaste. Cover the cake board with white sugarpaste and place the cake on top, making sure you have a neat join between the base of the cake and the board. Allow to dry overnight. Attach a fine band of orange ribbon around the base of the cake, and position a bow in each of the indents. Attach velvet ribbon around the board edge.

2 Strengthen the stems of the trumpet vine, if necessary, by taping an extra 18-gauge wire alongside each stem. Arrange the flowers on the cake, inserting the end of each stem into a posy pick. You might have to fill the picks with paste to help hold the stems in place. Arrange some of the foliage on the cake's surface.

TRUMPET VINE FAIRY

3 Make a tiny baby using a mould and some flesh-coloured flower paste. Dust some hair on the baby's

5 The hat is made from peach-coloured paste and cut out using a tiny blossom cutter. Attach the hat to the baby's head using a touch of egg white. Paint the rim with blue lustre colour.

6 Cut out a pair of wings using a tiny butterfly cutter and some white flower paste. Glue them on to the baby's back. Paint the surface with a design using a mixture of cornflower blue and lavender petal dusts mixed with alcohol.

LEAF HAMMOCK

7 Roll out some green flower paste and cut out a leaf using a scalpel and a template made from the outline on page 141. Vein using the hydrangea veiner, and soften the edges using a large celstick.

8 Using a scriber, make a hole at each end of the leaf. Rest the leaf on a pad of foam rubber to help keep the curved shape, and leave to dry. Dust the leaf with dark green and glaze using a ½ glaze. Leave to dry.

9 Model a tiny pillow using white flower paste and cut out a small rectangle of peach paste. Frill the edges of both. Place the pillow on the leaf, then the baby and then cover the baby's body with the peach flower paste blanket, making sure that the wings are in full view.

10 Tie some fine lace-making thread through the holes in the leaf and dust it with some green petal dust. Place a large piece of sponge on top of the cake just below the curving stem of the trumpet vine. Place the hammock on top, and then tie the thread on to the buds or leaves. Gently remove the sponge.

FANTASY BUTTERFLIES

11 Specimen butterflies could be made instead of fantasy ones, but I felt as the whole scene was one of fantasy they seemed more appropriate. Roll out some white flower paste on a grooved board, making sure the paste is very fine. Cut out the butterfly with your chosen cutter/veiner, and press the paste into the cutter to make sure that all the veins are marked on to the paste. Remove the paste, place it on a pad and gently soften the edges (do not frill them). Insert a 33-gauge wire into the underside of the body and dry the wings in a 'V' shape. (I find a piece of card bent into a 'V'shape holds the paste very well.) Repeat to make a second butterfly.

12 Paint and dust some markings on the butterfly wings and bodies using the lustre colours and a little alcohol.

13 Position the butterflies on the vine and cake, using the inserted 33-gauge wires to hold them in place.

Garden Flowers

THE GARDEN provides a constant source of inspiration and a never-ending supply of flowers to make; this section includes some of my favourites. I have a very small, untidy garden, but I still find that it gives me a huge amount of pleasure. Many garden flowers can be grouped together without much thought and still give a colourful, cheerful and at the same time informal arrangement.

Nasturtium

The nasturtium *(Tropaeolum majus)* is my favourite of all plants, and it is the first flower that I worked out how to make! The wild form, with orange flowers, is native to Peru where it is a strong-growing climbing plant. It has now been extensively cultivated, producing flowers in a wide range of colours.

Materials

Fine white stamens
18, 24, 26 and 28-gauge wires
Lemon, tangerine, red, aubergine, primrose, plum, dark green, holly/ivy, spring green and moss petal dust (blossom tint)
Nasturtium, pale melon and pale holly/ivy flower paste
Cyclamen or burgundy paste colouring
¼ and full glaze (see page 10)

Equipment

Pale green floristry tape
Nasturtium cutters (446–448)
Nasturtium petal and leaf veiners (GI)
Calyx cutter
Blossom cutter (F10)
Medium stephanotis cutter (566)
Fine pliers
Circle cutters (optional)

STAMENS AND PISTIL

1 Bend four fine stamens in half (to form eight) and add another stamen, which needs to be slightly longer than the others, to represent the pistil. Tape all of these together on to a 28-gauge wire using ¼-width floristry tape. Gently curl the stamens slightly, and then dust the tips with lemon petal dust.

PETALS

2 Roll out your chosen colour of paste (nasturtium has been used for the flowers illustrated) using a grooved rolling pin or board. Cut out three fringed (guitar-shaped) and two plain shapes using the nasturtium petal cutters.

3 Insert a moistened 28-gauge wire into the ridged area of each petal, making sure that the

wire is inserted to at least half the length of the petal. Cover the petals with a sheet of plastic while you are not working on them to stop them drying out. Vein all of the petals.

4 Working first on the three fringed petals, use a cocktail stick (toothpick) to frill only the upper curve of each petal. Nasturtiums don't have a very frilly edge, but I find that they can look a little stiff if left plain. Using a pair of fine scissors, cut the middle section horizontally

either side to represent fine hairs. (You will need to cut out small, deep 'V' shapes.) If these hairs are a little thick, place the paste back on the board and use the broad end of a dresden tool to flatten and thin the edges. Pinch the hairs from behind to display them on the upper surface. Allow the petals to firm up over a gentle curve.

5 Frill the edges of the remaining two petals, and then pinch them down the centre to reinforce the central vein. Allow these to firm up over a curve also.

COLOURING THE PETALS

6 Dust each petal from the edge towards the base using appropriate colours. (For the orange flowers, dust with tangerine and then a little red petal dust.) Colour the base of each petal with a touch of moss green.

7 The two plain petals have strong markings; paint these on using cyclamen or burgundy paste colour, a little water and a fine paintbrush. The lines radiate from the base, with the longest vein down the centre and those on either side getting shorter towards the edges.

8 Some varieties have burgundy shading; the petals illustrated here are dusted with a little aubergine petal dust on the centre.

ASSEMBLY

9 To assemble the flower, start by taping the two plain petals together with the stamens in front, curving towards them. Tape the three fringed petals in together, overlapping them as you feel necessary. As the flower is still slightly damp you can re-shape the edges if needed.

CALYX

10 Mix together a little pale melon and pale holly/ivy paste to create a creamy green, and roll a piece into a ball and then into a teardrop shape, trying to make this very fine as it represents the nectary which on the real flower is very slender. (The nectary, as the name implies, is where the nectar is stored.) Using your fingers and thumbs, pinch the larger end at the base to thin it out and turn it into the shape of a pointed hat. Place the 'hat' on the board and roll out the thinned area to make it a little finer.

11 Position the calyx cutter over the paste with one of the sepals closer to the nectary than the others, and then cut out the shape. Imagine the calyx as a person and broaden the 'arms' with a celstick. Place the calyx on a pad and soften the edges with a bone-end tool. Draw down a central vein on the inside of each sepal, and then,

using the pointed end of a cel-stick, open up the top of the nectary.

12 Moisten the inside of the calyx and then thread it on to the back of the flower so that the wire passes through the centre of the calyx and comes out just below the nectary, which should be positioned directly behind the join between the two plain petals. Stick down the sepals, making sure that each covers a join. Curl the nectary and then pinch the sides at the broad end with a pair of tweezers. Dust the tip of the nectary with a little moss and primrose petal dust.

BUDS

13 Roll out some paste the same colour as the flower, leaving the centre slightly thicker. (This can be done on a mexican hat board.) Cut out using the blossom cutter, and then gently frill the edges with a cocktail stick (toothpick).

14 Tape, hook and moisten a 24-gauge wire, and then thread on the blossom, pinching the thicker area of paste around the hook. Moisten the petals, and fold them together over the centre to form a neat bud. Make a calyx as for the flower, using the stephanotis cutter.

15 Tiny buds are made by forming a teardrop of pale melon paste, pinching the base to form a fine nectary, and marking the other end with a scalpel to form five sepals. Insert a hooked, moistened 28-gauge wire into the centre and pinch firmly to make sure it is secure. Curl the nectary and dust the bud with moss and primrose.

LEAVES

16 Tape over a 24-gauge or 26-gauge wire (depending on the size of the leaf), leaving a little at the end uncovered. Using pliers, hold the end of the wire and form an open round hook. Hold the hook halfway down and bend it so that it resembles a nail head.

17 Roll out some pale holly/ivy paste, leaving the centre slightly thicker. Cut out a leaf shape, either by using the veiner as a template and cutting with a scalpel, or using the circle cutters. Vein using the leaf veiners, and then soften the edges on a pad using a bone-end tool.

18 To fix the wire to the back of the leaf you can use egg white or edible glue (egg white mixed with flower paste to form a smooth consistency), but I find the most successful and quickest way is to heat up the end of the 'nail head' in a flame. As soon as the end turns red, place it on the centre of the leaf (in the thick area). The join will be instant as the heat caramelizes the sugar and cools very quickly to give a fairly firm join. Whichever method you choose, remember that each leaf is secured to its wire in a very small area only, and some might drop off! If this happens, don't panic as they can always be attached again. Allow the leaves to dry before you colour them with petal dust.

COLOURING THE LEAVES

19 Dust the edges with a mixture of plum and aubergine. Colour the whole surface of the leaf, working from the centre, with dark green, and then over-dust with holly/ivy. Glaze the leaves using a ¼ glaze. Allow to dry thoroughly, and then, using a scalpel, scratch away some of the colour to create the pale veins.

20 If you want to add some 'caterpillar bites' to the leaves (as in those illustrated), this is done by heating a metal cake tester until it turns red hot, and then piercing the leaf quickly in various places. Because the sugar caramelizes the hole has a brown edge which looks most effective.

SEED PODS

21 Roll a piece of pale green paste into a ball and insert a hooked 24-gauge wire. Pinch the base firmly to secure the paste.

22 Using a scalpel, divide the ball into three (they do not have to be equal parts). Pinch a series of ridges down each section using a pair of tweezers. Insert a fine stamen with the end cut off into the area where the three sections join at the top of the fruit. (This needs to be quite short to represent the pistil.)

23 Dust the ridges to various degrees with a little red and aubergine petal dust. Over-dust the whole thing with spring green. Dip into a full glaze and allow to dry, and then bend the stem into shape.

ASSEMBLY

24 The buds, flowers and leaves are all taped on to one 18-gauge wire to form the main stem. The flowers and

buds always come out from a leaf axil, and the leaves alternate down the stem. Tape the whole piece together with ½-width green floristry tape, adding extra wire to support longer stems.

25 Dust the upper surfaces of the main and smaller stems with a mixture of red and aubergine petal dust, and then over-dust the whole thing with dark green and holly/ivy.

Chinese Virginia Creeper

This creeper (*Parthenocissis hen-ryana*) has unusual silvery veins on dull green leaves that turn red during the autumn.

LEAVES

1 Roll out some pale green flower paste using a grooved board. Leave the paste in the groove and place a template on top. Cut around the template using a sharp scalpel.

2 Remove the paste and insert a 26-gauge or 28-gauge wire (depending on the size of the leaf). Place the leaf between the two sides of the appropriate size of veiner, and press firmly. Remove the leaf and place it on a pad. Soften the edge of the leaf using a large celstick. If any of the serrations around the edge are not clear enough, re-cut them using a pair of fine scissors. Allow to dry with a little movement in the edges. Work the base of each leaf between your finger and thumb to fine down and elongate it.

Equipment

Leaf templates (see page 143)
Large, medium and small hydrangea leaf veiners (GI)
Pale green floristry tape

3 Use the templates to make several different-sized leaves. You will need one large, two medium and two smaller leaves for each group. Make as many groups of leaves as you need, varying the size of group .

COLOURING AND ASSEMBLY

4 Tape the leaves together in groups of three and five. Dust the leaves that will be green first of all with dark green and then holly/ivy. Dust the edge, the base and a little of the central vein on each leaf with

Materials

Pale green flower paste
20, 26, 28 and 30-gauge wires
Holly/ivy, dark green, aubergine, red, tangerine, skin-tone and white petal dust (blossom tint)
Silver lustre colour (optional)
Clear alcohol (gin or vodka)
¼ or ½ glaze (see page 10)

aubergine petal dust. The autumnal shades are created using various combinations of tangerine, red, skintone and then aubergine.

5 Using a fine brush, paint in the silvery veins using white petal dust and a touch of green (and silver lustre, if you wish) mixed together with a little clear alcohol. Glaze the leaves using either a ¼ or ½ glaze (depending on your personal taste).

6 Make some tendrils by taping over a 30-gauge wire. Wrap the wire around a paintbrush handle to give it a twisted shape. Make several pieces and tape these together into groups.

7 Tape the various-sized groups of foliage together on to a 20-gauge wire using ½-width green tape. Start with the small groups, and then gradually increase them in size as you work down the stem. Add the tendrils at a leaf axil whenever needed. Bend the whole stem into the required shape, and then dust with the red, aubergine and green colours.

Montbretia

This popular garden hybrid *(Crocosmia)* originates from South Africa although it has also naturalized in Britain and France. It flowers during late summer and early autumn. There are many colour variations, from yellow to very strong reds. Its strong colours make it an ideal flower to use on a man's cake.

Materials

Freesia stamens
Tangerine, red, aubergine, lemon, moss and dark green petal dust (blossom tint)
Clear alcohol (gin or vodka)
24, 26 and 30-gauge wires
Melon and pale orange flower paste

Equipment

White and pale green floristry tape
Agapanthus cutter (516) or six-petalled freesia cutters (574, 575, 576)

STAMENS AND PISTIL

1 Paint the ends of three freesia stamens with tangerine and red petal dust mixed with a little clear alcohol or water.

2 To make the pistil, tape over the end of a 30-gauge wire with ¼-width white floristry tape, leaving a small flap of tape at the end. Using a pair of fine scissors, cut the flap into three. Twist each section between your finger and thumb to make quite fine strands.

3 Tape the pistil and stamens together, making the pistil slightly higher. Strengthen the

wire by adding a 26-gauge wire. Dust the length of the pistil and the stamens with lemon and tangerine petal dust.

FLOWER

4 Roll a ball of melon-coloured paste into a cone shape. Pinch the broad end of the cone between your fingers and thumbs to thin out the base and form a pedestal shape. Place the flat part of the paste down on the board and roll out using a small celstick. Try to form a tight, neat 'waistline' around the thick area of the pedestal.

5 Cut out the flower using the agapanthus cutter. Before you remove the paste from the cutter, rub your thumb over the paste against the cutter edge to make sure the petals have cleanly cut edges.

6 Place the flower on a board. Broaden each of the petals by rolling with the small celstick. If you want to make a larger flower, elongate the petals as well.

7 Open up the throat of the flower using the pointed end of the celstick. Press the base of each petal against the stick to help form a more graceful shape to the back of the flower.

8 Using the pointed end of a dresden tool, gently draw down a central vein on each petal. Pinch the tip of each petal between your finger and thumb to make a point.

9 Moisten the base of the stamens and pull them down into the centre of the flower. Neaten up the back of the flower and pinch off any excess paste.

COLOURING

10 Dust the flower with tangerine, working from the edges of the petals towards the centre. (Try to keep the centre pale.) Over-dust the edges with red. If you want a slightly darker flower, steam it and then dust it again (see page 10).

BUDS AND BRACTS

11 Attach a small cone of pale orange paste to a 30-gauge wire. Work the base of the cone between your finger and thumb to form a slender bud shape. You will need to make lots of buds in graduating sizes. If you wish you can mark some indents on each bud to represent petals.

12 There are two small bracts at the base of each bud and flower. Cut two small pointed pieces of green paste, vein down the centre, and then attach at the base of the flower or bud. (These can take a lifetime to complete; don't be afraid to leave them off if you haven't got time for them.)

ASSEMBLY

13 Start the stem by taping the smallest bud on to a 24-gauge wire. Continue to add buds down the stem, gradually increasing them in size and working from one side to the other.

14 Before you add the flowers, dust the buds with tangerine and red, leaving the base of each bud much paler. The spray illustrated on page 94 has quite dark buds; to achieve this, mix some red, tangerine and a touch of aubergine with a little clear alcohol, and then paint the colour quite heavily on to the buds.

15 Tape in the flowers, and then dust the base of each and the buds with moss and dark green. Strengthen the stem if needed with more lengths of 24-gauge wire.

Rambling Rose

This rose is based on several different varieties. It has the appearance of an old cottage-garden rose, with its almost untidy flower shape and dusky colour. All the petals are wired individually, which helps to give the finished flower a more irregular look.

Materials

Pale ruby, mid-green and pale green flower paste
18, 24, 26, 28 and 30-gauge wires
Plum, fuchsia, pink, white, lemon, primrose, red, dark green, moss, aubergine and skintone petal dust (blossom tint)
½ glaze (see page 10)

Equipment

Rose petal cutters (278, 277, 276, 551)
Ceramic silk veining tool (HP) or large rose petal veiner (GI)
Pale green floristry tape
Piece of bubble foam
Rose leaf cutters (B6)
Large rose leaf veiner (GI)
Rose calyx cutter (R11b)

FIRST PETAL LAYER

1 Roll out some pale ruby flower paste thinly on a grooved board. Remove the paste from the board and turn it over so that the ridge is on top. Cut out six to ten petals using the smallest cutter (278). Trim some of the petals to make them slimmer. Insert a moistened 30-gauge wire into the central ridge of each petal.

2 Vein each of the petals using either the rose petal veiner or by rolling over the whole surface of each petal with the ceramic silk veining tool. Place the petals on a pad and soften the edges gently using the rounded end of a medium cel-stick. Cup the centre of each petal and then curl back some of the edges using a cocktail stick (toothpick) and your finger and thumb. It is easier to assemble and tape together these petals before you colour them. Inter-link the petals as you feel they need to be; there is no particular order, except that I tend to use the slimmer petals at the heart of the flower.

REMAINING LAYERS

3 Roll out some more pale ruby paste on a grooved board and cut out approximately five petals using the next size of cutter (277). Insert a 28-gauge wire and vein, soften, cup and curl the edges of each petal as before. Allow to dry over some bubble foam to keep the cupped shape to the petals.

4 For the third layer, repeat step 3 using the next large cutter (276), again cutting out approximately five petals. Allow to dry over the bubble foam until firm enough to handle.

5 The last layer is the same as layers two and three, cutting out the petals using the largest of the cutters (551). Allow to dry as before.

COLOURING

6 Start by dusting the group of petals that are taped together. Colour all over with pink and white petal dust mixed together, then over-dust with plum and fuchsia to make the petals quite dark. The back of each petal should be a little paler.

7 Dust the other petals in paler shades, starting with the pale pink mixture and then over-dusting the centre of each petal on the back and front with the darker pink. Try to keep the edges of the petals much paler. If you are working on a pale-coloured or cream rose, dust a patch of lemon and primrose mixed together at the base of each petal on the back and front.

ASSEMBLY

8 Tape the larger petals around the smaller group that you have already taped, trying to position each petal to hide a join in the previous layer. Gradually tape in the other sizes until you have the size of rose you require. Remember this is a very informal rose with no definite shape. Once the flower has been taped together you can add extra colour if needed to the centre of the flower (the rose can look very flat if there is no depth created by the colouring).

LEAVES

9 I have made the leaves in various sizes and have coloured the smallest to resemble the new growth on each stem. Roll out some pale green paste using a grooved rolling pin or board. Cut out leaves in various sizes using the rose leaf cutters. Remember that the leaves can grow in groups of three or five and that the first leaf is usually larger than the others. For the new-growth foliage I have used the small cutter for all five leaves.

10 Insert a moistened 26-gauge or 28-gauge wire, depending on the size of the leaf. Place each leaf in turn into the double-sided rose leaf veiner and press firmly. Remove the leaf, place on a pad and soften the edges a little with a celstick. Pinch down the central vein, shape the edges and then allow to firm up for approximately 30 minutes before colouring.

11 Dust the smaller leaves to various depths using plum, skintone, red and aubergine petal dust. Dip into a ½ glaze, shake off the excess, and allow to dry.

12 The larger leaves are dusted with dark green and moss and a little aubergine or plum on the edges. Dust the back of each leaf with white and green petal dust mixed together, and then over-dust areas with aubergine and plum. Dip into a ½ glaze, shake off the excess, and allow to dry.

13 Tape the leaves together into groups of three or five. Start with the largest leaf and then tape two medium leaves below with their stems coming out at the same point. Finish the stem with two of the smaller leaves.

BUDS AND CALYX

14 The buds are made following the instructions on pages 14–15, except this time you will need to make a slightly untidy look when you spiral the petals. Dust them much darker than the flower, and then add a calyx.

15 Roll a ball of mid-green paste into a cone shape and then pinch out the base to form a hat shape. Roll out the paste to make it finer, though the paste should still be quite 'fleshy' when you finish. Cut out the calyx using the rose calyx cutter and then elongate and thin out each sepal using the celstick.

16 Place the calyx on a pad and cup each sepal. Dust the inside of the calyx with a mixture of white and green petal dust to make it paler. If you wish you can make some fine cuts in the edges of each sepal to give them their characteristic 'hairy' appearance. Moisten the centre and attach to the back of the rose or bud, trying to position each sepal so that it covers a join between the outer petals. The calyx would curl right back on a fully open rose, but on the buds it should fit tightly around the petals. Dust with dark green and moss petal dust.

Rue

This wonderful herb *(Ruta graveolens)*, with its beautiful soft blue-green foliage, is a favourite with flower arrangers. It was used during the Middle Ages, together with other herbs and flowers, in a 'tussie-mussie' (posy) to protect against contagious disease. By the sixteenth century, a tussie-mussie was an ornamental gift rather than a medicinal aid.

Materials

Very pale green flower paste
24 and 30-gauge wires
White, dark green, holly/ivy and pearl petal dust (blossom tint)
¼ glaze (see page 10)

Equipment

Triple-spreading E cutters (Zimbabwean cutters)
Pale green floristry tape

1 Roll out some flower paste using a grooved board or rolling pin. Remove the paste from the board, if necessary, and turn it over so that the ridge is on top.

2 Cut out lots of leaves of various sizes using the rue leaf cutters. Before removing the paste from the cutter, rub your thumb over the paste against the cutter edge to make sure the leaf has cleanly cut edges.

3 Insert a moistened 30-gauge wire into almost the full length of the central ridge of each leaf, work the edges with the broad end of a dresden tool, then place the leaf on a pad and soften the edges a little with a small celstick. Cup the back of each leaf with the rounded end of the celstick. Pinch a central vein down each one.

COLOURING AND ASSEMBLY

4 Dust each leaf with a little dark green petal dust. Over-dust with a mixture of holly/ivy and white. If you want to give a very soft effect, add a little pearl dust to the mixture. Dip into a ¼ glaze or steam (see page 10).

5 Tape over each of the stems, and then tape them together in groups of two and three. Tape these smaller stems together on to a 24-gauge wire to form a larger stem. Dust the stems with the soft green mixture and arrange the leaves attractively.

Chinese Witch Hazel

This is the most popular of the witch hazels, originating from western China. This plant (*Hamamelis mollis*) has one of the most exquisite perfumes and is one of my all-time favourites.

Materials

20 and 33-gauge wires
Red/brown flower paste
Aubergine, nutkin and black
petal dust (blossom tint)

Equipment

Yellow, green and beige
floristry tape
Tiny daphne cutter (466)

PETALS

1 Cut some ¼-width strips of yellow floristry tape, and cut several short lengths of 33-gauge wire. Tape over each wire and when you get to the end leave approximately 1.5cm (¾ in) of the tape untwisted. Trim the end, and then vein down the centre using the fine end of a dresden tool. You will need four petals for each flower. Tape the four petals together at the base using ¼-width green floristry tape. (There are some tiny stamens at the centre of the real flower, but it is not essential to include these as they do not affect the overall appearance.)

CALYX

2 Roll a small ball of red/brown paste into a cone, and then pinch the base out to form a hat shape. Place the flat base on a board and thin out using a tiny celstick. Cut out a calyx using the daphne cutter.

3 Open up the centre and mark a vein down the centre of each sepal. Moisten the centre and pull the wired stamens through. Curl the sepals back a little.

4 Dust the calyx and the base of the petals with a little aubergine and nutkin. You will need to make quite a lot of separate flowers to tape together into groups of three or four.

TWIG

5 Start by taping over a 20-gauge wire with beige tape, tapering the end to a slight point. Gradually build up the thickness, adding strips of absorbent kitchen paper where needed to help add bulk. As you work down the twig, tape in the groups of flowers. Join two or three stems together to make a larger piece. Dust with nutkin and a little black dust.

Smoke Tree

There are many cultivated varieties of this wonderful plant *(Cotinus)*. It takes its common name from the tiny flowers, which, from a distance, look like clouds of smoke. The leaves are an excellent choice to add depth to a spray or arrangement, especially during the autumn.

Materials

Pale holly/ivy flower paste
20, 28 and 30-gauge wires
Nutkin, aubergine, deep purple and black petal dust
(blossom tint)

Equipment

Rose petal cutters (276–280)
Poinsettia veiners (GI)
Pale green floristry tape

COLOURING

4 Dust the leaves while they are still damp. Dust in layers with nutkin, deep purple, aubergine and black. Steam the leaves when they are a little firmer (see page 10), and then re-dust to achieve a very dark colouring.

5 Tape each stem over with green tape and then group the leaves loosely into clumps, taping them together with ½-width tape. Tape the clumps together on to a stronger stem made from 20-gauge wire.

6 Dust the stems with the same dark mixture used for the leaves.

LEAVES

1 Although the tops of the leaves are very dark purple/brown in colour, their backs are green, which is why green paste should be used. Roll out some paste fairly thinly using a grooved rolling pin or board.

2 Cut out leaves of various sizes using the rose petal cutters. Cut either 30-gauge or 28-gauge wires (depending on the leaf sizes) into five short pieces each. Moisten the end of a piece of wire and insert it into the ridge down the centre of a leaf, inserting the wire to at least half the length of the leaf.

3 Place each leaf between a double-sided poinsettia veiner and press firmly. Remove the leaf and place on a pad. Soften the edges using the rounded end of a celstick or a bone-end tool.

Snapdragon

This cheerful summer flower (*Antirrhinum majus*) always brings back childhood memories, when I used to squeeze the flowers on both sides to make them 'snap'. There are many colours in the species, but there are also many hybrid forms. They grow mainly with pink, burgundy, white, yellow and orange flowers, although some are bicoloured.

Materials

Pale melon and mid-green flower paste
20, 22, 24, 28 and 30-gauge wires
Dark green, lemon and moss petal dust (blossom tint), plus chosen colours
¼ glaze (see page 10)

Equipment

Snapdragon plastic cutting sheet no. 7 (Asi-es)
Ceramic silk veining tool (HP) or metal frilling tool (Asi-es)
Pale green floristry tape
Medium and large stephanotis cutters (567, 566)

BOTTOM PETALS

1 Roll out some pale melon paste and place it over the top of the petal shape on the plastic sheet. Roll your rolling pin on top of the paste against the cutting sheet to cut out a petal. Remove the shape and place it flat on a board. Using a metal frilling tool or the ceramic silk veining tool, frill and at the same time vein each of the three petals at the top of the piece.

2 Moisten the edges of the cut-out 'V' shape on either side. Using your fingers, pinch the edges of each 'V' together (this will start to form the characteristic shape). Hollow out the area between the two joined edges using a bone-end tool or medium celstick. Draw down a central vein on this raised area and then pinch a ridge down each side of the vein using a pair of tweezers.

3 Tape over a piece of 22-gauge wire and bend a hook in one end. Moisten the hook and attach a sausage of pale melon paste over it. Moisten the underside and attach to the base petal. Pinch the two pieces together firmly to make sure they are secure. Pinch a ridge on the underside of the petal.

TOP PETALS

4 Roll out some more pale melon paste and cut out as before using the other shaped cutter on the cutting sheet. (I find that this petal is a little large so I usually trim it a little with a pair of fine scissors.)

5 Frill the edges of the two petals, again using either the ceramic silk veining tool or the metal frilling tool. Turn the petal over and mark a 'V' shape on the back using the fine end of a dresden tool. Turn the petal back over and pinch the ridge to

emphasize it a little more. Place the shape on a pad, again with the back of the petal facing up, and cup both of the frilled petals back.

6 Moisten the inside edges of this petal and place on top of the bottom petal. Pinch the two sides together as much as possible, creating quite flat sides to the flower. This is where speed is needed to join the paste as well as possible. Curl back the two petals on the top piece and allow to dry for approximately 30 minutes before colouring with petal dust.

BUDS AND CALYX

7 The small buds are cones of mid-green paste attached to the end of a hooked 28-gauge wire. Mark five indents on the surface to represent unopened petals.

8 The larger buds are made using pale melon paste. Attach a cone of paste to the end of a hooked 24-gauge wire. Pinch two pieces of paste at the top of the cone to represent the two upper petals. Moisten the underside and stick them down. Hollow out the small area between these two petals using the rounded end of the small celstick. Bend the bud so that it is slightly curved.

9 Roll out some mid-green paste thinly and cut out a collection of calyx shapes using either the medium or large stephanotis cutter. Place them on a pad and soften the edges of each of the sepals using the rounded end of a small celstick. Using the fine end of the dresden tool, vein the centre of each sepal. Moisten the calyx and attach to the back of the flower or bud.

COLOURING

10 Dust the raised area on the bottom piece of the flower with lemon petal dust. (Some hybrids have other colours on this part, for example there is a cream form with pink lips!) Dust the rest of the flower with your chosen colour of petal dust, making the back of each flower a little paler. If the colour is not dark enough, steam the flower (see page 10) and re-dust. Dust the calyx with moss and dark green. Allow the flower to dry and then steam to remove the dusty appearance. Leave to dry.

11 Dust the buds using the same colours as the flower, leaving the undersides very pale. (Sometimes the base of the flower has more of the pale melon colour showing.) The tiny green buds are dusted with the same colours as the calyces on the flowers and larger buds.

Bracts

12 Behind each of the buds and flowers there is a single bract, that comes out of the base of each short stem. These leaves can be cut out using a small leaf cutter or using a pulled method. I find it easier to attach a tiny cone of paste to the end of a moistened 30-gauge wire. Flatten the paste to make it finer and form the bract shape. Soften the edges if needed and draw down a central vein on each. You will need to make these in graduated sizes to use down the stem. Dust with moss and dark green petal dust. Glaze using a ¼ glaze.

Leaves

13 The leaves are made in the same way as the bracts using a longer piece of paste on a 30-gauge or 28-gauge wire, depending on the size of the finished leaf. Dust with moss and dark green, making the leaves darker than the bracts. Tape the leaves together to form a small stem using ½-width green floristry tape. You will need a few of these leaf groups to tape on to each stem.

14 Once the flower dies and falls off, it leaves behind the pistil and ovary. To make the pistil, tape over the end of a 30-gauge wire using ¼-width white tape. Leave a flap of tape at the end and cut it in half. Twist each piece between your finger and thumb to make it finer. Dust with the flower colour. For the ovary, attach a ball of green paste at the base of the pistil. Flatten the sides, so that it has three flat, almost triangular-shaped, sides. Add a calyx as for the flower.

Assembly

15 Start by taping a few of the small green buds on to the end of a 20-gauge wire using ½-width green tape. Attach a couple of the bracts underneath these. Gradually work down the stem, increasing the size of the buds and adding a single bract to each one. When you have achieved enough length with the buds start to introduce the flowers, again taping in a bract at the base of each of the stems. Once you have added your flowers you can start to tape in a pistil and ovary or two, again along with a bract. The last things to tape on to the stem are the groups of leaves. Although a lot of these grow on a stem I usually only give a suggestion of them. Bend the whole of the stem into shape and then dust over the main stem and the smaller stems with the green petal dusts.

Green Hellebore

Hellebores flower during the winter months and included in the family (*Helleborus*) is the ever-popular white Christmas rose. Hellebores have been used in the past to ward off evil spirits and although the plant is highly poisonous it has also been used for various medicinal purposes. If you are planning to work from the real flower, handle with extreme care!

Materials

20, 24, 26 and 28-gauge wires
Tiny white seed-head stamens
Moss, primrose, dark green,
holly/ivy, aubergine, plum,
white and lemon petal dust
(blossom tint)
Pale melon, pale green and
dark green flower paste
Clear alcohol (gin or vodka)
½ glaze (see page 10)

Equipment

Pale green floristry tape
Large stephanotis cutter (566)
Large Christmas rose
cutter (282)
Christmas rose round
veiner (GI)
Horse chestnut leaf
cutters (SC)
Large briar rose leaf
veiner (GI)

PISTIL AND STAMENS

1 To form the pistil, use ¼-width pale green tape. Twist five pieces of tape to make fine strands. Tape these together on to a 28-gauge wire. Curl the tips back a little.

2 Take a good bunch of tiny white seed-head stamens, bend them in half and position them around the pistil so that they are a little shorter. Tape

around the base of the stamens down on to the wire to hold them in place. Colour the tips of the stamens with primrose and lemon petal dust. Dust a little mixed moss and primrose down into the centre to add depth. Dust the tip of the pistil with a touch of aubergine. Curl some of the stamens using a pair of tweezers.

NECTARY (PETALS)

3 These small pieces are actually the flower of this plant; each petal is a nectary. The large 'petals' are actually tepals. Roll out some pale green paste and cut out two shapes using the stephanotis cutter. Place them both on a pad, soften the edges with a celstick, and then draw down a central vein on each using the broad end of a dresden tool. Moisten the base of each petal and then pinch each one together at the base using the tweezers.

4 Moisten the centre of one of the shapes and place the other one on top so that the top petals are in between each of the petals below. Moisten the centre and carefully thread the stamens through the centre. Pinch the paste to secure the flower behind the stamens. Dust with a mixture of moss and primrose petal dust.

TEPALS

5 What appear to be the 'petals' of this flower are actually tepals. Roll out some pale melon paste using a grooved board or rolling pin. Turn the paste over so that the thick ridge is on top, if necessary, and cut out five tepals using the Christmas rose cutter.

6 Insert a moistened 28-gauge wire into each tepal, holding the thick ridge firmly between your finger and thumb. Place each tepal in the double-sided

Christmas rose veiner and press firmly. Remove and place on a pad.

7 Soften the edges using the rounded end of a celstick, and cup the centre slightly. Shape each tepal between your finger and thumb to create a pleasing effect. Allow to dry for approximately 30 minutes.

COLOURING AND ASSEMBLY

8 Mix together moss and primrose petal dust to form a lime green. Dust each tepal from the base on the back and front, leaving the edges much paler. Over-dust the base on the front with a little more moss green. Dust a little aubergine and plum on the edges and at the base on the back of each tepal.

9 Tape the tepals tightly around the stamens and the

flower. Overlap the tepals, if needed, but do not spiral them. Add two 24-gauge wires to the main stem and tape over with ½-width green tape. Holding the stem just behind the flower, bend the wire to form a curve in the stem. Tape two or three small leaves (see below) at the bend in the stem. Dust the stem with aubergine and plum petal dust.

BUDS

10 Attach a cone of pale melon paste on to a taped, hooked 20-gauge wire. Make a 'cage' with five 24-gauge wires (see page 10). Insert the bud, point first, into the 'cage' and close the wires firmly into the paste, keeping them as evenly spaced as possible. While the wires are still in place, pinch the paste out from in between them to form the tepals. Remove the 'cage', and then twist the sections of the bud together to form a neat shape.

11 Dust with the lime green mixture and a little aubergine and plum.

12 Hold the wire behind the bud and bend it to form a curve in the stem. Add a couple of small leaves (see below) at the bend, as for the flower.

LEAVES

13 Roll out some dark green paste using a grooved rolling pin or board. Cut out the leaves either freehand or using the horse chestnut cutters. Insert a 24-gauge or 26-gauge wire (depending on the size of the leaf) into each leaf, inserting the wire to at least half the length of the leaf.

14 Place each leaf in the rose leaf veiner and press firmly. Remove the leaf and place it back on the board. Create a serrated edge using the fine end of the dresden tool, cutting into the edge of the leaf at an angle. Place on a pad and soften the edges a little with a celstick.

15 Pinch the leaf down the centre to reinforce the

vein. Allow to dry over a slight curve. You will need to make one large, two medium and two small leaves for each leaf group required.

16 Dust heavily with dark green, and then over-dust with holly/ivy. Paint a central vein on the leaf using white and a touch of green mixed with a little clear alcohol. Allow to dry and then dip into a ½ glaze, shake off excess, and leave to dry again.

17 Tape the leaves together with ½-width green floristry tape, starting with a large leaf, then adding a medium leaf on either side, and lastly adding two small leaves. Dust the stem with aubergine and plum.

18 Make some smaller leaves in the same way to use behind the flowers and buds. The larger leaves grow at the base of the plant.

Trailing Tropaeolum Cake

The bold colours of nasturtium make it a wonderful subject for a man's birthday cake. I have used it to decorate this very simple cake, allowing the flowers to be the main focus of the design. As this plant attracts a lot of insects it seemed a good idea to include a caterpillar!

Materials

30cm (12 in) long octagonal cake
Apricot glaze
1.5kg (3lb) almond paste (marzipan)
Clear alcohol (kirsch or vodka)
2kg (4lb) sugarpaste, coloured with a little melon and egg yellow paste colouring
Fine willow green ribbon to trim cake
Green satin ribbon to trim board
Nasturtium paste colouring
Dark green, holly/ivy, white, moss, primrose and lemon petal dust (blossom tint)
Pale green flower paste

Equipment

Sugarpaste smoothers
40cm (16 in) long octagonal cake board
Pale green floristry tape
2 posy picks

Flowers

13 nasturtium flowers (see page 88)
11 large and 7 small nasturtium buds (see page 89)
3 nasturtium seed pods (see page 91)
80–90 nasturtium leaves, assorted sizes (see page 90)

PREPARATION

1 Brush the cake with apricot glaze and cover with almond paste. Allow to dry overnight. Moisten the cake with clear alcohol and cover with yellow sugarpaste, using sugarpaste smoothers to achieve a good finish. Cover the cake board with sugarpaste and place the cake on top, making sure there is a neat join between the base of the cake and the board. Allow to dry.

2 Attach a length of willow green ribbon around the base of the cake, and a length of green satin ribbon around the board edge.

PAINTED DESIGN

3 Make a paper pattern from the design on page 141, and scribe it on to the top and sides of the cake. Mix a little clear alcohol with some nasturtium paste colouring and add a touch of white petal dust. Paint in the flower petals using long brush strokes.

4 Dilute some dark green petal dust (again adding a little white), and paint in the leaves and small buds. Paint in the calyces using a mixture of the green dusts and a touch of lemon. Outline any areas of the design if needed using a darker shade of the appropriate colour.

FLOWERS

5 Tape the nasturtiums into loose stems, and then combine together in two groups, one large and one small. Bend the wires of the flowers in the larger spray at an angle of 90° and tape together to form a handle. Insert two posy picks into the cake (one on the top left-hand edge and the other on the right-hand side at the base of the cake). Position the flower sprays into the picks, and then curl and move the stems around to form a pleasing display.

CATERPILLAR

6 To add a bit of fun to the design I have made a tiny green caterpillar using pale green flower paste. Mark the surface of the paste with a scalpel to form the divisions. Dust the caterpillar with moss green and primrose and, before the paste dries, bend it into shape. Attach to the base board using a little egg white.

Cottage Garden Wedding Cake

'Old-fashioned' flowers, like full-blown roses, are currently very popular in bridal bouquets, and here I have combined them with snapdragon in fairly informal sprays. This cake would be particularly suitable for a couple whose wedding reception was to be held in a cottage-style garden.

Materials

20cm (8 in) and 30cm (12 in) oval cakes
Apricot glaze
2kg (4lb) almond paste (marzipan)
Clear alcohol (kirsch or vodka)
3kg (6lb) sugarpaste, coloured with a touch of mint green paste colouring
Fine magenta ('beauty') ribbon to trim cake
Green velvet ribbon to trim board

Equipment

Sugarpaste smoothers
25cm (10 in) and 38cm (15 in) oval cake boards
Celcakes split ring separator
Posy pick

Flowers

TOP
1 large rambling rose and 2 buds (see page 96)
3 pieces of rue (see page 99)
2 large stems of snapdragon (see page 102)
3 stems of large ivy (see page 22)
1 long stem of small rambling rose leaves, plus several shorter stems with larger leaves (see page 97)

MIDDLE
1 large rambling rose,
1 rose bud and 1 half rose (see page 96)
1 main stem of small rose leaves, plus several larger stems (see page 97)

BOTTOM
2 large rambling roses (see page 96)
1 small and 2 large stems of snapdragon (see page 102)
2 large pieces of rue (see page 99)
5 stems of large ivy (see page 22)
Several stems of rambling rose leaves (see page 97)

PREPARATION

1 Brush the cakes with apricot glaze and cover with almond paste. Allow to dry overnight. Moisten the cakes with clear alcohol and cover with pale green sugarpaste, using sugarpaste smoothers to achieve a good finish. Cover the two cake boards with sugarpaste and place the cakes on top, making sure there is a neat join between the base of each cake and its board. Allow to dry overnight.

2 Attach a length of fine ribbon around the base of each cake, and a length of green velvet ribbon around each board edge.

FLOWERS

3 Wire up a small bouquet for the top tier of the cake, following the suggested arrangement on page 112. Make a second, larger, bouquet for the base board, then make a small spray of rambling rose to use on top of the bottom tier to help disguise the cake separator.

4 Place the split ring separator on the centre of the base tier and arrange the small spray of rambling rose inside, positioning part of the rose flower on the outside and part inside. (Some of the leaves and the bud should also be placed on the outside.) Insert a posy pick into the top tier and place the spray in position. (You might find it easier to set the cake up before doing this to get a better idea of where to position the spray.) The larger spray is simply placed next to the base tier with its handle bent to balance the whole piece.

Cottage Garden Spray

This spray has been wired up into an informal version of a reversed 'S' shape. Using a limited number of flowers and plenty of foliage, a spectacular arrangement can still be made. Here the spray is displayed in a coffee pot, perhaps for a wedding table.

Flowers

1 small and 2 large stems of snapdragon (see page 102)
1 large rambling rose and 2 rose buds (see page 96)
1 long stem of small rose leaves, plus several short stems with larger leaves (see page 97)
3 stems of rue (see page 99)
3 stems of large ivy (see page 22)

Equipment

Fine pliers
Pale green floristry tape
Wire cutters
Florists' staysoft

SPRAY

1 To form the basic outline of the spray, bend the ends of the three stems of snapdragon at an angle of 90°, making the smaller stem shorter in length. Tape the three pieces together using ½-width floristry tape. Trim away excess wires.

2 Tape the large rose into the centre to form the focal point, which should be slightly higher than any of the other flowers. Tape in the long stem of small rose leaves, plus a few shorter stems of larger leaves to fill in around the main flower. Add the two rose buds to the left-hand side of the spray.

3 Fill in the large gaps with rue, which will also help to outline the shape of the spray.

4 Tape in the stems of large ivy to complete the spray. Neaten the handle by taping over with floristry tape.

Large Summer Arrangement

This is an extension of the Cottage Garden Spray (page 112), with the addition of several daisies; it could be used to carry the floral theme on to the wedding couple's table. Being large, it is, however, very time-consuming to make.

Flowers

4–5 stems of large ivy (see page 22)
6 stems of rue, various lengths (see page 99)
5 stems of snapdragon, various lengths (see page 102)
3 large rambling roses (see page 96)
3 half rambling roses and 3 rose buds (see page 96)
3 long stems of small rambling rose leaves, plus several stems with large leaves (see page 97)
5 large daisies and 5 daisy buds (see page 120)

Equipment

18-gauge wires
Pale green floristry tape
Florists' staysoft
Painted clay pot (see Note)
Fine pliers
Wire cutters

PREPARATION

1 First of all, strengthen any of the long stems by taping an 18-gauge wire alongside the flower stem. (To support some of the heavier flowers and foliage, you might need a few 18-gauge wires.)

THE ARRANGEMENT

2 Place a clump of staysoft in the pot, making sure it is firmly pressed in.

3 Start by arranging the ivy and rue in the staysoft to form the height and width of the spray. (The height should be at least one and a half times the height of the pot.)

4 Add the snapdragons, using most of them to fill in the gaps in the outline.

5 Use the large roses to fill in the focal area, and add the half roses and buds along with the foliage towards the edges of the arrangement.

6 Finally, add the daisy flowers and buds, spaced around the arrangement, trying to keep it as informal as possible. Add any extra foliage at this stage, if needed, to complete the piece.

Note

The pot used for the arrangement illustrated was one of a pair tied vertically together with rope and string (available from most good florists' shops). I separated the two and, in so doing, was left with a pot with small holes in its sides. I have made good use of one of the holes by inserting a large piece of ivy and a daisy in it at the base of the arrangement.

Scented Winter Arrangement

The hellebores and witch hazel in this arrangement are usually in flower during late winter and I often pick them and bring them indoors, where the scent from the witch hazel soon fills the room.

PREPARATION

1 Place a clump of staysoft in the jug. (If you are worried about damaging the inside of the jug, place the staysoft in a plastic bag before you put it in the jug.) If any of the stems need extra support, tape an 18-gauge wire alongside the main stem.

THE ARRANGEMENT

2 First of all, form the curves of the arrangement by placing the two twigs of witch hazel into the staysoft. Add the two hellebore buds next to the witch hazel. To add depth, add the hellebore foliage next.

3 Add the hellebore flowers, using one of them as the focal point. Try to position the flower heads so they each face in a slightly different direction. Start to add some of the trailing ivy to form the outline of the piece.

4 Fill in any gaps by threading in the ivy berries and extra foliage. Once everything is in position, stand back and take a look at the arrangement and, if needed, move or 'relax' the flowers a little.

5 To display the arrangement, place it on a pewter plate, which adds balance to the whole piece.

Wild Flowers

WILD FLOWERS have an instant appeal as
they often bring back memories of childhood
summers and Sunday-afternoon walks.
British wild flowers are very understated yet
have a simple beauty that is hard to match.
If this section of the book is slightly shorter
than the first three, it is certainly not for want
of subject matter, but rather because I
covered wild flowers in detail in an earlier
book, and I wanted to devote more of this
book to other types of flowers.

Daisy

The daisy *(Leucanthemum)* has always been a popular subject with flower makers. The only problem with it is that the petals often break when the flowers are being wired into a spray. In this version the petals are all wired individually, making them easier to use.

Materials

20, 22, 28 and 33-gauge wires
White, lemon and pale green flower paste
Lemon, primrose, moss, spring green, dark green and skin-tone petal dust (blossom tint)
¼ glaze (see page 10)

Equipment

Fine pliers
Large-mesh sieve
Narrow daisy petal cutter (613)
Pale green floristry tape
Rose leaf veiner (GI)

CENTRE

1 Bend an 'L'-shaped hook in the end of a 22-gauge wire. Hold the hook halfway down with pliers and curl it back inside itself to form a coil. Bend the whole coil over so that it is at right-angles to the wire and forms a ski-stick shape. Attach a ball of lemon paste to the end and flatten, then allow to dry.

2 Cover the dry paste with another layer of lemon paste. Push the paste against a large-mesh sieve to texture the surface, then indent the centre slightly using the small end of a bone-end tool.

3 Dust the paste with primrose and lemon petal dust. Add a little moss green to the indent in the centre and around the base and edges.

PETALS

4 Roll out some pure white paste on a finely grooved board and cut out lots of petals (you will need approximately 20–30 for each flower).

5 Insert a moistened 33-gauge wire into the very base of the thick ridge down the centre of each petal. Pinch the base firmly to make sure that it is secure.

6 Broaden each petal by rolling with a celstick. Mark several veins on each petal using a dresden tool, and curl the petals a little. Allow to dry for approximately 30 minutes.

7 Tape the petals around the daisy centre using ½-width green tape, leaving a little of the wire showing underneath the centre.

Calyx

8 Roll a ball of pale green paste into a cone shape, and then hollow out the broad end using the rounded end of a small celstick. Moisten the centre, and thread on to the back of the flower. Thin down the back, if needed, and remove any excess paste. To form the scaled effect that the daisy calyx has, press the pointed end of the daisy cutter into the paste many times until the whole calyx is covered.

9 Dust with dark green and a little spring green. Dust the top edge of the calyx at the base of the petals with a little skin-tone petal dust.

Bud

10 Attach a cone of white paste on to a 20-gauge wire, inserting the wire into the pointed end. Indent and slightly cut into the surface using a sharp scalpel to give the impression of unopened petals. Allow to dry, and then add a calyx as for the flower.

Leaves

11 Roll out a small amount of green flower paste using a grooved rolling pin or board. Cut out basic leaf shapes using a scalpel. Insert a 28-gauge wire into at least half the length of each leaf.

12 Cut a serrated edge on each leaf with the scalpel, cutting into the edge and flicking each piece away.

13 Vein the leaves using a rose leaf veiner. Soften the edges with a celstick and shape the whole leaf using your fingers. Pinch down the back of the leaf to reinforce the central vein. Allow to dry for approximately 30 minutes.

14 Dust with spring green and add depth with dark green. Dip into a ¼ glaze, shake off excess, and leave to dry.

15 Tape the leaves alternately down the stem of each bud and flower. Dust the stem with spring green and dark green.

Common Ivy

This form of ivy (Hedera helix) has flowering and non-flowering stems.

Materials

Pale holly/ivy flower paste
20, 26, 28, 30 and 33-gauge
wires
Dark green, moss, aubergine,
primrose, black and holly/ivy
petal dust (blossom tint)
½ glaze (see page 10)
Fine white stamens

Equipment

Ivy cutter/veiners (HH)
Pale green and beige floristry
tape
Common ivy templates (see
page 00)
Large ivy veiners (GI)
Tiny calyx cutter

NON-FLOWERING STEMS

1 The leaves on the non-flowering stems are neat in shape with three to five lobes. Roll out some pale holly/ivy flower paste using a grooved board or rolling pin. Cut out various-sized leaves with the ivy cutter/veiners. Insert a moistened 26-gauge or 28-gauge wire into each leaf, depending on size. Place the leaf on a pad and soften the edges a little with a cel-stick. Pinch down the centre to make a central vein, and allow to firm up a little before colouring.

2 Dust the leaf while it is still slightly damp, starting with aubergine on the edges. Dust the main part of the leaf with dark green, and then over-dust with holly/ivy. Allow to dry thoroughly.

3 Dip the leaf into a ½ glaze, shake off the excess, and allow to dry. To create the pale veins that the leaf has, scratch away some of the glaze and colour, and actually scratch into the sugar, following and adding to the main veins on the paste.

4 Tape the leaves on to a 26-gauge wire using ½-width beige tape. You can start the stem with a tendril if you wish, but on real ivy this tends to be a very small leaf forming. The size of leaf varies on each stem, and sometimes two leaves develop at the same point.

FLOWERING STEMS

5 The leaves on flowering stems are made in exactly the same way as for non-flowering stems, except that they are cut out with large, heart-shaped leaf templates made from the outlines on page 142. Vein with the large ivy veiner. Use a heavier gauge of wire, and when you colour the leaf use less aubergine petal dust and a little moss green as well as the other two greens to make a brighter leaf colour. Glaze and scratch as before.

FLOWERS AND BUDS

6 Cut a length of 33-gauge wire into short pieces and bend a tiny hook on each. Attach a tiny ball of green paste to the end and insert five tiny white stamens. Allow to dry.

7 Roll out a small piece of paste, leaving the centre slightly thicker. Cut out a calyx shape using the tiny calyx cutter. Place it on a pad and stretch each petal using strong strokes with a small celstick. Moisten the centre and pull the stamens through so that the two fit tightly together. Curl the petals back. You will need to make a lot of these flowers to make up a flower head.

8 Dust the centre of each flower with moss green and primrose mixed together. Tape a collection together with the stems all coming out at the same point.

9 To make the buds, attach a tiny ball of paste to a hooked 33-gauge wire. Mark some indents on the surface to give the impression of unopened petals. Tape buds together in clusters.

BERRIES

10 Cut short lengths of 30-gauge wire. Roll a ball of green paste and insert the wire so that it almost comes out at the other end, forming a sharp point. Pinch the point if it is not sharp enough. Using a pair of tweezers, pinch five lines around the top part of the berry to form a pentagon shape.

11 Tape over each stem with ¼-width green tape. Dust the berries to various degrees of ripeness, using a little aubergine and black to colour the top part of each berry, and moss green on the sides. The more mature the berry, the blacker it should be. Tape the berries into clusters and steam (see page 10) to take away the dusty appearance.

ASSEMBLY

12 Start a stem with either a cluster of buds, flowers or berries, and then tape in a small leaf. Work down the stem, adding larger leaves and a 20-gauge wire to add bulk. Dust the stem with the green petal dust. Add other clusters and smaller stems to the main one if you wish.

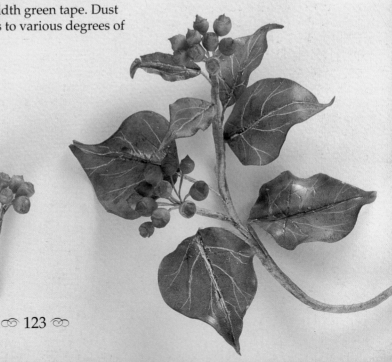

Columbine

Often called 'granny's bonnet', the columbine (*Aquilegia vulgaris*) can have dark purple, pale violet/pink or white flowers. These plants were once used to cure sore throats, which is very strange as they are highly poisonous! They are, however, one of the most attractive flowers during the late spring and early summer months.

Materials

Fine white stamens
20, 24, 28 and 30-gauge wires
Bluebell, lavender, cornflower blue, violet, dark green, vine green, plum and primrose petal dust (blossom tint)
Pale melon and pale holly/ivy flower paste
¼ glaze (see page 10)

Equipment

Pale green floristry tape
Fine pliers
Daisy petal cutter (89)
Ceramic silk veining tool
Rose calyx cutter (R11b)
Oak leaf geranium cutters
Frilled geranium cutter
Aquilegia leaf veiner (GI)

STAMENS

1 Bend a group of fine white stamens in half and tape alongside a 24-gauge wire. Dust the tips of the stamens with primrose, and then curl back some of the tips using pliers. Dust the centre of the stamens with a little vine green.

PETALS

2 Each of the petals is formed in a tubular shape.

Roll out some pale melon paste and cut out five petals using the daisy petal cutter. Roll with the veining tool to broaden and vein.

3 Using a cocktail stick (toothpick) to support the petal, roll it into a tubular shape. If the paste starts to dry out use a little egg white to

stick the two edges together. Roll the base of the petal very finely between your finger and thumb. Thin the upper edge of the petal by frilling with a cocktail stick. Curl the fine base into shape. Allow to dry a little before colouring.

TEPALS

4 Roll a ball of pale melon paste into a cone shape and then pinch around the base to form a hat shape. Roll out the

paste around the thick area at the centre, still leaving the paste quite 'fleshy'. Cut out the shape using the large rose calyx cutter.

5 Divide the calyx shape into five separate pieces using a sharp scalpel. Insert a moistened 30-gauge wire into the base of each tepal. Roll the base of each tepal between your finger and thumb to make it finer. Broaden and vein at the same time using the ceramic silk veining tool. Place each of the tepals on the pad and soften the edges. Curl the base of each of the tepals back and give the tips a sharp pinch. Allow to firm up.

Colouring and assembly

6 Dust each of the petals and tepals with a mixture of equal proportions of bluebell and lavender. Add depth by dusting into the tubes, at the base of the petals and down the centre on both sides of the tepals using a mixture of cornflower blue and violet.

7 Tape the tepals around the stamens using ½-width pale green floristry tape. To stick the petals in place you will need to mix up a glue; mix a little egg white with some flower paste and work it with the broad end of a dresden tool to form a smooth paste. Apply a little of this glue to the base of the stamens in between the tepals. While the glue is still wet, position the five petals in between the tepals.

8 Tape a length of 20-gauge wire on to the main stem to make it both longer and stronger.

9 For a seed-head, insert a 30-gauge wire into the base of a teardrop-shaped piece of pale holly/ivy paste, pinch a ridge down one side with your finger and thumb, thin down the tip to make it very fine, and curl as illustrated. Make another four, and then tape together with the curled tips on the outside, using ¼-width tape. Dust with plum, vine and dark green.

Leaves

10 Roll out some holly/ivy paste using a grooved rolling pin or board. Cut out one large and two small leaves using a combination of the two sizes of oak leaf geranium and the frilled geranium cutters. Insert a moistened 28-gauge wire into almost the full length of each leaf. Vein using the aquilegia leaf veiner.

11 These leaves are actually quite flat on the edges, but I prefer to give them more movement. Work on the edge using the broad end of the dresden tool. Pinch the leaf down the centre and allow to dry a little before colouring.

12 Dust the edges with plum. Colour the main part of the leaf with dark green, and then over-dust with vine green. Dip into a ¼ glaze, shake off excess, and leave to dry.

13 Tape the leaves together into threes using ½-width green tape.

Oak

The best known and most loved tree in Britain is without doubt the majestic oak (*Quercus*). Oak is always a good piece to use on a man's birthday cake, a retirement cake, or even on an autumn wedding cake.

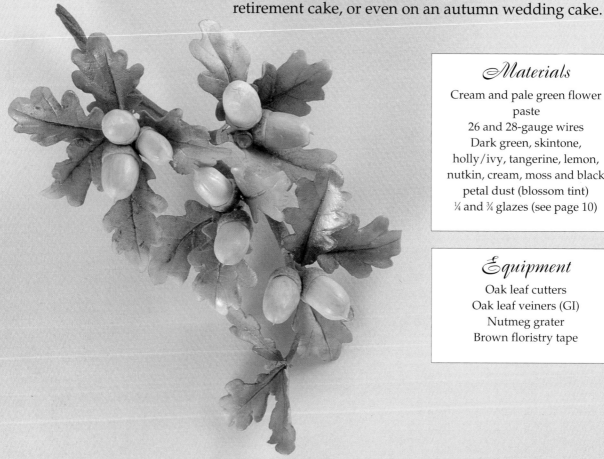

Materials

Cream and pale green flower paste
26 and 28-gauge wires
Dark green, skintone, holly/ivy, tangerine, lemon, nutkin, cream, moss and black petal dust (blossom tint)
¼ and ¾ glazes (see page 10)

Equipment

Oak leaf cutters
Oak leaf veiners (GI)
Nutmeg grater
Brown floristry tape

LEAVES

1 Decide whether you want leaves in autumn colours or green. If you plan to make autumn leaves, then it is better to work with cream flower paste. Roll out some paste using a grooved rolling pin or board, and cut out leaves using various sizes of oak leaf cutters.

2 Insert a moistened 26-gauge or 28-gauge wire (depending on the size of the leaf), making sure the wire is inserted to at least half the length of the ridge. Place each leaf into an oak leaf veiner and press firmly.

Remove the leaf, place it on a pad and soften the edges with a celstick. Allow to dry for approximately 30 minutes.

COLOURING

3 Dust the leaves to various depths of colour. Start dusting down the centre of each leaf with dark green, holly/ivy and moss. Dust in from the edge of each leaf with cream, lemon, tangerine, skintone and nutkin (try to give variation in your colouring). Dip each leaf into a ¼ glaze, shake off the excess, and leave to dry.

ACORNS

4 Roll a ball of cream flower paste into an acorn shape (quite straight sides with a rounded top). Insert a hooked, moistened 26-gauge wire into the base. Pinch a tiny sharp point at the tip. Mark the sides of the nut using a scriber or the back edge of a scalpel. (These long markings should be very light and straight, continuing down to the base of the nut.) Dust the nut with cream, tangerine and a little moss green. Dip the acorn into a ¾ glaze, shake off the excess, and allow to dry.

5 To make the acorn cup, use a smaller piece of green paste. Roll into a ball, and then hollow out using the rounded end of a celstick. Thin out the edges of the cup by pressing them against the sides of the celstick. Leave the tool in the cup and roll the sides of the paste against a nutmeg grater to give a textured surface.

6 Moisten the centre of the cup and attach to the base of the acorn, making sure that it fits neatly. Pinch off any excess paste. Dust the cup with cream, moss, nutkin and a little black in places. Make some extra cups, but this time insert a moistened 26-gauge wire into the base of each one. Quite often the nut has fallen off and it looks interesting in a spray if you have the odd cup in amongst the full acorns. Dust the inside of the

cup a dark cream/brown, leaving a pale area at the centre. Paint with ¾ glaze and allow to dry.

7 Sometimes there are some tiny brown nuts at the base of the larger ones. These are made in the same way as before, colouring them with nutkin and a little black.

ASSEMBLY

8 Tape two or three acorns, with or without empty cups, very tightly together at the base. Add the smaller nuts as required, again keeping them tight in with the other nuts. Tape a group of leaves in various sizes behind each clump of nuts.

Notes

Both the shape of the acorn and the oak foliage vary from one species of oak to another. There are many species; though often thought of as a traditionally British tree, only two species of oak are native to Britain – the sessile and the English oak. The oak is a common sight in parks and large gardens, where it supplies a habitat and food source to many animals, birds and insects.

Medlar

Medlar (*Mespilus germanica*) is a shrub that has quite small flowers and huge green-brown apple-like fruits. It makes quite an unusual and interesting subject to use on a cake, either by itself or with other autumn fruits in a large arrangement. Because the fruit is very large I have scaled it down to make it more suitable to use on a cake.

Materials

Fine white or brown-tipped
stamens
20, 26 and 30-gauge wires
Clear alcohol (gin or vodka)
Primrose, moss, nutkin, spring
green, dark green, white,
holly/ivy, skintone, champagne, lemon, tangerine and
black petal dust (blossom tint)
White, mid-green and brown
flower paste
¼ glaze and ½ glaze (see
page 10)

Equipment

Pale green and brown floristry
tape
Heart-shaped cutter (330)
Rose calyx cutters (526, 249,
248)
Styro-foam ball
Large rose leaf veiner (GI)
Large rose veiner (Asi-es)

shaped cutter. Cut five short lengths of 30-gauge wire, moisten the end of each and insert into the thick ridge of each petal.

3 Frill the edges using the broad end of a dresden tool, or work them with a cocktail stick (toothpick). Cup the centre of each petal with the small end of a bone-end tool. Pinch the base and then curl back the

and nutkin petal dust. Allow to dry, and then dust in the centre with a mixture of primrose and moss green.

STAMENS

1 Take a group of stamens and bend them in half. Tape a short length of 26-gauge wire alongside using ¼-width green floristry tape. Open up the stamens a little using tweezers. If using white stamens, paint the tips with a mixture of alcohol

PETALS

2 Roll out some white flower paste thinly using a grooved rolling pin or board. Cut out five petals with the heart-edges of each petal. Allow to dry slightly over a gentle curve.

4 Dust the base of each petal with a mixture of primrose and moss green. Dust the whole of each petal with champagne petal dust.

5 Tape the petals evenly around the stamens. If the petals are still damp you can now gently re-shape the edges if needed.

Calyx

6 Roll a ball of green flower paste into a teardrop shape and pinch out the base to form a hat shape. Roll out the base using a small celstick. Cut out the shape using the largest rose calyx cutter (248). Vein and pinch down the centre of each sepal, forming the tip into a long, sharp point. Dust the inside of the calyx with white and moss green petal dust.

7 Moisten the centre of the calyx and position it on to

the back of the flower, trying to cover a join in the petals with each of the sepals. Curl the tips of each sepal back. Dust the back of the calyx with dark green and moss.

Bud

8 Roll a cone of white paste and insert a hooked, moistened 26-gauge wire into the broad base. Using a 'cage' made from five 30-gauge wires (see page 10), indent the bud to give the impression of unopened petals. Pinch the tip into a sharp point. Add a calyx as for the flower using one of the smaller cutters (this will depend on the size of the bud). Dust the calyx as for the flower.

Fruit

9 Roll a large ball of brown flower paste. Flatten it slightly. Roll out some more of the brown paste and cut out a shape using one of the smaller calyx cutters. Moisten the back of the

calyx and place on to the surface of the ball. Using the pointed end of a celstick, embed the shape into the ball. Open up the centre a little more and then insert a taped, hooked and moistened 20-gauge wire, making sure the hook is hidden inside the fruit.

10 Texture the surface of the fruit by rolling over with a styro-foam ball. Make fruit in various sizes for each branch.

11 Dust the whole of each fruit with nutkin brown petal dust. Shade in areas and add depth to the centre of the fruit using some more nutkin mixed with black. To add a mossy effect dust in places with spring green. Dip into a ¼ glaze, shake off excess, and leave to dry. You might find the fruit needs dusting gently again after glazing to give a denser appearance.

Leaves

12 Roll out some mid-green paste using a grooved rolling pin or board. Cut out the leaves using a sharp scalpel (these vary in size and are oval in shape with a point at the end). Insert a moistened 26-gauge wire into the central ridge to at least half the length of each leaf.

13 Vein using the large rose leaf veiners (you will need the Asi-es veiner for the very large leaves). Place on a pad and soften the edges using a large celstick. Pinch the leaves down the centre and dry over a gentle curve until firm enough to dust.

14 Dust the edges of each leaf to various degrees with lemon, tangerine, skintone and nutkin brown. Colour the main body of the leaf with dark green, moss and holly/ivy. Dip the leaves, one at a time, into a ½ glaze, shake off excess, and leave to dry.

ASSEMBLY

15 Tape a group of leaves behind each flower and fruit using ½-width brown floristry tape. Arrange these together to form a branch, adding extra leaves as needed. Dust the branches with nutkin brown and a little black.

Old Man's Beard

This plant *(Clematis vitalba)* is a member of the large Clematis family. 'Old man's beard' is the name given to the hairy seed-heads that the plant produces in autumn.

Materials

White silk thread
24, 28 and 33-gauge wires
Lemon, moss, primrose, dark green, aubergine, skintone and nutkin petal dust (blossom tint)
Holly/ivy flower paste
½ glaze (see page 10)

Equipment

Pale green floristry tape
Simple leaf cutters (225-232)
Clematis montana veiner (GI)

SEED-HEADS

1 Wrap some silk thread around two parted fingers eight times. Remove from your fingers and twist the loop into a figure-of-eight shape, then bend the shape in half to form a smaller loop. Thread a 33-gauge wire though the centre of the loop of silk, bend it over the thread, and tape over the base of the silk and down on to the wire using ½-width tape.

2 Cut the silk and open it up. Dust the very centre with nutkin petal dust to represent the seeds. Moisten the centre and the very tips of the thread with egg white, then pull back the silk and twist the ends around the wire. Allow to dry, and then tease the silk open again. (The egg white will stiffen the silk to hold it in position.) Dust with lemon.

LEAVES

3 Roll out green paste using a grooved board. Cut out different-sized leaves using the leaf cutters. The leaves grow in groups of three or five, the top leaf tending to be larger, so for each group you will need one large leaf and two or four smaller ones.

4 Insert a moistened 28-gauge wire into each leaf. Vein with the clematis veiner, then make cuts in the edges with scissors.

5 Dust the leaves with moss and primrose, adding depth with dark green. Dust the edges with aubergine. Glaze using a ½ glaze. Tape the leaves together in groups.

6 Tape over each of the stems with ¼-width green tape. Group the seed-heads in separate stems of two and three. Tape the leaves and seed-heads on to a main stem (24-gauge wire), noting that the leaves grow with two sets opposite each other. Dust the stems with aubergine and skintone.

Lazy Daisy and Busy Bee

Daisies are a wonderful subject for a summer birthday cake. The flowers could also be wired up as a daisy chain and displayed around the base of the cake, and if the bumble-bees are not to your taste, there is an alternative brush embroidery design on page 143.

Materials

20cm (8 in) long octagonal cake
Apricot glaze
750g (1½lb) almond paste (marzipan)
Clear alcohol (kirsch or vodka)
1kg (2lb) white sugarpaste
Fine willow green ribbon to trim cake
Green velvet ribbon to trim board
Holly/ivy, dark green and white petal dust (blossom tint)
Royal icing (optional)

Equipment

Sugarpaste smoothers
30cm (12 in) long octagonal cake board
Bumble-bee ink stamp
Green floristry tape

Flowers

5 daisies and 4 buds (see page 120)

PREPARATION

1 Brush the cake with apricot glaze and cover with almond paste. Leave to dry overnight. Moisten the almond paste with clear alcohol and cover with sugarpaste, using smoothers to achieve a good finish.

2 Cover the cake board with sugarpaste, and place the cake on top, making sure you have a neat join between the base of the cake and the board. Allow to dry for 2 days.

3 Attach a length of fine green ribbon around the base of the cake, and a length of velvet ribbon around the board edge.

SIDE DECORATION

4 The bumble-bee design is created using an ink stamp that I bought from a National Trust shop. Mix together holly/ivy, dark green and white petal dust on a saucer with a little clear alcohol, to form a fairly thick consistency. Apply the colour to the ink stamp using a broad paintbrush (trying not to paint too much on to the surface of the stamp as this will make the design smudge on the cake surface). Press the stamp in the desired places, using a firm press-and-release motion. To give the cake a little humour, if desired, paint a series of 'Z's above the bumble-bees. Use the green paint mixture again and a very fine paintbrush.

THE SPRAY

5 This is probably the easiest spray I have ever put together! Simply bunch the flower and bud stems attractively, and fasten together at one point using ½-width floristry tape. Rest the flowers diagonally across the cake surface. If you wish to secure the spray, pipe a little royal icing under the stems.

Autumnal Fruit and Nut Cake

This unusual design would be ideal for a birthday cake. The cake has an interesting texture; along with the oak, ivy fruit and seed-heads of old man's beard, it gives it quite a rustic look.

Materials

20cm (8 in) heart-shaped cake
Apricot glaze
750g (1½ lb) almond paste (marzipan)
Clear alcohol (kirsch or vodka)
1kg (2lb) sugarpaste, coloured with holly/ivy paste colouring
Dark green, holly/ivy and tangerine petal dust (blossom tint)
Pearl and pastel green lustre colours
Green velvet ribbon to trim board

Equipment

Sugarpaste smoothers
30cm (12 in) heart-shaped cake board
Large and small hydrangea leaf veiners
Round-headed grooved cocktail sticks (toothpicks)
Posy pick

Flowers

1 large and 1 small Autumnal Spray (see page 137)

PREPARATION

1 Brush the cake with apricot glaze and cover with almond paste. Leave to dry overnight. Moisten the almond paste with clear alcohol and cover with green sugarpaste, using sugarpaste smoothers to achieve a good finish. Cover the cake board with sugarpaste, and place the cake on top, making sure you have a neat join between the base of the cake and the board.

DESIGN

2 Using the ridged side of the hydrangea leaf veiners, emboss the cake's surface in the desired areas. Mark some stems on the cake with the fine end of a dresden tool to link the foliage together. Once the leaf design is completed, texture the whole surface of the cake and board with the rounded ends of a bunch of grooved cocktail sticks (toothpicks). The surface of the cake then becomes recessed, while the leaf design stands proud.

3 Dust the leaf design with variations of dark green, holly/ivy and tangerine, and then over-dust with the lustre colours. Dust around the base of the cake with a mixture of dark green and holly/ivy.

4 Attach a length of velvet ribbon around the edge of the board.

5 Wire up the sprays as described on page 137, and position on the cake. The large spray should be inserted into a posy pick pushed into the top left-hand corner of the cake, while the small spray simply rests on the cake board.

Autumnal Spray

There are two sprays on the Autumnal Fruit and Nut Cake (page 134); the instructions given here are for the larger one. The smaller spray is simpler in form, the flowers simply being taped together at one point.

Large spray

6 pieces of oak, plus extra foliage (see page 126)
3 stems of old man's beard (see page 131)
3 pieces of berried common ivy with foliage (see page 122)
1 piece of flowering common ivy with foliage, plus 2 clusters of ivy buds (see page 122)

Small spray

2 stems of non-flowering ivy foliage (see page 122)
1 clump of oak with acorns (see page 126)
1 clump of oak without acorns (see page 126)
3 clumps of ivy berries (see page 123)
2 flowering ivy stems (see page 122)
1 stem of old man's beard foliage (see page 131)

Equipment

24-gauge wires
Green floristry tape
Fine pliers
Wire cutters

1 To strengthen all the stems, tape on additional lengths of 24-gauge wire using ½-width floristry tape. Decide on the size and shape of the spray and then gather together five stems (here I have used three pieces of oak and two stems of old man's beard). Bend each stem to an angle of 90°, and then tape them together using ½-width floristry tape. This will form a handle to the spray.

2 Add the focal point in the centre of the spray. In this case I have used a clump of oak. Add another two clumps of oak to fill the gaps around the centre.

3 Finally, tape in the ivy berries, flowers and foliage, spacing them mainly around the focal point. Cut off any excess wire from the handle to cut down on the bulk, and tape over with full-width tape to neaten.

4 For the smaller spray, simply gather the pieces together attractively and tape at one point.

Granny's Bonnet Birthday Cake

'Granny's bonnet' is yet another common name for aquilegia, so it is an obvious choice for a grandmother celebrating her birthday during late spring or early summer!

Materials

20cm (8 in) oval cake
Apricot glaze
750g (1½ lb) almond paste
(marzipan)
Clear alcohol (kirsch or vodka)
1kg (2lb) champagne
sugarpaste
Cream and white (optional)
royal icing
Soft pine ribbon to trim board
Violet, lavender and deep purple petal dust (blossom tint)

Equipment

Sugarpaste smoothers
30cm (12 in) oval cake board
Crimper
Nos. 0 and 42 piping tubes
(tips)
Thick card
A4 plastic file pocket
Florists' staysoft
Small cake card
Glue gun and non-toxic glue
stick

Flowers

8 aquilegia flowers and 5 buds
(see page 124)
3–5 aquilegia seed-heads (see
page 125)
Many clumps of aquilegia
foliage (see page 125)

PREPARATION

1 Brush the cake with apricot glaze and cover with almond paste. Leave to dry overnight. Moisten the almond paste with clear alcohol, and cover the cake with sugarpaste, using sugarpaste smoothers to achieve a good finish.

2 Cover the cake board with sugarpaste, and crimp the edge. Place the cake on the board. Allow to dry.

3 Pipe a shell border around the base of the cake using cream-coloured royal icing and a piping bag fitted with a no. 42 piping tube. Attach a length of ribbon to the edge of the board.

SIDE DECORATION

4 Trace the leaf design on page 143 several times on to a piece of tracing paper. Cut a piece of thick card to fit into an A4 plastic file pocket, and insert it, with the tracing paper, into the pocket so that the traced design shows through.

5 Pipe over the lace work, using white or cream royal icing and a piping bag fitted with a no. 0 piping tube. Allow the lace to dry, and then colour each piece while it is still on the file pocket using first of all violet and then a mixture of lavender and deep purple petal dust.

6 Scribe a fine line on to the cake, either freehand or using a template, to help position the embroidery and lace. Pipe the embroidery just above the scribed line using a no. 0 piping tube. (This piping can be piped freehand, or you can trace the embroidery design from page 143, scribe it on to the cake, and then pipe over it.) Using the pointed end of a cel-stick, create the eyelet holes and then pipe around the edge of each one. Allow to dry, and then petal dust over the embroidery with appropriate colours.

7 Attach the lace to the cake with royal icing, piping two tiny dots on to the cake's surface for each piece of lace, and gently holding the lace in position until it will stay in place.

FLOWERS

8 Attach a lump of florists' staysoft to the small cake card using a glue gun. Arrange the flowers in the staysoft, trying to make the display quite informal. You might find bending the base of each wire into a hook before inserting it into the staysoft will help to hold the stems a little more firmly. Remember to reserve one stem to place on the other side of the cake to complete the design.

Templates

Stargazer Lily
(page 17)
leaves

petals

*Anemone
Leaf*
(page 33)

Mothering Sunday Cake
(page 46)
anemone plate design

Trailing Tropaeolum Cake

(page 108)
painted top design

*Trumpet Vine
Christening Cake*

(page 83)
leaf hammock

Blue Gum Blossom

(page 68)

Frog Down Under
(page 80)
designed by Annemieke Mein

Common Ivy
leaves of flowering stem
(page 122)

*Lazy Daisy and
Busy Bee*
(page 132)
daisy embroidery design

*Chinese
Virginia
Creeper*
(page 92)

*Granny's Bonnet
Birthday Cake*
(page 138)
lace leaf and embroidery

Index